PARENTING WITH PURPOSE

& AFRICAN WISDOM

'The proverbs of the people reveal the wisdom they have'
African (Congolese) Proverb

Gladys K. Mwiti, PhD

OASIS INTERNATIONAL LTD

Parenting with Purpose & African Wisdom

ISBN 13: 978-1-59452-736-4
ISBN: 1-59452-736-9

Published by Oasis International, Ltd. in partnership with and with permission from Arba Publications, Nairobi, Kenya. For more information, go to arbapublications.com.

Oasis International is a ministry devoted to fostering a robust and sustainable pan-African publishing industry. For more information, go to oasisint.net.

18 19 20 21 22 23 24 25 BPI 10 9 8 7 6 5 4 3 2 1

ENDORSEMENTS

Parenting with Purpose and African Wisdom is one of the best books on parenting I've read. The African wisdom in this book will benefit non-Africans as well as Africans. I was particularly struck by the author's insight on the need for fathers to mentor their sons to become men -- the missing Gaaru. That's a message that needs to be heard in the West as well as in Africa. Parenting with Purpose and African Wisdom is practical, direct, helpful, compassionate, and biblical. I recommend it most highly.

Larry Stone, former Vice President of Thomas Nelson Publishers, President of Rutledge Hill Press, Editorial Manager of The Africa Study Bible, author of The Story of the Bible, father, and grandfather, USA

Parenting is getting challenging every day and both parents and children are losing hope. Parenting with Purpose and African Wisdom will instill hope in a unique way. Dr. Gladys K. Mwiti has blended the Bible, psychology and African wisdom to provide guidance in parenting. With these three, there's hope for generations to come.

Mrs. Rahab Mwangi, MA Counseling; Director, Chara Care and Counseling, Kenya

Dr Gladys Mwiti has written a book for all seasons on parenting, an increasingly challenging social phenomenon in contemporary times. A tour de force, *Parenting with Purpose and African Wisdom* is predicated upon expert psychotherapy and family counseling and contains key elements of African wisdom, spiritual integrity and contextual realities. I strongly endorse the book as an instructive companion for any and all involved in parenting in all its aspects, and highly recommend it as essential reading for parents, teachers, counselors and spiritual guides seeking to be relevant in parenting matters.

Rev. Dr. Samuel Kobia, Chancellor, St Paul's University, and Senior Advisor to the President of the Republic of Kenya on Cohesion, Peace and Conflict Resolution, Kenya

Parenting with Purpose and African Wisdom is a most compelling, insightful and exciting title on parenting grounded in the African context. A must read for all prospective and new parents across generations and cultures.

Prof Margaret Kobia, PhD, CBS, Chairperson, Public Service Commission and Associate Professor of Management and Entrepreneurship, Kenya

Parenting is a discipline in which children find their identity, security, memory, hope and responsibility. In this light Dr. Gladys Mwiti provides thoughtful ideas in *Parenting with Purpose and African Wisdom,* reminding us that each parent should endeavor to do their best while partnering with God in order to pass on lasting legacies. Her extensive experience in counseling parents and their children plus her value-based training in Clinical Psychology make the book a suitable manual for all parents.

The Most Rev. Dr. Eliud Wabukala, EBS, Archbishop of Kenya & Bishop of All Saints' Cathedral Diocese

Gladys Mwiti manages to integrate modern science and traditional wisdom. There is much to be learned from both – not only African readers can profit greatly from the knowledge and experience that has been developed from generation to generation, as from Western scientific knowledge. An important and helpful book for everyone parenting, educating or teaching children!

Prof. Dr. Ulrich Giesekus, Psychology and Counseling,
Liebenzell International University, Germany

Dr. Gladys Mwiti covers all the important and key aspects of parenting, giving young mums like myself practical and solid advice on how to tackle the often confusing and sometimes lonely journey of parenting. It's a joy to read. Her ability to weave in African wisdom and spiritual faith adds more gravitas to her words and down-to-earth advice that will become a great reference time after time. If you want to become the best parent possible, read this book!

Neva K. Read, Author; Founder and CEO,
Afya Organics Pty Ltd. Sydney, Australia

Parenting with Purpose and African Wisdom is a very informative, practical and much-needed resource for parents and all resource persons working with parents and children in today's multifaceted and complex society. The author draws from her extensive professional counseling practice, Christian principles and African traditional childrearing practices.

Amb. Prof. Ruthie C. Rono, Deputy Vice Chancellor,
Academic Affairs. United States International University – Africa, Kenya

We should not be surprised that this tremendously practical, helpful, entertaining and encouraging book on parenting with purpose is written by a strong Christian wife and mother who was raised in a simple Kenyan village by an amazing mother she describes as "illiterate, purposeful and confident." As a young girl, Gladys Mwiti did her homework by lamplight in a four room house with a corrugated tin roof and mud walls and has now become an internationally respected and loved author, speaker, psychologist and CEO.

This parenting book is rich in wisdom learned through scripture, African proverbs, and Gladys' keen observations of what has worked in her life and in that of others. Many books focus only on the day-to-day challenges of parenting. But Gladys shows us how our parenting tactics can flow from our long term purpose as parents. That purpose is captured in the question, "What kind of person does God, the Creator, desire my child to become?"

Bradford M. Smith, Ph.D., Lausanne Movement Catalyst for Global Mental Health and Trauma Response, and Director of the Institute for International Care and Counsel, Belhaven University, USA

One of the tragedies of our time is the diminishing emphasis on value systems that define the present and future of any society. If our children represent the future we look forward to, there is need more than ever before to rethink our priorities as parents as far as our children are concerned. Dr. Gladys Mwiti captures this obligation in her compelling book on parenting by drawing invaluable wisdom from her Christian, professional and family background. The church in particular needs to embrace the contextual approach employed by Dr Gladys Mwiti in developing culturally sensitive approaches to ministry that employ the fusion of Christian witness and biblical cultural values. The book is a blessing to not only the Christian reader but to the society at large.

Rev. John Maromba, Superintendent Minister, Lavington United Church, Nairobi, Kenya

FOREWORD

In a generation where the family is under attack and mere tolerance becoming a gauge in everything that human beings engage in, Dr. Gladys Mwiti has dedicated to release a book on parenting with a purpose. The book provides the basis for understanding that parenting is not for the faint-hearted, for it takes passion, focus, and commitment. It cannot be an instant undertaking or as easy as counting one to five, but calls for patience and purpose. Consequently, you will discover pathways for purposeful parenting that deliver results at the end.

Since parents are not likely to predict how each of their children may rise to an identity of their own, the book urges the reader to consider specific parenting characteristics that will open up the growth of their children in the manner that God desires. It is for this reason that potential and continuing parents are invited to initiate a clear plan of action that will ensure that their children get to their optimal level of growth. Drawing different examples from various individuals and herself on purposeful parenting, Dr. Mwiti reminds that parenting for positive results in life is a possibility in all social and economic contexts. The book interweaves various case studies of successful individuals whose upbringing embraced some of the characteristics discussed in this book that any interested parent can study carefully.

The book calls all those with children to consider a very fast dying virtue in parenting, namely partnership. Drawing from African traditional communities where child raising was a concern for the whole village, the book presses the objective that it is only partnership that will ensure our generation is able to parent both males and females to transition to responsible men and women. Indeed, partnership in purposeful parenting calls for deliberate inclusion of those who matter in parenting circles so as to inculcate in the children long lasting values.

This book engages a reader with twelve characteristics for purposeful parenting, among them, prayer, obedience, sexual purity, work ethic, integrity and self-discipline. Dr. Mwiti's passion for God, counseling and church ministry is evident in the manner she centralizes all in purposeful parenting. For any potential parent or anyone currently parenting, this is a book worth reading. It will help you pick the characteristics that have shaped the lives of others, and will shape your parenting journey.

Rev. Prof. Peter Mageto
Deputy Vice-Chancellor, Academic Affairs
Kenya Methodist University

PREFACE

PARENTING WITH PURPOSE

If you dream of moving mountains tomorrow you must start lifting small stones today.
~ *African (Mauritanian) Proverb*

Whoever walks in integrity walks securely, but he who makes his ways crooked will be found out.
~ *Proverbs 10:9*

The African proverb: "*If you dream of moving mountains tomorrow you must start lifting small stones today,*" reminds us that parenting happens in small steps. *Moving mountains* stands for accomplishing great exploits, and successful parenting is exactly that. Tiny, whining babies eventually become tall, strapping men and sniffling toddlers become beautiful, accomplished women. Who would have known!

I recently listened to a gentleman preparing himself to campaign for Presidency in the United States of America's next elections. The whole group of aspiring candidates was asked: "What would you have done with baby Hitler if you were present at his birth?" The man said: "I would have killed him." Someone else made a comment: "I would have adopted him and given him all the love I could and parented him to become a responsible adult." The moral of course is that none of us knows what kind of adults babies will become, but we know the meaning of the word parent.

Literally, it means faithfulness in doing good things, some of them small, like wiping running noses and cleaning after babies, and then seeing the little ones blossom to become responsible adults.

The Biblical proverb: "*Whoever walks in integrity walks securely, but he who makes his ways crooked will be found out,*" underlines the need for integrity in all matters, even in parenting. Parents of integrity can be described as honest, truthful, honorable, reliable, and upright. These people live with confidence and assurance that God will honor the work of their hands. However, for those who choose to live crooked lives, the result shows in the lives of their children. An old idiom says: "*No fruit falls far away from the parent tree,*" meaning that children are very much like their parents. Someone said: "I looked at the father, then at the son, and I thought, '*The apple doesn't fall far from the tree.*'"

Most parents would like to see their children succeed in life, turn out right, make good friends and take up fruitful careers after winning academic and sporting awards through school and college. They dream of young men and women, of whom the parent can say: "There goes my son! That beautiful, successful young woman is my daughter!" However, for many parents, the journey is long and hard. It is difficult to imagine that the little, new born baby who keeps mother and hopefully father awake all night, will one day become an Obama or Mother Teresa. The two seem as far removed from one another as day is from night: the baby boy and the man, the girl child and the saint.

In this world of shortcuts to greatness, thirst for instant riches, desires for pain-free beauty, even instant tea and coffee, one wishes there could be instant well-behaved children, drug and alcohol-free youth as well as instant happy homes. However, the law of nature demands that anything lasting must be created slowly, surely and purposefully. This is the central theme of this book- that truly successful children have, as one of their key ingredients, purposeful parenting.

This book is not a recipe for success, but merely a presentation of principles that make for parenting that delivers results most of the time. Let us explain a few statements here. We cannot assume that every well-parented child will blossom to the expectations of the parent or succeed at all life stages strictly following the parent's time-line. In every family, God, the Eternal Creator, chose to place unique individuals sharing genetic make-up. Yet out of this inherent milieu, he forms different personalities who respond to the same parenting in different ways. There are the early bloomers who make the parents proud and happy. Then there are the late bloomers who test the parents' patience to the letter.

We also have the apparent non-bloomers who end up fallen and miserable, soaked in drugs and wrong living. Finally, we have blooming that can be classified as all sorts of shades and mixes of these three, the stragglers, who somehow make their way to the finishing line with a kaleidoscope of skirmishes enough to write a full adventure novel. It is difficult to explain how all these variations can easily be found in the same household. When patterns of child development baffle age-old wisdoms, mystified parents are left wondering: "Alas! What did I leave out here?"

The point is that no parent can predict how each child, in their unique individuality is likely to turn out. However, borrowing from the farmer, the role of the parent is to plant and tend the seedling faithfully: water, weed, fertilize the plant, and remove weevils and other nasty creatures that feed on the young and juicy sapling. The parent's duty is to shield the crop from marauding animals and flying pests. Then after doing what one can, the rest is left to the Lord of the Harvest, who is the child's creator and protector.

In the next chapters, I attempt to encourage parents to pursue parenting with purpose. Purpose can be defined as the reason for which anything is done, created or exists. A sense of purpose sets direction in parenting and weathers any challenges that would discourage commitment to this task. We do not sway from planting even if the weather masters predict a storm. In the same vein, we should not sway from weeding even if weeds surround our little plants and various roots and creepy creepers threaten. Do not falter in your determination to water your plants even if the rain does not fall on the land. Keep up the purpose of regularly checking on your plants, and your attitude, believing that the Lord of the Harvest will surely reward your labor.

Wikipedia defines wisdom as the ability to think and act using knowledge, insight and understanding. The western tradition places wisdom among the four cardinal virtues: habits or disposition to perform an action with the highest degree of adequacy under any given circumstance. The four cardinal virtues include prudence or wisdom - the ability to judge between actions; justice or protection of the cause of the vulnerable; temperance or the practice and exercise of self-control, also called restraint; and courage, also called strength and endurance. These are learned attributes that are gained through listening, learning, self-monitoring, personal discipline and constant practice.

To whom does one listen? From whom do we learn? Who reminds us to practice self-discipline? Who has the greatest responsibility of shaping behavior? From time immemorial, the primary role of raising children has belonged to parents or guardians, not to schools, places of worship or any other institution outside the family. Any parent or guardian who expects someone else to parent their child misses out on the Creator-given role that, although difficult and challenging, is one of the most rewarding endeavors in life.

In Africa, one of the traditional ways of learning and passing on wisdom was through proverbs or wise sayings. This increased understanding of people and their motives, as well as events and situations and their implications. Africans are religious people and the Biblical book of Proverbs also encourages the need to apply perception and judgment for one to identify the optimal course of action.

Wisdom requires temperance or the control of one's emotional reactions or passions so that sanity prevails as a constant guide to decision making. In short, wisdom in this context demands that parents utilize instructions from the Creator, appreciate the giftedness or unique abilities of their child, listen to knowledge of the wise in their community, and use optimum judgment to help shape the life of their child. As we dialogue through these pages, we shall strive to listen to various people define marks of successful parenting and the wisdom that exemplifies such indicators. So keep reading, thinking, meditating and assessing your own parenting against the questions we ask.

With these few remarks, African style, let us begin the adventure of asking: "What does parenting with purpose look like?" The curious reader may seek to know: "Is the writer a purposeful parent?" I shudder in my boots, sorry, shoes, because many a time, I ask myself the same question. However, I write because I too seek the answer. So, I am riding with you in our *matatu*, towards "Parenting with a Purpose." For the non-Kenyan reader, I said: "We're riding together in the *matatu*, not *matata*!"

The former are Kenya's notorious public transporters, the ride of common folk. The latter means trouble in Kiswahili. So, together in the *matatu*, let us go!

Gladys K Mwiti, PhD

CONTENTS

CHAPTER 1

PURPOSE IN PARENTING

THE MEANING OF PURPOSE

If you close your eyes to facts, you will learn through accidents.
~ *African Proverb*

Commit to the Lord whatever you do and your plans will succeed.
~ *Proverbs 16:3*

The African proverb: *"If you close your eyes to facts, you will learn through accidents,"* reminds us that it is wise to seek out knowledge on any important task we undertake. Parenting, for example, is never taught as a subject in a classroom. Although it involves bringing up another complex human being and preparing them for life, and although the process can never be repeated if one messes it up, little preparation for this task is ever undertaken. As parents, most of us bring up our children by trial and error. The proverb reminds us to be aware of the fact that we often have no clue how to bring up our children. This reality will remind us to seek to learn skills from a position of humility, with a learning posture that wants to do the right thing. Failure to do this can land us into accidents that curtail our children's healthy development or mark their lives negatively forever.

The Biblical proverb: *"Commit to the Lord whatever you do and your plans will succeed,"* reminds us that the author of parenting is God. Humbly asking him for wisdom is the beginning of parenting according to God's plan. He gives us strength to remain focused on the task however challenging it might be some of the time, and above all things, he causes our hearts to rejoice as we see our children developing into responsible adults. Parents know that the joy of motherhood or fatherhood is so unique that it can never be replaced with anything similar on earth.

This chapter explores purpose in parenting. The word purpose means intention, aim, resolution and determination. The active verb "to purpose" means to aim, to intend, to resolve or to plan. Purposeful parenting can be assumed to mean having determination or plan in mind as the parent sets out in the project of parenting. Basically, purposeful parenting presupposes a plan, sense of direction and action towards that direction. The direction is determined by the destination that the parent has in mind regarding each child in particular and for all the children in the family in general.

Since purpose is a destination, it answers the question: "What kind of person does God, the Creator, desire my child to become?" This question presupposes a value destination, meaning that arrival at some destination is not the aim but that what matters most is what kind of destination it will be. For example, parents hope that their children will grow up and get married. Often, the quality of marriage is influenced by the quality of personalities that make up the marriage, and these personalities are often shaped right from birth: by the nature of parenting they received from birth and how much those parents partnered with the Creator. To this end, in partnership with God through seeking his wisdom, parents determine the destination of their parenting, live it dynamically and enrich it with ingrained value systems that will inform the being-ness of each child.

Besides keeping us focused on our destination to bring up holistically balanced children, purposeful parenting also reminds us that we should not give in to fear. The very anxiety of how children will turn out in our complicated society that gets even more complex each day is enough to scare even would-be parents as well as individuals already with children. I have heard young people say: "I do not want to be a parent. It is just too complicated. Too much work!" Then, some parents say that they are afraid that after doing the best, the dangerous environment of modern society will erode all the gains of dedicated parenting. Can anyone really succeed in bringing up well-adjusted children in this day and age?

Focusing on the task at hand and determining to make small gains with time may make the journey less arduous, as will remembering that these small steps of constant commitment make for success. Hence, as we seek to succeed as purposeful parents, what does success look like? How do we know we have done or are doing the right thing? Success is hard to measure in a world where the markers are often placed on wrong posts and eyes are focused on the flashy and transient things of life. Sometimes the pointers form shifting guideposts manned by shifting personalities. This is why we need wisdom in parenting. What then is wisdom and how is it obtained?

The expectation that the primary role of childrearing, upbringing and training belongs to parents or guardians does not negate the critical role played by support systems of extended family, friends and other networks to which the family belongs. However, childrearing as mentoring, training and behavior shaping cannot be passed over carelessly to anyone except those with the primary responsibility over the wellbeing of the child or young person.

In many countries, traditional childrearing focused on

teaching and training a child to become the best individual within cultural definitions of "best," to fear God, mind the welfare of others and carry the legacy of a good family name. Children relied on their parents or guardians for the development of character, values and life goals. Indeed, parents and guardians partnered with teachers and demanded that their children keep school rules and become responsible people.

Today, however, the focus in many societies has changed. Many define children's success as making good grades in school and preparing for a good career. All else is sacrificed and deemed less important to studying in a good school and aiming to get a good job that pays a lot of money. It is easy for parents to forget that good grades are secondary to good character and passing exams and attending a good school are less important than developing to become a responsible member of society. This is because values and character outlast good school grades, great careers and even riches and property. For a parent or caregiver, ability to focus on what matters most in life and so balancing the demands of purposeful parenting requires wisdom and purpose.

Purpose in Parenting and Value Systems

By labor comes wealth.
~ African (Yoruba) Proverb

Lazy hands make a man poor, but diligent hands bring wealth.
~ Proverbs 10:4

The African (Yoruba) proverb: "*By labor comes wealth,*" comes from the Yoruba people, an ethnic group of south-western and north-central Nigeria as well as southern and central Benin in West Africa. The wise saying reminds Africans that it is predestined that to earn anything, one must work for it. Wealth gotten in other ways soon flies away. This is the law of nature. Work ethic therefore is one of the major values that purposeful parenting should pass on to children.

Similarly, the Biblical proverb: "*Lazy hands make a man poor, but diligent hands bring wealth,*" reminds us that God's word praises hard work and condemns laziness because it is a source of hunger and poverty. One of the most quoted passages from the book of Proverbs is Ch. 6:6-7 – "*Go to the ant, you sluggard; consider its ways and be wise! It has no commander, overseer or ruler, yet it stores its provisions in summer and gathers its food at harvest. How long will you lie there, you sluggard? When will you get up from sleep?*" The word *sluggard* is defined as a lazy individual who refuses to work and yet wants to eat and have other needs met by others!

I am a Kenyan national and Meru by tribe. Tribe here refers to the people group that God chose as the crucible where he would place my earthly roots. The tribe or people group for each individual is God's idea because he not only preselects the womb where he fearfully and wonderfully forms us but also the people group where we shall be shaped. One of my mother's value destinations for us as a family was the determination to turn out young adults with a strong work ethic - diligently valuing hard work and the fruits of honest labor. My mother's core value of enterprise, which in this case means energy and initiative as a personal value, was passed on to us through training, reminding, shaping and sometimes "hand' discipline. She did not merely preach hard work, but she modeled the same.

The Meru people believe that hard work and industry pay dividends. I learnt very early in my life that if I visited a friend and found her working in the coffee farm, picking or pruning or weeding, I was not to expect her to vacate the farm and come home to entertain me. I was to put my bag down and join my friend at work. When it was done, we could then go home and enjoy a well earned cup of tea. Without this work ethic, the temptation would be to keep my friend company by sitting on a log or standing around talking but all the time watching her work. Among the Meru people, this is considered rude. Only laggards watch others work. Lazy fellows, it is believed, fall back and slide into poverty. Practice makes perfect even if practice is laggard behavior. One then eats the fruit of laziness that eventually translates to poverty and begging.

Hence, believing that hard work pays, my mother purposed to communicate and model diligence and the discipline that goes with it. She made it very clear to each one of us, repeating the message at each level of development: You will succeed at all you do. From school, no child of mine will bring home a failing grade. You will obey your teachers. You will go to Sunday School and learn to obey God. You will become skilled at the use of the *panga* (machete) meaning that you will learn to work in the garden, to grow food with your own hands, to reap and to bring home the harvest. "You see children," said my mother, "you have to excel both at the use of the pen and use of the *panga*, for I do not know what you'll end up holding in you adult life. If you fail at using the pen for a living, you will not fail at the *panga*." Her destination for her children was diligence as a lifestyle.

Purpose in Parenting and Motivation

He who fears the sun will not become chief.
~ *African (Ugandan) Proverb*

The sluggard says, "There is a lion outside!" or "I will be murdered in the streets!"
~ *Proverbs 22:13*

The African proverb: "*He who fears the sun will not become chief,*" can be translated literally. Becoming a chief of one's village was something to be envied in traditional Africa. This high honor was conferred to people who had done well through hard work and integrity of life. Fearing the sun refers to laziness because hard work in Africa is often done *jua kali* – meaning "under the hot sun." No one can therefore *fear the sun* and expect to go far. The sun could be anything that would discourage one from doing their best in every situation. Loving and obeying God, learning to work to earn good grades, cleaning up after one self, planting and harvesting from the garden, keeping oneself clean, living a productive life with integrity and confidence, and becoming a blessing to others is the only way one can progress through life without regret. No one can expect progress if all he does is avoid difficult life challenges.

Similarly, the Biblical proverb: "*The sluggard says, 'There is a lion outside!' or 'I will be murdered in the streets!'*" rules out excuses as a way of getting by in life. Growing up in a responsible manner is working against the natural tendency to be lazy and sluggish. This section on "Purpose in Parenting and Motivation" explores the need for parents to encourage and inspire their children to internalize the work ethic and supervise them towards the goal of becoming responsible from a very early age.

My mother understood the purpose of motivation Maslow-style. She made her demands pleasurable, clearly communicating that her purpose of instilling enterprise was not a law to be obeyed with pain and regret but a joy to be lived. She helped us to perceive hard work as fun, liberally rewarding success but never sparing the rod for anyone that entertained mediocrity. Mediocrity merely means consistently getting stuck to middle level qualities, neither very good nor very bad, becoming satisfied with common-place living and average achievement when one is capable of doing better. It borders closely to what God told the Church in Laodicea: "I know your works: You are neither cold nor hot! So, because you're lukewarm, neither hot nor cold, I will spit you out of my mouth" (Rev 3: 15-16).

My mother purposed that anything worth doing was worth doing well. In this regard, she gave us duties and supervised them. She rewarded success, trained the ignorant and disciplined the headstrong. It is only after her death in 1999 at 74 years of age that I realized that she demonstrated the gift of psychology: the study of human behavior. This illiterate, purposeful, confident village woman knew the meaning of behavior reinforcement. She rewarded improvement on specific achievements and encouraged each child to perform to their best ability.

As an example, contrary to my father's desire, she had purposed that all her daughters must go to school and compete at the same level as their brothers. My father was sometimes influenced by other men in the village who thought that girls were good enough only for marriage. Such men would often barter their daughters at drinking meetings, promising the young ones off to old men, some already married to one or two women.

My mother stood her ground with determination and

my father, who was by now a polygamist with another family, finally relented, agreeing that all the children could go to school. However, there was a condition. My mother had to find the means to provide for our needs through primary school, and he would take over in high school, if we passed the determining major national examination. My mother took the challenge, and she made sure that we would indeed sit and pass the exam. She would train us to be diligent, disciplined, and competitive, and she modeled the same.

Among the animals in our home: the goats, sheep, pigs, and dogs, and the occasional visiting rats and porcupines, were chicken. From as early as I can remember, my mother fattened a cock that would be presented as a reward to any of us who achieved the best position in their class at the end of each term. The individual, boy or girl, who won the cock was given the freedom to enjoy chicken stew with rice or whatever else, in a feast with friends. We all desired to win the fat bird and hence worked hard for the same. This healthy competition made learning fun because she secretly found other ways to reward anyone who was less endowed. I look back today and see this purpose and diligence written all over me, ingrained by an illiterate woman who was a teacher, motivational speaker, counselor and behavioral psychologist, all rolled into one.

Purposeful Parenting and Determined Destinations

A child who is carried on the back will not know how long the journey is.
~ African (Nigerian) Proverb

An army of sheep led by a lion can defeat an army of lions led by a sheep.
~ African (Ghanaian) Proverb

In all your ways acknowledge Him (God) and He will make straight your paths.
~ Proverbs 3:6

The Nigerian proverb: "*A child who is carried on the back will not know how long the journey is,*" discourages dependency. Africans believe that a child's sense of responsibility should increase with age. This is why many African communities had rites of passage where a child graduated through developmental phases. After completing one age group, the child was expected to never again indulge in behavior associated with that stage but to instead engage in more mature behavior.

Some parents may be tempted to "carry" a child too long. For example, a mature man of 40 years may still be living in his father's house with his mother still cooking for him and doing his laundry. Unless that man is disabled or underdeveloped, he should already be out of his "mother's kitchen".

To lead children and young people through various phases of maturation needs the courage of a lion or lioness, and not the hesitating, uncertain spirit of a sheep, and so the Ghanaian proverb: "*An army of sheep led by a lion can defeat an army of lions led by a sheep.*" I admire women in Africa who have never been to school or college but have brought up children who have worked hard and studied to become medical doctors, lawyers or successful business people, men and women living with integrity and bringing up their own children. These mothers can be described as "lions" leading sheep by the fact that they never went to school while their children have studied well through their mothers' leadership and persistence. These mothers are true lionesses because many face insurmountable difficulties yet they persist on, leading their children with purpose.

Such mothers testify to the fact that they depended on God for wisdom, and so the Biblical proverb: "*In all your ways acknowledge him (God) and he will make straight your paths.*" They acknowledge the fact that parenting is a God-given responsibility and so look up to him for wisdom and strength. God in turn honors the labor of their hands, removes obstacles from their pathway or gives them power to overcome them, and finally brings them to his appointed goal for each of their children.

Purposeful parenting determines the direction family leadership desires to take and identifies the gifting in each child that needs to be fanned into a flame. Purposeful parenting uses words, examples and stories to paint the destination and then ingrains action and motivation into the training. Purposeful parenting involves supervision. Mention of the word supervision may make some parents straight away think: "O Yes! I supervise my child's homework." Good! This is one part of supervision. However, there is more to purpose than academic success.

Purposeful parenting begins with a plan in mind, and then, translates that plan into a process. For example, a parent may determine that the children will learn to take care of themselves so that they can begin to live independently as they grow older.

Too many of our children may be academic giants but dwarfs in cleaning their environments, cooking and managing their own hygiene and laundry. For some of them, even making their beds is a challenge. Etiquette, time management, good manners, table and dining rules are foreign to many.

Once, a young woman visited us and watched me set the table for a meal. She observed me in silence and innocently asked: "You mean that you guys eat at a dining table? Do you set it like this for each meal?" She owned up that she could not remember her family ever sitting together at mealtime. She continued: "The food is placed on the table, and you just serve yourself and eat it anywhere you please: watching TV, in your bedroom or wherever. Please teach me how to set the table." I did so gladly.

Purpose in Parenting and Training for Independence

By crawling a child learns to stand.
~ African Proverb

Discipline your son, for in that there is hope; do not be a willing party to his death.
~ Proverbs 19:18

The African proverb: *"By crawling a child learns to stand,"* indicates that growing up has to happen and that no child should be spared its pains or be neglected such that they lose the capacity to develop normally from stage to stage. Training a child to live independently and imparting skills with patience and persistence sets the young one on the path of healthy maturation. Someone has said that the problem with life is that it is so *daily*, so is parenting. If parents were to imagine that they are needed year after year until a tiny, newborn baby becomes a responsible adult, many would *freak* out of the challenge. However, there is joy in parenting and one can say that determination and focus contribute to that delight.

The Biblical proverb: "*Discipline your son, for in that there is hope; do not be a willing party to his death,*" reminds us that keeping on the course of engaged parenting creates hope for the child but neglect can lead to disaster. Death here would refer to unrealized goals or destruction brought about by loss of direction or falling into destructive behavior. Purposeful parents determine the skills they want to pass on to their children and then slowly, and with resolve, train the young ones in that direction.

My mother, as mentioned earlier, was determined to train us to live independently. She often quipped: "If you fail using the pen, do not fail using the *panga*. How do I know which one you will end up with?" The *panga* is a tool used in the garden for weeding and slashing. This statement meant that she expected us to learn how to do household chores and work in the garden, make good grades in school and still take active part in church and family activities. There was to be no shirking of any responsibility.

She did not teach us to set the table because we had no table to set. All we had as a table was a small, rickety affair that we used to study and read on. An oil lantern would stand at the center as the dim, flickering light had to be shared by all. If you needed to make your bed at night, all you had to your use was the lantern, which was christened *nishikie nitandike*, meaning "hold it for me as I make my bed" in Kiswahili.

This makeshift lantern was a rusty, small metal tin with a tight cover. You'd make a hole in the middle and insert a long piece of rag, then fill up the tin with kerosene or paraffin as we called it. Lighted, the smoky flame provided light, but since it was open, any breeze or sudden wind would blow it off. This is why someone needed to hold it high, away from the beddings, while another person made the bed. So, there was no table to set in our home, but our mother taught us how to manage each assignment over and beyond academics.

In our home, the day began the evening before. My mother taught us to manage the day, beginning in the evening after school and projecting to early the following morning. After school, there was no dilly-dallying on the way home. Yes, you could join as many after-school activities as you wanted but after it was over, you went home and got there before sunset because there was a long agenda you had to complete while it was still light. Evening chores were assigned with clarity, and included bringing water from the river, splitting firewood and helping with cooking. The smaller children would have the duty of shutting in the chickens and locking the door of the pigsty. She was present to do these duties with us and supervised us as well. Afterwards, we would wash up, eat dinner and then retire to the table room to do homework. The only activity that my mother could not supervise was school assignments. Since she could not read and write, she trusted us to do our work and do it well. However, all the other duties were supervised as she worked along us, encouraging and urging us on.

She may have been illiterate, but she checked our books for completed and assessed homework and class tests. My sister Mary, four years older than I, recently reminded me how mother would ask for our books and check how we performed on class tests. For example, Math teachers often gave surprise quizzes that they called Mental Work. Mother knew how to monitor such tests in the Math exercise books, and to tell our performance, she only needed to count the red tick marks and compare with the number of crosses.

Woe to anyone who consistently brought home more crosses than ticks! Out would come the rod, a carefully cured branch that was stringy like a whip. "Were you sleeping in class? Didn't you have enough to eat? Are you sure you've memorized your multiplication tables?" Those were the days when Mental Work demanded you know your 12x12 multiplication tables off-head, and you subtract and add in your head! After homework, my mother would distribute duties for the following day.

My earliest memory is that of the voice of my mother praying early in the morning. It was normal for her to call upon God to partner with us and bless all our activities for the day. Our main house was a square structure with a corrugated iron roof and mud walls polished bright with a mixture of cow dung and ash, and repaired every school holiday by all of us mixing the ingredients and plastering away. The house was divided into four rooms: the parents' bedroom, the boy's room, the girls' room and the table room. Four boys and four girls occupied each room, two to a bed.

Since we had no ceiling, I heard my mother wake up to pray each day at 5a.m. She prayed for everyone by name, even for sick cows and lost cats as well as sick neighbors. After one hour and mentioning us all by name, she would call each of us by name to sit and pray with her. "Gladys, sit up. Susan, wake up. Silas, are you still asleep? Sit up." Discipline and obedience carried itself even in prayer because we knew that you did not talk to God while lying down or covering up your head with a blanket. "God is more important than your school headmaster. Do you talk to him while seated?" Those were the days when you stood ramrod straight when talking to anyone in authority, man or woman. "So, sit up to talk to God or kneel by your bed."

After prayer, the next task was to complete our assigned tasks before preparing for school, eating breakfast, walking four miles and making it in time to ring the school bell at 7.30 a.m. Bell ringers were usually in class six, and because we were known to keep time, my siblings and I passed the bell-ringing task from one to the other. It was usually known that when one of us graduated to class six, we would take over the responsibility. None of us died from waking up early to fetch water from the river down the valley and filling up the storage, or picking coffee, pruning or weeding the coffee trees, and feeding the pigs. And rarely was work left undone or incomplete. I remember once, when I was still very young and tiny for my age, and it was my duty to lock up the pigsty in the evening. The huge mother pig had 10 piglets and those little things were downright sneaky, squeaky, mischievous and playfully evil. They did not like getting locked up and once in their pen, they would creatively make small holes in the fenced wall through which they would wriggle out into dark night.

On that day, in the gathering dusk, a few of them disappeared into the bean garden. I was mad, but I knew that I had to trace each sneaking piglet, otherwise I could not retire for the night. My big brother finally came to my aid, and after getting scratched by the thorny fence many times and scrambling in the dark with the aid of the oil lantern, all the piglets were finally safely locked away. That evening, I learnt the tenacity of staying on the job until it was done even if it meant slipping several times on the wet floor of the sty. Whoever has kept pigs knows how stinky that slough can be!

Purpose in Parenting and the Gift of Trust

Nobody is born wise.
~ African Proverb

Wisdom will save you from the ways of wicked men, from men whose words are perverse.
~ Proverbs 2:12

The African proverb: "*Nobody is born wise,*" reminds that parents should not be quick to judge their children negatively because learning is a continuum. Along the path of maturation many of us do foolish things, sometimes out of rebellion where we know better and choose to dissent, or where we are acting totally out of ignorance. Parents face the challenge of training children and then setting them free trusting that they will remember to do as they have been taught.

Nobody becomes perfect instantly. We learn through failure but when we falter, we get up and keep learning. This reality should humble us as parents from judging our children too harshly when they falter. Harsh judgment can discourage or communicate mistrust. It is true that releasing children to start managing their own lives using the skills we have taught them can be scary, but slowly release them we must, because if we do not, they will not learn.

The Biblical proverb: "*Wisdom will save you from the ways of wicked men, from men whose words are perverse,*" underscores that purposeful parenting imparts wisdom so much needed by our children in making life choices. When we set young ones free more and more to make their own decisions, they mature and build skills for making wise choices. Success in decision-making increases the courage to walk in paths yet untrodden and to try new experiences yet untried, and still do all that with internalized wisdom. Such understanding increases the ability to negate destructive peer influences from "*wicked men, from men whose words are perverse.*"

As we grew older, my mother would ask us to organize our duties. The control however remained. She set limits on when you came home and warned you to be responsible. I remember, however, that one of the greatest gifts my mother gave me in her training was the gift of trust. She never grilled me like some mothers did, asking: "Where did you go? Who was with you? Who was the boy? I know…you girls run wild when your mothers are not looking! Are you lying to me again, young lady? You said you were going to Nell's but I know you were with that good-for nothing boy whose father drinks all the traditional beer in the village! I know how you girls can lie with your eyes wide open!" Such prophecy ends up being self-fulfilling and produces what the parent fears most.

Children brought up with no autonomy cannot learn to control their time and activities. So, it is necessary to ask children's help to create a roster that includes all in various duties according to their age and ability. Even three year-olds can set the table and put away their shoes. However, at whatever age, children's work needs to be supervised and output rewarded. Purpose is all about planning and following through on the process. Process presupposes communication and discipline. Purposeful mothers make it clear to the children where the young ones are headed and then use encouragement, urging, reminding and when necessary the rod of discipline to keep children on track.

As the young ones grow older discipline changes into instruction, discussion and guiding with respect. It does not make sense ever to physically discipline adolescents or young adults if the growing up years have been spent right and a relationship of mutual respect established. Sometimes as parents, we forget that we are the mature ones, the wise ones. Trust is not total release of a child to do and live as they please. It involves clearly communicating expectations, agreeing on boundaries, and expecting the child to adhere to the same. This adherence creates trust.

For example, an adolescent girl may ask: "Mum, can I go out with my friends?" Mother: "Where are you going and with who?" Girl: "We're just taking a walk in the market with my friend Mary. Then, we will visit Rehema." Mother: "It's now 2 pm and you know you are not allowed to be out after dark. What time will you be back?" Girl: "I'll be back by 6pm, I promise." Mother: "Alright. Enjoy yourself and see you later."

If this young woman comes home by 6pm as promised, trust will be multiplied. If the young one does not come home as promised, then the mother firmly seats the young one down and objectively, without anger and name-calling, asks for an explanation. Once again, she communicates expectations clearly. This firmness creates respect and reminds the youth to be more responsible next time.

Case Study on Parenting with Purpose

Justice Martha Koome, a Justice of Kenya's High Court, shares her story on her experience of parenting that was purposeful and determined. I asked her how her parents shaped her life. She responded that her mother trained her through discipline and sheer hard work, with an emphasis that "nothing comes easy, not even food!"

Justice Koome adds: "From the earliest I could remember, maybe from age three or four, I had to work hard, from fueling or keeping the fire going as food cooked to fetching water with a small container. I graduated from these smaller duties to eventually taking up more roles. My mother was the sole breadwinner, without regular income except from produce from her peasant farming. I learnt that I had a responsibility to support her in everything she did, be it in the garden or at home."

Justice Koome explains that her mother taught her that "education will change your life from being a perpetual peasant to financial independence." She kept reminding her that education cannot rot, using the Kimeru words *kithomo gitioraga*. Surrounded by many unemployed people, Justice Koome's mother told her children never to give up or get discouraged since their destinies were different and special.

Justice Koome adds that her mother modeled values that would shape the little, hard working girl into a Justice of Kenya's High Court and a woman of great humility in spite of her many achievements. "My mother did not pretend to be what she was not. All she owned and whatever she did was open to all of us. This is the greatest thing l learnt from my mother and I have tried to pass to my children, that whatever they can see on my face is also what I have in my heart."

This transparency was firmly rooted in a life of disciplined Christian faith: "My mother taught me to pray all the time and to present all my needs to God. She led us in prayer and she always made passionate petitions, citing our individual names and needs before the Almighty."

Justice Koome adds that lessons in industry and productivity began very early: "My mother taught and modeled lessons in time and self-management, on forming good habits and routine, beginning with creating time for prayer, cleanliness, work and more work." Justice Koome concludes that learning was reinforced through stringent discipline: "My mother always scolded and disciplined us whenever we failed in our chores or committed other misdemeanors. The biggest punishment was to be denied supper and one had to sleep hungry!"

I am sure that many readers looking at Justice Koome's final statement would say, "Ouch! How can a parent allow a child to sleep hungry?" Somehow, however, this mother's determination as a single parent paid dividends.

The little three-year old child, who carried water from the river in a little container, collected firewood and tended the fire, learned skills that Kenya enjoys today as she continues to serve the nation from the lofty position of Justice, a title that she holds with poise, dignity and great humility.

CHAPTER 2

PARENTING AS PARTNERSHIP

A child is a child of everyone.
~ African (Sudanese) Proverb

Whoever loves discipline loves knowledge, but he who hates correction is stupid.
~ Proverbs 12:1

The Sudanese proverb: *"A child is a child of everyone,"* is a simple yet profound saying that reminds us that the business of raising the next generation is a collective responsibility. Indeed, Africans believe that a pregnant woman is carrying "our baby" because progeny is our business. This is because our people will be annihilated if we do not give birth and if we do not take care of the ones we birth. This essentially is the meaning of the proverb that a child belongs to all of us because new life assures us that as a people, we shall survive and not die off.

The Biblical proverb: *"Whoever loves discipline loves knowledge, but he who hates correction is stupid,"* once again underlines the fact that discipline and knowledge are related, and the best way to learn is through a multiplication of good teachers, committed trainers, loving parents, and wise mentors. The Bible consistently reminds that we are blessed if we do not *walk in the counsel of the wicked* (Psalm 1:1), and if we heed correction, we are described as prudent and wise.

In the last chapter, we discussed the topic "Purpose in Parenting", emphasizing that we should start the process of parenting with the end in view. What is the goal and destination for which we trust God on behalf of each child and depending on their specific gifting and personality? What is the desired outcome? What qualities do we as parents hope to ingrain in the child? What kind of guidance and input is needed for this to happen?

Africans cite and underline the saying that: *"It takes a village to raise a child."* A village in this case refers to a collection of personalities whose involvement is critical in the balanced upbringing of every child. Boys to men and girls to women do not just happen. It takes a *Harambee* process, a united action to ensure holistic maturation of each child. In this regard, we can conclude that males are born but men are made. Similarly, females are born but women are made. Where this critical aspect of partnership in parenting is missing, we end up with adult boys and males running the affairs of the world as well as grown up girls and females trying to deliver what only women can. Both genders fail horribly because boys and girls in adult bodies can only be males and females, never men and women.

What do I mean by adult boys and males, and grown up girls and females? One can measure an individual's maturity by the kind of fruit produced by their behavior: sense of responsibility, life goals, level of self-discipline, patience, maturity, commitment, values and ethics, and so on. The number of bank accounts one has or the size or model of car they drive can never be a measure for maturity, nor can the clothes we wear or the crowd we command. Not even the level of education can determine the level of maturity. The reality is that only those who have attained the level of true being with maturity can be described as men and women and can, in turn, produce other men and women out of their growing children.

Let me emphasize that none of us will ever be a perfect man or woman, meaning that none of us will ever attain the maturity to parent a child on their own. We are all in the process of becoming and so we need to live with discipline and constant self-examination. Meanwhile, we do not stop parenting, but do so with the humility that seeks partnership to compliment our efforts to bring up responsible children.

The Meaning of Partnership

Two ants do not fail to pull one grasshopper.
~ African (Tanzanian) Proverb

The way of a fool seems right to him, but a wise man listens to advice.
~ Proverbs 12:15

The Tanzanian proverb: "*Two ants do not fail to pull one grasshopper,*" means that one ant, much smaller than a grasshopper, attempting to capture the larger insect for food will have difficulty, but two ants working together can pull the grasshopper to the desired location and a meal will be assured. The basic moral of this proverb is that Africans believe that working together in as many activities as possible, people accomplish more. Similarly, parenting demands partnership. African parents are not supposed to ignore or take their primary role for granted, but they should also seek other adults around them who can reinforce the principles of growing up that they communicate to the children.

The Biblical proverb: "*The way of a fool seems right to him, but a wise man listens to advice,*" reminds us that wise people become wiser by listening to others. Fools however think they know everything and they do not pay attention to what others say or seek to check their way of life or behaviors against the opinion of others. Listening to others is not a weakness unless the listener is so weak that they sway this way or that following other people's opinions. Listening with wisdom IS wisdom, and partnership is choosing to walk with others in wisdom.

The word "partner" is defined as a person who takes part or engages in some activity in common with another, or an associate, one who plays on the same side. A partner can also mean a support or mast or other upright structure that strengthens another. In this regard, partnership in parenting refers to a deliberate decision by parents to include close relatives, friends, teachers, pastors, neighbors and so on in the training and mentoring of their children. This inclusion does not mean abdication of parental responsibility but it involves creating a wall of love and protection around the child.

The first partner in parenting is, of necessity, the child's maker or creator. The book of Judges tells a story of the birth of Samson, born during a period of depravity in Israel's history. The Philistines had taken Israel captive and God purposed to deliver them from the hands of their oppressors. For this reason, a child, who would become God's instrument of deliverance, was promised to a couple, Manoah and his wife. The man desired to obey God in bringing up the child, and so he prayed to God: "O Lord, I beg you, let the man of God sent to us come again and teach us how to bring up the boy who is to be born," (Judges 13:8). Manoah realized the giver of this child of purpose had a prescription for his bringing up.

Just like Samson, every child has a God-given purpose as to why he was created and sent into the world. This is why, according to psychologist Victor Frankl, humanity's search for meaning is a preoccupation for anyone who dare seek to ask the three existential questions: "Who am I? What am I doing in the world? Where am I going?"

True answers to these questions can only come from the Creator who sees the beginning and ending of every individual. God only can help the individual towards the search for these answers. For this reason, the first partner in parenting should be the Creator. I am convinced that as soon as a parent knows that a child is on the way, their prayer, like that of Manoah, should be: "Help me, Holy God, to seek your wisdom in parenting this child."

Identifying Partners in Parenting

If you want to travel quickly, travel alone. If you want to go far, travel together with others.
~ African Proverb

A simple man believes anything, but a prudent man gives thought to his steps.
~ Proverbs 14:15

The African proverb: "*If you want to travel quickly, travel alone. If you want to go far, travel together with others,*" reminds us that some people may find partnership with others burdensome. "Why should I wait for others to go with me when I know that their opinions will slow me down? It is better to make decisions alone and move on." The proverb agrees that indeed, one can walk faster alone, but eventually, exhaustion takes over. Whereas in the company of others, there will be mutual encouragement, even help in carrying heavy loads when the burden becomes unbearable.

Someone has said that *it takes a flock to fly*. Scientists have noted that flying in hazardous flights, the northern bald ibises fly in a V-formation and take turns to lead the flock. The lead bird faces the greatest wind resistance and when tired, drops back and another one takes the lead position. Without this partnership, one bird, flying alone, would never make the long, dangerous journey.

Using the Biblical proverb: "*A simple man believes anything, but a prudent man gives thought to his steps,*" in this discussion on partnership in parenting reminds us that the assumption that parenting is easy and no one should tell me what to do smacks of simplicity or naivety and foolishness. One may ask: "What's so difficult about becoming a father? You just get children and they grow up! What's so complicated about that?"

Mothers may also say: "In this day and age, who needs anyone to tell them what to do? What don't I know? Then, if I don't know something, there's Google! Check up parenting tips on the Internet and mind my own business. I don't need *anyone* breathing down my neck telling me how to bring up my child!" However, a prudent, careful, cautious, sensible, far-sighted and wise person will think twice before dismissing the need for the wisdom of others in childrearing. Africans believe that "*One finger cannot kill a louse*!"

Who are our partners in parenting? The days of automatic partnership in parenting are fast disappearing. In the days when our African communities were more intact with less mobility and possessing rich values of family and community, an adult man the age of my father was also my adopted dad. Likewise, I respected and listened to adult women who were the age of my mother. Away from home and community to the classroom, the teachers took it upon themselves to discipline the child, as did the pastor at church and village elder in the market or by the way side.

In those days, parenting and training of parents were accomplished through teaching, modeling and shaping of behavior, the older to the younger. There was also goodwill since the village shared the joy of making sure that children were raised up well. These systems were strengthened by leadership systems at family and community level. Today, things are not that automatic.

Parenting with the end in view assumes that parents are deliberate in order to create the kind of support their children need to mature. This approach can be referred to as intentional creation of a parenting community. The tragedy is that some parents who are convinced they know better count it as interference when someone else tries to guide their child. In this regard, today, adults are wary to correct and guide other people's children. Indeed, some parents have been known to tell off anyone, including teachers, who dares to discipline their young ones.

Similarly, in days past, older people used to be careful how they walked and behaved, fully aware that children would be watching and seeking stable and accountable role models. In a fast changing society, partnerships in parenting can no longer be taken as an automatic process. Each parent must deliberately determine which adult they should involve in complementing the training of their child. After identifying such adults, the next step is to become proactive in making sure that the partnership happens.

Practical Application of Partnership in Parenting

Knowledge without wisdom is like water in the sand.
~ African (Guinean) Proverb

Wisdom is more precious than rubies, and nothing you desire can compare with her.
~ Proverbs 8:11

The African proverb: "*Knowledge without wisdom is like water in the sand,*" emphasizes the difference between knowledge and wisdom. Africans believe that knowledge can be learned through teaching of facts and internalizing the same. However, if that knowledge is not used with understanding, intelligence, perception, maturity and good judgment, it becomes foolishness. Water does not seep into the sand. It runs off and leaves the sand dry. Many learned people live foolishly and many individuals without school learning live their lives with wisdom and diligence.

The Biblical proverb: "*Wisdom is more precious than rubies, and nothing you desire can compare with her,*" reminds us that to have good judgment and acumen is more precious than great riches. The gains of wise parenting are so valuable that they should be sought above all else so that nothing should be spared to bring up children who can make prudent decisions and order their steps with care. Parenting with partnership is wisdom.

How can this partnership be possible in our busy world? Who should be my partners in parenting my children? Where will the wisdom to shape and model our children come from? What qualities should we seek to help ingrain values and underline integrity in our children? How do we select a helping environment wherein to socialize and shape their behavior in positive ways?

Parenting begins in pregnancy where every parent has the responsibility of creating the right environment for the expected child. This environment should be holistic, involving the mother's physical health, emotional wellbeing and spiritual fortitude. For example, the food the mother eats while pregnant makes for purposeful parenting. Research indicates that, besides ensuring the physical health of the unborn child, mother's diet influences the cognitive and intellectual development of the fetus.

Other studies indicate that stress and emotional upheavals around a pregnant woman impact the affective or emotional status of the unborn child. Similarly, a peaceful serene environment makes for the fetus' emotional wellness. This being the case, partnerships that enhance peace in pregnancy will improve the holistic development of the child. Besides the general environment, cooperation and love between mother and father create a warm, supportive home for the child.

In our society with a growing number of single parents, we encourage that the parent seeks the close presence of a relative or other-gender mentors, someone of good character and solid values, the kind who may be found leading a church small group such as a Bible Study. These caring adults can provide gender balance around the growing child. Deliberate action may be necessary to create this enriched input in single-parent homes. Indeed, experience indicates that children who receive this enrichment end up better prepared for life and living.

Besides the needs of the body and mind discussed above, parents also need to cooperate with spiritual mentors in child rearing so that the young ones become acquainted with God at an early age. Erroneously, some parents argue that they do not have to introduce their child to faith at all, that the young one will make their own choice along the way as they mature. "They'll choose their own faith when they are older," the parent states. I choose to differ.

Holistic child development requires a balance between physical, mental, relational, spiritual, academic and social development. We do not leave the healthy feeding of our children to chance, allowing them to eat what they want to and when they want to. Responsible parents take charge of the diet of their children. Similarly, we do not leave little ones free to choose to go to school or stay at home if they want to. We reinforce mandatory schooling, stipulated in the law of the land. We go to the extent of guiding the children's socialization, mandating that our young ones do not hang out with the wrong crowd. So, we dictate their diet, education and also shape their social connections. Children of responsible parents grow within ever-widening but present limits.

Partnering with God in Parenting

He who learns, teaches.
~ African (Ethiopian) Proverb

For these commands are a lamp, this teaching is a light, and the corrections of discipline are the way of life.
~ Proverbs 6:23

The African proverb: *"He who learns, teaches,"* reminds us that teachers first must be learners. A learning posture earns one the privilege to teach, for teaching others is not a right. Africans assume that children will learn anyway and the failure of parents to teach and train them does not suggest that someone else will not teach them. A common Kiswahili saying states *"Asiyefunzwa na mama hufunzwa na ulimwengu."* This means that whoever is not taught by his mother will be taught by the world. There is no lack of teachers and trainers when parents fail to nurture their children as well as shape their behavior. Indeed, in our current society, parents compete for the attention of their children, and training them demands that the parent understands the challenges they face by learning about their world.

The Biblical proverb: "*For these commands are a lamp, this teaching is a light, and the corrections of discipline are the way of life*," reminds us that the equipping of parents begins with obeying God's command. Obedience to his instructions is like having light shed on our way so that parenting does not become groping in the darkness, but there is instead a sense of direction. Just as God corrects us and disciplines us as his children, we also teach our young ones with the same commitment. This seriousness, intent, faith and spirituality mean that we rear our children to recognize, obey and worship God. This teaching and training cannot be left to chance.

Just as parents carefully choose the school the child should attend, so should they choose the faith within which to bring up the child and then go ahead to model the same life. Young children like the joke: "Monkey see, monkey do," which ceases to be jest when we realize that children "hear" more what adults do than what they say. This means that every parent has the responsibility to model a life of faith to their children as well as choose spiritual mentors and a spiritual community with which to seek parenting partnership for these children. Parents need to show the way to obey God by living according to the same tenets of faith.

A child who honors God will learn to honor the parent, and the parent who honors God will receive the wisdom to guide the child to holistic maturation. A story is told of a young boy who was taken by his mother and father to buy his very first Bible. As they walked into the bookshop, the child looked up at his mother and said: "Mom, can I have a Bible just like yours? That's the one I want." His dad laughed and asked: "Why do you want a Bible like your mother's? Why can't you have one like mine?" Quipped the youngster: "Because Mom's Bible is more interesting. You see, I see her reading hers all the time. You hardly touch yours!"

Identifying Adult Role Models

A pretty face and fine clothes do not make character.
~ African (Congolese) Proverb

He who thinks he is leading and has no one following him is only taking a walk.
~ African (Malawian) Proverb

The integrity of the upright guides them, but the crookedness of the treacherous destroys them.
~ Proverbs 11:3

The African proverb: "*A pretty face and fine clothes do not make character,*" reminds us that true character must originate from within and people should not be esteemed by what they show on the outside. Looks can deceive, but true moral fiber begins from the motives of the heart, perceptions of the mind and values that build character. In identifying role models, the warning is that external looks should never be used to determine the quality of role models.

Another mark to determine the worth of role models is that each of us needs to be truthful in our self-evaluation. The proof of leading is in the quality of the following. Genuine leaders will command genuine following, and so the African proverb: "*He who thinks he is leading and has no one following him is only taking a walk."* People are able to tell the fake from the real, and do not follow anyone blindly except if they are blind themselves or have selfish reasons to follow an impostor.

This African warning on the kind of role models that parents should seek out for their children is underlined by the Biblical proverb: *"The integrity of the upright guides them, but the crookedness of the treacherous destroys them."* Eventually, truthfulness, veracity and reliability of upright people becomes a blessing to themselves and to those who follow them while dishonest, corrupt and fraudulent people and those who follow them are destroyed by the very deceitful lives they have chosen to live.

With these wisdoms in mind, parents should seek out adults who not only model a life of active faith but also help mentor the child to live a godly life. Often, while speaking to parents' meetings, I ask a question that many find difficult to answer. "For the men here today who already have sons, carefully think of five men, yourself included; five men you would like to point out to your son as role models. Imagine telling your young man: 'Son, as you mature, I want you to walk close to these five men. Watch how they walk. Note their values, their morality, their sense of discipline and their integrity. Copy their manners. Check out their honesty and truthfulness, my son. You will make me a proud father if you become just like these men.'" I now ask the men to raise their hands if they can find five such men, with themselves as part of the five. Many end up with two. Others sadly shake their heads and say: "I can't find any!"

I repeat the same model search with mothers. "Think of five women, with yourself as one of them. Five women you would like to point out to your daughter to model her life after. Imagine telling your daughter: 'As you mature, my beloved one, I want you to walk close to these women. Watch how they walk. Note their values, their morality, their sense of discipline and their integrity. Copy their manners. Check out their honesty and truthfulness, my daughter. You will make me a proud mother if you become just like these women.'"

At the end of this exercise, we all with tears in our eyes wonder: "Where have all the heroes gone? Where have all the heroines gone?" As we read our newspapers and watch the paparazzi, each would-be hero and heroine comes crashing to the ground like Humpty Dumpty who sat on a wall, had a great fall – and no one could put together again. The great question for us as parents is: "With whom are we partnering in parenting our children?" Heroes and heroines still abide. The challenge is for parents to partner with God and live in such a way that we can become men and women that our children can model their lives after.

We also seek after God as the first partner in our parenting and then look for other true heroes and heroines in the right places, people who can serve as role models for our children. Raised in such a community, our children will find the stability to blossom into the best people they were created to become.

Individuals who can become role models for our children will rarely be on the front page of newspapers or in the flashy magazines of our day. They may never feature before television cameras or appear on the latest list of "Who is who". The craving of society is always fed by stories of transient personalities who seem to have it all together but often rise up, fall and eventually wither to nothingness before our very eyes. Such people capture our attention and that of our children, and their posters may be hanging on the walls of our children's bedrooms. That they may be druggies or alcoholics, adulterers or fornicators is never ever mentioned, and when they fall and exit the stage of glamour and fame, hardly anyone remembers them because others rise and take their place.

For modeling and shaping the character of our children, we need role models who persist over time and have the being-ness of plan and purpose. We need adults who have identity and a purpose, having the conviction of who they are, whose they are, and where they are going.

We seek for men and women who are humble enough to need the Creator God as a partner in their lives. We need people who are not too big for their ego. These will be solid parenting partners a father can point out to his son and say: "Son, follow closely after that man as you follow after me. I too will not lead you astray because I seek to follow after Christ." And, the mother will say: "My daughter, if I am too busy for you, if there is anything you cannot tell me, and in case I pass on before you, you can safely walk by the side of this woman. She will not lead you astray." Such are parenting partnerships.

Case Study on Partnership in Parenting

Sharing her story in the book *Life Journeys, Seeking Destiny* (Footprints Press, 2010), Eva Muraya, entrepreneur and marketer, tells how her mother and grandmother partnered in her upbringing. Eva explains that her parents divorced when she was five years old and an only child. With her father's absence and the fact that her mother had to work, care of the young child fell into the hands of both her mother and her grandmother.

Eva remembers growing up under the watchful eye of her grandmother. Under the older woman's care and supervision, this successful woman reveals that by 11 years of age, she was already comfortable doing various domestic chores that included taking care of younger children in her extended family as well as "tilling the land, harvesting crops and preparing meals." This is the setting where a stringent work ethic was instilled in her. As if writing her memoir on her grandmother, Eva remembers her as a woman who modeled and taught the young maturing woman "virtues of love and hard work, integrity and an irrepressible sense of humor. She showed me how to maintain my dignity."

Ms. Muraya went on to boarding school and did not see her mother as much as she wanted to. However, the older woman, whom she describes as beautiful, with a wonderful temperament and great resilience, made sure that at every school play or performance that her daughter featured in, she would be sitting at the front pew, cheering and encouraging, to the point of giving a standing ovation even when young Eva "forgot her lines." She continues to admire her mother, a woman who led a tough life but "never lost the zeal for life. From her, I learned to rise no matter how hard the fall."

Between a resilient mother and a committed grandma, Eva Muraya rose to become a woman who is leaving footprints for others to follow, a renowned entrepreneur and marketer. One can suppose that lessons in resilience learnt from her mother made Eva survive her husband's passing away in a tragic road accident. Lessons in hard work and enterprise from her grandmother must have catalyzed Ms. Muraya's founding of Color Creations, a brand that is creating waves in Kenya and beyond.

CHAPTER 3

PRAYER IN PARENTING

DEFINITION OF PRAYER

A house that is built by God will be completed.
~ African (Ethiopian) Proverb

Many are the plans in a man's heart, but it is the Lord's purpose that prevails.
~ Proverbs 19:21

The African proverb: "A *house that is built by God will be completed,*" reminds us that God is a builder not of houses but of lives, and that he completes what he is allowed to build. We say allowed to build because he does not build lives alone but in partnership with parents. From conception, God is in partnership because he is the giver of life and nurtures the same if the parents do their part. When a child is born, parents or caregivers need to continue that partnership, and God is ready to do his part as parents do theirs.

The Biblical proverb: *"Many are the plans in a man's heart, but it is the Lord's purpose that prevails,"* reminds us that as much as a parent may have plans, wishes and desires for their child, God's plan for each of his children are above human dreams. The reason is that he alone can see ahead into the life of our children and he alone has the purpose for their creation. The parent is in the life of the child for just a few years but beyond that, the young adult takes over control of their personal life. With the myriad dangers in our world, partnership with the all-knowing, all-protecting, all-covering God is the only safe way to bring up children so as to ensure that his presence covers them through life.

Prayer is defined as communion with God or an earnest request addressed to Him. Prayer begins with acknowledgment that there is someone bigger, wiser, more knowledgeable and far more powerful than us human beings, someone who is willing to listen and to get engaged with us. We have already looked at parenting as an enterprise that should have a purpose, beginning with the end in view. We have also discussed the fact that no single individual is perfect, and so the need to create partnership in parenting by bringing in other individuals so as to create fertile ground around the maturing child. Now, we emphasize the need to involve the child's maker, the Almighty God, in parenting. This should be done proactively and with determination.

No one knows the pain of prayer more than a parent whose child is going astray. I have often sat down with many a parent who is saying: "Dr. Mwiti, I have done everything but nothing is working. She keeps running away from home and many days go by before I know where she is. She won't tell anyone where she has gone and never says where she has been when she finally shows up! What am I to do? She's driving us crazy!" A mother says: "It's my son. He is an alcoholic. He can't stop drinking. Sometimes he stops, then, he is at it again. We don't know how to help him."

Another one bemoans: "My daughter is failing in her education. She keeps promising to do better, but all in vain. If she keeps on this way, she'll not graduate. What am I to do?" A father is confused. "My young son is keeping bad company. We don't allow them to use the Internet at home. But I just learnt that he's been watching pornography with the neighbor's son and his friends every weekend. What are we to do?"

The list of parents' woes is endless. How do they respond to the challenges of parenting? Some will tighten rules at home in a bid to control their children. Others will blame one another. An angry father may beat up his child to try and "knock some sense into him." A mother may lock her son out of the house, or just withdraw into a guilt trip of self-blame: "It's me. I must have failed somewhere! Where did I mess up?"

Manoah – A Parent in Prayer

A wise man never knows all, only fools know everything.
~ *African Proverb*

Buy the truth and do not sell it; get wisdom, discipline and understanding.
~ *Proverbs 23:23*

The African proverb: "*A wise man never knows all, only fools know everything,*" is a moral that reminds us that maintaining a learning posture indicates maturity and wisdom. This means that investing and devoting our energy in gaining wisdom in parenting is a worthy pursuit. Where does our focus and commitment lie? In acquiring and using riches or in learning and using wisdom so that wealth, if God chooses to give it, can be used right?

The Biblical proverb: "*Buy the truth and do not sell it; get wisdom, discipline and understanding,*" teaches the same moral that wisdom is precious and supreme above all things, and should not be sacrificed for anything. The merchant in Matthew 13: 45-46 sold everything to buy a pearl of great value. Although Jesus was talking about the kingdom of heaven, we can apply the same analogy here that parents should not spare anything when it comes to seeking and learning how to partner with God in parenting. In essence, the effort will ensure that their children are part of God's kingdom whose benefits persist even after parents depart.

Manoah was such a man. He chose to partner with God by praying for guidance long before the birth of his son. No parent should wait for his child to go astray and then begin to pray. Similarly, there is no guarantee that every child prayed for, will automatically succeed in everything in life. Prayer simply invokes God's presence in the task of parenting. It indicates the parent's willingness to partner with the Almighty in the onerous process of bringing up another human being.

The reality is that every child is brought up in a society that is full of good opportunities as well as difficult challenges. Many parents worry about what good positive parenting will accomplish when schools, neighborhoods and other homes are alive with bad influences. "What's the use of training my child when such few parents take time to train their children? My good work will be undone as soon as my child sets foot outside my door! What's the use of even trying?"

The suggestions in this book are meant to help parents build a strong foundation right at home, a basis against which their child can evaluate other exposure to the contrary. Dr. James Dobson, a clinical psychologist and encourager of positive parenting urges parents to do their best in ingraining right values in their children and to leave the outcomes of their effort to the Creator.

Parenting is very much like planting the seed: we do our best in planting, weeding and watering the seed, and then leave the outcome to the Creator. Prayer then is a deliberate invitation of God in thanksgiving for the privilege of parenting, submission to His guidance in the journey of bringing up the child, request for wisdom to set a clear path for the young one, and patience and persistence in the task that never ends whatever age the child may be.

Learning expands great souls.
~ African (Namibian) Proverb

**The father of a righteous man has great joy;
he who has a wise son delights in him.**
~ Proverbs 23:24

The African proverb: "*Learning expands great souls,*" teaches the moral that heroic, noble people become better if they are not too proud to keep learning. Some of the world's most famous people are humble and ask questions about things they do not know. They are forever in a learning mode, and that spirit of searching for truth and incorporating the same into their lives expands their hearts, and they become wiser with time. On the other hand, fools assume that the little they know is all that is needed and they plough their way through life leaving tragedies in their path. God is the greatest teacher and learning from him forms the greatest knowledge of all.

The Biblical proverb: "*The father of a righteous man has great joy; he who has a wise son delights in him,*" reminds us of the joy of a parent who lives to see the outcome of imparting the truth he knows to his children. The joy is many times that of a proud farmer who stands looking over his healthy crop heavily laden with fruit; the evidence of committed breaking ground, planting, weeding and protection from pests of all kinds. Such is the joy of a father who watches his adult son become a righteous, responsible, wise man. The father's heart is full of thanksgiving to God for the gracious gift of a son, a son who has become a mature, dependable man.

The gift of children is the fulfillment of adults, and so, it is difficult to imagine the longing of a childless woman.

Jane, not her real name, got married at a beautiful wedding. She and her husband Tom planned to start a family immediately, but the first year went by and no child was forthcoming. They did not worry, but kept waiting patiently. When the second year ended with no conception, there was fear, with questions: "What is the matter?" By the third year, their friends started asking: "Are you going to keep us waiting for ever?" The assumption was that the couple was planning to start a family later. Their families too began asking difficult questions: "Is there something wrong with the young woman you brought to us?" questioned Tom's family. Tensions entered the loving relationship.

Finally, Jane broached the subject, "Tom, let's see a doctor." "You can go if you want," answered the young man. As impatient as he pretended to be though, he was beginning to feel afraid of the unknown. What if he was the problem? A visit to her gynecologist declared Jane fertile and with nothing that would hinder conception. She was relieved, but obviously scared for Tom. "It's your turn, my dear," she told him. After putting the visit off for many months, Tom finally agreed to see the doctor. He came home with the news and a sigh of relief: "I too, am OK Jane. The doctor just said to be patient. We may get a surprise soon." Their families did not believe them. "If both of you are okay, then what's the problem?" they wondered.

A full five years after their marriage, Jane missed her periods. She stayed a few more weeks before daring to go for a pregnancy test. When she did, she could not believe it when the doctor said: "Jane, you're six weeks pregnant." When finally the couple held a healthy baby girl in their arms, they could not stop giving thanks to God. No wonder her name is Zawadi, meaning God's gift. After that, they did not have any problem conceiving their next two healthy children. What was all the waiting about? They wondered. And, the answer was always: "Zawadi. We waited for God's gift." They would then look at their beautiful daughter and smile, remembering all the doubts, all the fear, all the waiting.

Not every man and woman is blessed like Jane and Tom. Some wait, and there is no child. They struggle with fertility treatments and all manner of methods to ensure conception. Some accept their status and adopt children, which is another form of "conception." Whatever way God uses to bring a child into their lives, the parents' attitude should be one of humility and thanksgiving. Parenting will always remain a privilege to biological and adoptive parents. It is never a right to be taken for granted or gloated over, and so the need for humility and thanksgiving, and persistence in responsible, purposeful parenting.

Prayer as Submission and Request for Wisdom

The ruin of a nation begins in the homes of its people.
~ *African proverb*

By wisdom a house is built, and through understanding it is established.
~ *Proverbs 24:3*

The African proverb: "*The ruin of a nation begins in the homes of its people,*" represents basic reality that emphasizes the importance of parenting as the bedrock of any nation, and so the need for parents to seek God's wisdom in undertaking this critical role. The greatest threat to any nation is not an enemy from without but decay from within. This begins with the destruction of values and poverty of rearing and mentoring of the next generation.

The Biblical proverb: *"By wisdom a house is built, and through understanding it is established,"* is a reminder that God-given wisdom is the only way to establish stable homes and stable nations. In the Bible, the word house can refer to a family or a nation. Seeking God's wisdom in raising children will give us fervent men and women who contribute to the establishment of strong nations.

Seeking wisdom in parenting is admission that knowledge without God's wisdom is useless. This submission is a position of obedience and meekness where someone looks up to, and with humility yields power and control to another. From this position of humility, the parent requests for wisdom and know-how in order to guide the child into God's plan and purpose.

The way the Almighty has ordered his world is that none of us has power to see into the future. How wise then, is the person who acknowledges this blindness and requests the Almighty to guide both child and parent into the unknown! This submissive request for wisdom is an ongoing and non-ending process, not only because the future is a mystery, but also because children's personalities are another enigma.

This is especially so because children are very different and every parent soon finds out that they cannot cut and paste a parenting style from one child to the other. Hence, parental blindness is double-fold: they cannot tell the future, and they are dealing with fresh molding clay every time they hold a new baby in their arms. How much then, does the parent need the humility that says: "God, show me how!"

I'll never forget the challenges I faced in weaning our second-born baby. Every mother remembers that weaning is not as easy as simply switching the baby's diet from liquids to solids and everything is smooth all the way. It's not that simple. Our first-born daughter loved mashed avocado. Then came our son. Every time I mashed avocado into his food, he spat the stuff into my face as though he was shouting: "I'm not my sister! Please, leave out avocado. I hate the stuff!" He could not speak, but my! Could he spit!

This is a simple but clear reminder, that our children are different in many ways. It follows that every parent needs all the help they can get from the children's creator. So, our role as parents is obedience and meekness towards God as well as consistent request for wisdom: "God show me how to bring up this child."

Once again, this request for wisdom never ends however old the child might become. Mrs. Odero narrated to me how untidy her teenage daughter, Minnie, was. The young lady was tidy and careful with her personal things all through her later childhood into her teens. Then, everything changed. Minnie's bedroom that she shared with her younger sister, Debra, became a nightmare. Her clothes were thrown all over the floor. She got into the habit of eating in the bedroom and leaving food all over the place. Dirty plates would be discovered under the bed days after, with mold covering the leftovers.

Debra hated what her sister was becoming: selfish, irritable, lazy, and dirty. Mrs. Odero lectured and threatened, but there was no change. She decided to keep quiet, pray and wait. It was a wonder that in spite of the laziness, somehow, the young lady kept up her grades. The family celebrated the day she left home to go to college after passing her high school exams very well. At the end of the semester, the whole family dreaded her coming home. "Mom, do I have to share my room with Minnie again? I wonder how her college roommate survived the semester!" moaned Debra.

Finally, Minnie came home, and all were struck with her change of mood. She was happy, pleasant to be around, and very cheerful. Debra stayed out of the bedroom while Minnie unpacked. Finally, the young one could not keep outside any longer and finally decided to go to bed. Expecting to find clothes and other personal belonging scattered all over the floor, Debra was shocked to find her older sister snoring away, and the room looking spic and span – everything was neatly put away and the room was even tidier than before. The following day, everyone waited for the untidiness to resume, but Minnie was a changed person. Up to today, their mother cannot tell what changed Minnie, but they all knew that their sister "came back" to herself, and they were grateful to God for that.

Prayer for Patience and Persistence

However long the night, the dawn will break.
~ African Proverb

A man's wisdom gives him patience; it is to his glory to overlook an offense.
~ Proverbs 19:11

The African proverb: "*However long the night, the dawn will break,*" is a quiet reminder that persistence and endurance in parenting are jewels worth seeking for and nurturing. This is because rearing children is a long, arduous and yet joyous engagement because the outcomes create joy however long the waiting period. Watching young ones mature rewards every labor, and the benefits are like precious stones that have been sought with commitment and tenacity.

The Biblical proverb: "*A man's wisdom gives him patience; it is to his glory to overlook an offense,*" is a reminder that patience and self-control are related. Knowledge that a child will not remain young and foolish forever is wisdom that contributes to restraint. How many times I hear parents state: "When he did that, I felt like killing him." Killing here is used lightly, an African way of saying, "I felt like taking my son bodily and *shaking the life out of him*."

Many parents are often so angered by naughty children and disrespectful youth that their anger threatens to overflow. What is it that wins the day? The parent's silence, self-control and maturity, restraint that may look like weakness but actually is strength. Many parents realize that these values are not inborn because our fallen nature threatens to take over when our authority in challenged. This is why we must pray to God to imbue us with patience and persistence.

Every parent reading this book must have many stories of tested and tried patience as well as proven outcomes of persistence. We shall examine the role of patience and persistence later, but let me emphasize here that giving up is often a welcome solution to parents who do not cultivate "stay ability" or staying power in child rearing. Which mother does not know how their patience has been tested, or is being tested as they toilet-train their baby! What of the challenge of eradicating bad habits before they take root? Then, there is homework supervision. How long does it take for Junior to sit down and do his homework?

We often talk to mothers who are juggling work, school and parenting. The child's father may be absent. There are those who are working far away from home, even in international locations. Women married to such men tell of the struggle of making decisions alone. They have to train the children, supervise them and say Yes and No for both parents. Their other responsibilities await them as they spend time shaping the lives of the children. The kind of persistence needed here is more of tenacity: the resolve and determination to succeed in parenting, and not give up until the journey is done.

Then, one of the parents may be actually present but absent! There are two types of present-absent here. The father may be around but never within the household or engaged in the child's life. Some taking care of their children are single parents raising children without the support of the child's mother or father. Life is especially challenging for single parents. They multitask, jumping from feeding the baby, to checking that the math homework is on course, and still, such parents may be in school, with a paper due for a university class in a few days time.

One wonders, "Where do such parents get all this strength from?" Parents who pray know the answer to this question. It is not that they have strength enough and to spare. No, they often feel like giving up, but they go on anyway. This is steadfastness and determination. One day, they will look back and ask themselves: "How did I really make it?" Some will know that even the time to pray was non-existent. They just threw single sentence prayers into the air, and God heard and honored their request. Their children turned out all right.

Case Study on Prayer in Parenting

Munene was the last born of five siblings. When he was 13 years old, his parents separated. After separation, one of his brothers stayed with his father, while two girls left with his mother. None of the parents seemed to want him and so he was taken in by his unmarried Aunt, his father's sister, who became like a mother to him. Having no children of her own, Aunt Lydia loved the boy as if he was her own child. However, the more she cared for him, the more he acted out.

By his 18th birthday, the young man had been expelled from several schools for poor performance and truancy. He was often angry and oppositional. Several times, he was caught smoking cigarettes and keeping company with boys who broke school rules and bullied new students. Aunt Lydia was always called to school to meet with teachers who declared that they had done all they could for Munene.

Eventually, the young man dropped out of school altogether. He often shut himself up in his room, refused to shower and to talk to anyone. Someone referred Aunt Lydia to a psychologist and specialist in working with troubled youth. All through the years of struggle, Aunt Lydia, a prayerful woman, never stopped asking God to intervene in the life of her troubled nephew. She also hoped that the psychologist would be a believer in God's power to change and transform lives.

During his sessions at the clinic, Munene poured out his anger and feelings of rejection, voicing the questions that had plagued his troubled adolescence. "Why did my parents reject me? Why did they start fighting as soon as I was born?" He went on to narrate that from early childhood he had never known the love of his father. The older man never as much as played with the boy, often seeming to avoid him or behave as if he was not in the room. "What did I do to earn his hatred?" The young man harbored deep feelings of low self-worth, perceiving himself as a non-entity. This is because his father behaved as if he did not exist. "Then my mother," mused the youth, "I can understand a man rejecting his son. But, why would my mother throw me away?" Aunt Lydia prayed without ceasing, and the therapist continued to work with the youth.

Eventually, Munene was strong enough to sit for his high school examinations from home. Therapy continued. Several months later, when the high school results were released, Munene had passed well enough to join university. Aunt Lydia threw a party to celebrate this milestone and women from Lydia's church showered Munene with gifts. He cried as he felt so much love and acceptance from the mothers. Over the years, the young man joined university and graduated with a degree in economics. By now, he was quieter and more peaceful. At university, he had joined the Christian Union group and eventually, began to worship in his Aunt's Church. He also volunteered to work with young people, especially targeting troubled youth.

Munene never discovered all the answers to the many questions in his life. However, one day, in his young adult years, he learnt that his mother had been unfaithful, conceiving him out of wedlock. His father's rejection was a projection of anger against the product of an unfaithful union and his mother's negative response was a result of shame and guilt. Munene was a constant reminder of her adultery. At the end of the day, the young man grew up as his Aunt's son. He loved her for her patience and believing in him. She in turn thanked God for answered prayer. She often mused how easy it would have been to give up, but somehow, God gave her strength to hold on.

CHAPTER 4

PARENTS AS PASSERS OF LEGACIES

DEFINITION OF LEGACY

Wisdom is like fire. People take it from others.
~ African (Hema - DRC) Proverb

Wealth, when used, comes to an end; learning, when used, increases.
~ African (Swahili) Proverb

Blessed is the man who finds wisdom … for she is more profitable than silver and yields better returns than gold.
~ Proverbs 3:13-14

The African (Hema) proverb: *"Wisdom is like fire. People take it from others,"* comes from the Hema people of the Democratic Republic of Congo (DRC) and underlines the *preciousness* of wisdom. It is only in Africa where we talk of people *taking fire* from others. Elsewhere in this book, I discuss the reality that in a traditional village, someone may not have a matchbox and so people depend on one another for live embers to light a fire early in the morning.

Normally, the night before, the last person to exit the fireplace pushes a log into the hot ashes. The wood piece smolders slowly through the night leaving hot rich coals ready to be scooped out and used to light a healthy fire the next day. However, alas, if someone forgot to hide that log in the hot ash, or if something puts off the remains of the fire at night, the fireplace is cold and lifeless the next morning. With nothing to light the fire, the individual will have to make her way to the neighbor's house, bearing a piece of broken pot to bring the fire home. The request is: "Good morning, neighbor. My fire did not last through the night. Could I please have some of yours?" Several hot coals later, the fire is passed on to the home and the cold fireplace comes alive.

The African proverb compares wisdom to precious fire. Those without do not pretend that they can do with a cold fireplace. They humble themselves and seek it from the wise. The second African (Swahili) proverb: "*Wealth, when used, comes to an end; learning, when used, increases,*" comes from *Swahili*, also known as Kiswahili, a Bantu language and the first language of the *Swahili* people. The language is used in the African Great Lakes region and other parts of Southeast Africa, including Tanzania, Kenya, Uganda, Rwanda, Burundi, Mozambique and the Democratic Republic of the Congo. The wise saying underlines that wisdom comes from using the knowledge we have acquired because we become wiser if we practice truths of life. Wealth if used reduces, but when knowledge and learning are used, they increase and grow into wisdom. This is the secret of passing wisdom to children because wealth can end in poverty but wisdom cannot. It multiplies when used for living.

The Biblical proverb: "*Blessed is the man who finds wisdom … for she is more profitable than silver and yields better returns than gold,*" summarizes the reality that blessings abide for anyone who discovers the benefits of wisdom and invests in acquiring it more than attaining the accolades of wealth. The Bible of course underlines the fact that true wisdom comes from obeying God's law. He alone is the source of true insight. This is clarified in Psalm 19:9b-10: "*The ordinances of the Lord are sure and altogether righteous. They are more precious than gold, than much pure gold; they are sweeter than honey, than honey from the comb.*" These are the legacies parents of purpose seek to pass on to their children.

A legacy is defined as money or property left to someone in a will, or anything handed down from an ancestor to a descendant. In the context of this book, we want to emphasize the second meaning and expand on the definition to include: *Anything of precious value that a parent determines worthy to pass onto the child.* The proverb above about taking fire from other people is a truly African expression of this desire.

The reason for alluding to "anything of precious value passed on by a parent to a child" is that, first, not everyone will have concrete valuable items to leave to a child, especially in Africa, where many people live a hand-to-mouth existence. Secondly, tangible treasures quickly vanish in the hands of a child who has no lasting principles. History is littered with stories of treasures that have been left in the hands of naïve descendants. These are said to have blown away their inheritance over only a few months. All too soon, the wealth that their parents took many years to gather disappears.

Other families have been left embroiled in court cases over the management of the dead parents' estate. Instead of unity in sorrow, there is hatred, murder and competition between kin. Sometimes, some children have wished the quick passing away of rich parents so that they can inherit the wealth that has been denied them. In some cases, the parent has been too busy making the money to really invest in a relationship with the children, leaving behind bitterness and anger because money that cannot buy love created a vacuum of despondency.

On the other hand, many lazy sons, who are more intent on drugs, alcohol, flashy living and womanizing than in working hard as the parent has done, surround hardworking fathers. It follows that legacies must be defined by attributes beyond money and property. They must be seen to mean non-tangible values and principles that prepare human beings for living, not mere existence. Someone has said that it is indeed easier to make money than to grow children who have what it takes to live and thrive in a competitive world. Our focus in this chapter is values that build and foundations that last.

A wise man in the book of Proverbs gave various pieces of advice to his son, emphasizing on the foundations of life. For example, he pointed out some critical values like the legacy of obedience. In a society where breaking the law is becoming a norm, obedience assumes a critical meaning. How can *lawmakers* break the very law they created? Lawyers steal from clients. Doctors cheat patients after swearing the Hippocratic oath to treat the ill to the best of one's ability and to preserve a patient's privacy. Teachers assist students to cheat in examinations and policemen, stewards of the law, steal from the public. In times like these, obedience becomes a critical legacy for parents first to live themselves and then to model and pass on to their children.

THE LEGACY OF OBEDIENCE

He who refuses to obey cannot command.
~ African (Kenyan) proverb

Ears that do not listen to advice, accompany the head when it is chopped off.
~ *African Proverb*

My son, keep your father's commands and do not forsake you mother's teachings.
~ *Proverbs 6:20*

The African proverb: "*He who refuses to obey cannot command,*" is a reminder that legitimately commanding others is not a right but a privilege that must be earned through first becoming an adherent to the very demands we make on others. For parents, children watch us very closely to see if we also obey what we prescribe. The words "*cannot* command" in this proverb do not mean that *disobedient parents* cannot demand obedience from their children, but that even if they demand it, children will rebel quietly from within. It follows that disobedience has consequences.

This is the central meaning of the second African proverb: "*Ears that do not listen to advice, accompany the head when it is chopped off,*" in that disaster follows the disobedient and anyone else related to them also suffers the consequences of deliberately refusing to listen, learn and adhere to laws of life.

This is the warning contained in the Biblical proverb: "*My son, keep your father's commands and do not forsake you mother's teachings.*" Parents are instructors to their children on rules that govern living. Indeed, Proverbs 1:23 adds that like a lamp, these commands light up one's way, and the teachings add more light to the steps of life. When the child is corrected to ensure obedience, there is nothing strange because discipline is the way of life. Anyone growing up without restraint ultimately brings sorrow to his parents.

Legacy assumes that parents have a set of values that they desire their children to adhere to and that they live by example, modeling the same. We live in a world where many parents do not seem to have any set of values or morals, making it very difficult for their children to know how to live. Many years ago, a young man was referred to our clinic for drinking and running wild. During our sessions, when I asked him how he financed this drinking habit, he related how he had made a habit of blackmailing his father. The young man quipped, "My father gives me whatever I ask,"

"How is that?" I asked.

"Because he knows that I know," and he smiled.

"What do you know?" I persisted.

"Let me tell you a story," he responded.

"One day, I sneaked out of the house at 3 a.m. in the morning. My brother and I had this habit of creeping out through our bedroom window, crawling over the roof of our apartment and then scrambling all the way down the drainage pipe. We would bribe the watchman to open the gate for us and later let us in when we got back. One day, I was in a crowded nightclub, dancing with my girlfriend. Through the dim lights, I looked across the crowded room, full of other dancing couples. Guess who was looking directly at me across the room? My Dad! He was dancing with his girlfriend, a young girl, about my age. Our eyes locked for a moment, and then the two quickly melted into the crowd. That was several months ago. None of us, neither Dad nor I, have ever discussed that incident. I've never mentioned it to my Mom either. However, since then, I make all sorts of demands for money from my Dad, and I make sure that I ask in my mother's presence. Dad always hands me what I want. If he dares hesitate, one look from me reminds him that I know! So you see, I know what I know and he knows that I know!"

The point here is that purposeful parenting needs to go beyond supplying children with food, ensuring a roof over their heads and giving them a good education. Well-parented children are those who are receiving a set of values and morals to live by. And home is the place where such are ingrained, where such legacies are passed on.

Obedience involves role modeling, the process of a parent clarifying and then living a set of values and morals and then requiring the same of the child. A father narrated this story. His young adult son walked into the house and the older man noticed that the young man's lips were dry. "Come here, John," he commanded. "Tell me, have you started smoking? I have always warned you never to touch cigarettes. Those lips are the lips of a smoker!" "What if I have?" retorted the youth. "Who asks when you go out drinking?" The father said that he was shocked into silence. Here, we are not advocating for rudeness from children towards their parents. We want to emphasize the need to face the reality that true obedience has to be modeled, not just commanded.

If a mother steals with a child strapped on her back, what do you expect of the child?
~African Proverb

A woman who pursues a man for sex loses her spiritual beauty.
~ African Proverb

Now my sons... do not let your heart turn to her ways... many are the victims she has brought down; her slain are a mighty throng. Her house is a highway to the grave, leading down to the chamber of death.
~ Proverbs 7:25-27

The African proverb: *"If a mother steals with a child strapped on her back, what do you expect of the child?"* is a rhetorical question that reminds us that children begin internalizing their parents' values very early. In this proverb, the word steal does not necessarily mean pilfer or pinch something belonging to another person. Rather, it points out the reality that children are *copycats,* more or less implying the fulfillment of one of the common sayings repeated by children: *Monkey see, monkey do!* Young ones absorb the values of their parents, good or bad, hence history has an uncanny way of repeating itself.

The second African proverb: *"A woman who pursues a man for sex loses her spiritual beauty,"* is a reminder that true beauty is from within, and that is so fragile that once lost, it is difficult to reclaim. Immorality is one sure way of losing the inner beauty that makes a woman glow, however ugly or beautiful she may be on the outside.

The Biblical proverb: *"Now my sons... do not let your heart turn to her ways... many are the victims she has brought down; her slain are a mighty throng. Her house is a highway to the grave, leading down to the chamber of death,"* refers to the adulteress, the subject of the whole of Proverbs 7. Who is an adulteress? Other meanings of this word are a *wayward wife* and *a prostitute*. These are women who commit adultery or fornication. Adulterers are married people who sexually move outside their marriage beds and fornicators are single people who seek out others for sex.

The proverb warns sons but the Bible is written in a figurative manner because the same refers to women, and could easily read: *"Now my daughters… do not let your heart turn to his ways… many are the victims he has brought down; his slain are a mighty throng. His house is a highway to the grave, leading down to the chamber of death,"* The focus this time would be the *adulterer*, the *male prostitute*. Sexual morality is a legacy worth passing on to children in a clear, discernible manner.

Recently, the *Sunday Nation*, a Kenyan newspaper, carried the story of Nollywood's Desmond Elliott, a Nigerian film star. In an interview on morality among other film stars, he emphasized that, unlike many popular movie stars who have a bevy of women hanging around them, and others who marry and remarry several times, he has managed to stay true to his wife. Asked to explain, he said: "When a woman chases after me, I run for my wife."

Elliott narrated that, just like with other film stars, some women want to sleep with him, but he is determined to safeguard his marriage and not to have an affair. "At the end of the day, I know I have to go back home... I run because I have ambitions which I don't want women to ruin for me." Sexual morality is a value worth protecting. One day, when Desmond looks in the eyes of his children, he can say: "I determined that adultery would not ruin my ambitions. You too must run from adulterous women."

In our time and age, only a morally upright parent can discuss the value of morality with his child. As much as sexual immorality seems to be the norm, young people passionately long for adults who can model faithfulness and sexual uprightness. In particular, they desire to know that their own parents can model this hope for them and their children.

Parents should never give up instructing their children on how to live with sexual integrity in a permissive society. Instruction assumes knowledge - where the teacher has more awareness on a subject than the student. This is because when a parent tells a child to resist the temptation of sex outside wedlock as God commands, the youth may ask: *Why?* The parent cannot answer: "*Because I said so!*" or, "*Because God commands it.*" An intelligent, curious youth will desire to know more. When answers are not forthcoming from parents, or when parents do not link a child with a trusted source of information, the young one seeks their own teacher - other children who may know more of myths than truth, the Internet, pornography, or sexual perverts.

To ensure that the parent knows more than the child, the parent needs to seek *to know more* than the child. For example, with all sorts of information on sex in our society, parents should know enough to critique messages that enter our space - from the media, school system, music, movies, television, novels, advertisements, social media, and much more. There are some critical questions for which parents need to find answers. For example, the current argument in many forums today is that youth need to be taught that there is something called "*Safe Sex*" so long as they commit themselves to "*safe practices.*" First, there is no safety in breaking God's law, just as there is no safety in breaking the Highway Code or the Law of Gravity.

Let us assume for a moment that sex outside wedlock can be safe and examine some arguments that have been used to vouchsafe or argue in support of Safe Sex. Parents need to check out some of these arguments and determine if they are true or mere myths. For example:

1. Stop trying to teach your children sexual integrity because *ALL teens and young adults are sexually active.* Are they? Many research surveys report those *who are* sexually active, not those who are not. Once I read a study that indicated that 42% of teenagers in the sample said that Yes, they have lost their virginity. The recommendation was: "*Therefore, teach adolescents to use condoms and the pill because they will have sex anyway.*" The researchers left out a critical fact, that 56% of the sample said: "*No, they have not had sex.*" Another 4% did not mark the item, or the response was not clear. The 56% indicated another majority method of 'safe sex' that was left out: *No Sex or Abstinence* was already working for majority of the study sample.

2. Sex can be safe because *condoms protect against unintended pregnancies and sexually transmitted diseases.* Do they? Combined with over 30% of condom failure when used 100% by adults, how will children who forget pencils and books at home remember to carry a condom 100% of the time?

3. *Teen pregnancy and Sexually Transmitted Disease (STD) rates would decline if we would provide teenagers easy, free and confidential access to condoms in schools.* Check out studies in nations like USA that have had *Safe Sex* campaigns for many years. Has this happened? Have STDs declined?

A 2014 report by Center for Disease Control indicates that only a fraction of STDs are reported in America. CDC adds that of the reports received, indications are that STDs have become a significant challenge facing USA. The report estimates that nearly 20 million new sexually transmitted infections are reported every year, half among young people 15-24 years old. These new infections account for an additional national health burden of $16 billion. The report adds that each infection is a threat to the health and wellbeing of each individual and carries the risk of future infections that could lead to complications of fertility and ectopic pregnancy.

New strains of STDs are always popping up through mutation. Indeed, medical research is not able to keep pace with these new species that do not respond to any known medication. In 2013, a new strain of Gonorrhea called A8806 popped up in Hawaii and has also appeared in Norway, Australia and Japan. The strain is not responding to known antibiotics and seems to have more fatality power than the AIDS virus.

Gonorrhea has the capacity to mutate and form unknown strains that are a step ahead of medical research. This STD is most common among 15-24 year-olds. Symptoms include infections in the genitals, rectum, and throat; a burning sensation during urination; increased discharge in both women and men; and for women, vaginal bleeding in between periods. With these scary truths about sexual immorality and more, I wonder which parent would leave sexual education to charlatans who may care more for other gains than the holistic health and wellbeing of our children.

Legacy of Industry and Hard Work

You are beautiful, but learn to work, for you cannot eat your beauty.
~ African (Congolese) Proverb

As a door turns on its hinges, so a sluggard turns on his bed. The sluggard buries his hand in the dish; he is too lazy to bring it back to his mouth.
~ Proverbs 26:13-14

The Africa proverb: "*You are beautiful, but learn to work, for you cannot eat your beauty,*" is a tongue-in-cheek wise saying appreciating the gift of beauty. However, it reminds beautiful African women and their daughters, and by extension, handsome men and their sons, that it is easy for an attractive person to be drunk with narcissistic self-admiration and spend all the time engrossed in showing off their physical attributes. Such people end up with misplaced energy. Instead of settling down to studies, housework, farm work or regular employment, they spend time seeking for admirers and never seem to have enough of adoration.

With time, drunk with the effect they have on people, they fail to tell the fake, manipulative or abusive admirer from the real one. Finally, in the foolishness of self-absorption, they lack the perception to avoid exploitation. Wisdom and good judgment should remind them that work is a necessity because personal needs of food, shelter, education, training, and later on industrious work must be met and this can only happen through consistent conscientiousness.

The Biblical proverbs: "*As a door turns on its hinges, so a sluggard turns on his bed. The sluggard buries his hand in the dish; he is too lazy to bring it back to his mouth,*" emphasize a literal understanding of this wisdom, in that a lazy person loves to sleep, and snores and turns this way and that just like a door attached to its hinge. Just like hard work, idleness can become a habit that affects the whole individual – spiritually, mentally, physically, academically, socially, and, so on. That is why instructing children in industry cannot be dismissed as of no essence.

Industry also means hard work or steady endeavor. Other words are constant diligence, systematic effort or habitual employment. Employment here does not mean working for someone but refers to keeping busy or occupied. The opposite of industry is laziness and indolence. It is also unwillingness to work, sluggishness or nursing a laggardly, lazy-bone attitude. Indolent people avoid hard work. They seek lots of gain for minimum pain.

One may argue that society has many wealthy people who do not have to lift a finger, and yet they drive big cars and live in posh homes, all because they have learnt to defraud, bribe, extort and steal. However, Solomon was quite aware of such people, and shortcuts to wealth were as common in his day as they are in our society where people are quick to argue that the end justifies the means. So, Solomon concludes: *"The wages of the righteous bring them life, but the income of the wicked brings them punishment,"* Proverbs 7:16.

Any parent who truly loves his child will model industry, diligence and hard work. He will clarify that the only treasure that is worth boasting about is that which is honestly gathered, for this brings no sorrow with it. Wealth that is dishonestly gained or hurts another brings with it curses and death, and many a parent have passed curses on to their children. It follows that a little that is honestly gained will bring with it blessings to the family. However, much gained through corruption and fraud will reap curses and pain for many generations. Industry, hard work and diligence are worthy legacies to pass on to our children, complete with the patience and pain that accompanies steady work and the sweat of honest enterprise.

Steadiness presupposes the ability to withstand the peer pressure of running after quick riches. Parents committed to the value of systematic work will remind children that as the young ones steadily climb up the ladder of life, they should not compare themselves with those who ride up fast as if on a roller coaster. This is because those who excel slowly through diligence will often meet the fast riders plummeting downwards through the great fall that certainly follows the cheat and defrauder. Some of these people rise fast, fall hard and even die miserably. Those who may not fall or die leave riches that cause destruction to those who inherit them. As we emphasize the legacy of hard work, we bemoan the many lazy young people in our society. Some of them lack parents and adults to model hard, steady work. However, other youth and young adults are downright disobedient and refuse to work. It seems that I hear more stories of young men than young women who will not work. What is a 30 year-old man doing sleeping all day in his father's house? He eats, showers, watches television, and repeats the same story that he cannot find work.

Others get jobs, but quit soon thereafter complaining that the pay is too little. There is some truth that our education curriculum is sometimes unrealistic, preparing our children for white-collar jobs in clean offices away from the toils of the common man. Not all of our children will end up in these offices. A good number will have to learn to create wealth in farms, cottage industries, building sites, and so on.

This reality suggests parents' involvement in the kind of curriculum taught in our schools. It must be practical, relevant, realistic, and rewarding. What happened to 4-K clubs where children used to compete raising horticultural produce in school? Where are our polytechnics – vocational colleges that used to absorb children not gifted in academia and train them in other skills such as masonry, carpentry, electrical works, plumbing, vehicle mechanics, sewing, pottery, and so on. Alas! Many of them have been taken over as university campuses. This could be costly short sightedness. Parents can advocate for realistic change.

Legacy of Training for Living, Working and Thriving

He who fears the crying of a child will cry himself.
~ African (Swahili) Proverb

By trying often, the monkey learns to jump from the tree.
~ African (Baganda) Proverb

Go to the ant, you sluggard; consider its ways and be wise! It has no commander, no overseer or ruler, yet it stores its provisions in summer and gathers its food at harvest.
~ Proverbs 6:6-8

The African (Swahili) proverb: "*He, who fears the crying of a child, will cry himself,*" is a reminder that parenting and child instruction will always involve discipline, and correction brings tears. Therefore, the crying of a child when corrected should not stop the parent from insisting that learning happens consistently. Discipline is not punishment and is never meted to inflict pain and shame on the child. Later on in this book, we discuss this difference at length. The African (Baganda) proverb: "*By trying often, the monkey learns to jump from the tree,*" comes from the Baganda people of Uganda. It is encouragement that persistence in training our children will always bear fruit. Habits, both good and bad, take root with much practice.

The Biblical proverb: *"Go to the ant, you sluggard; consider its ways and be wise! It has no commander, no overseer or ruler, yet it stores its provisions in summer and gathers its food at harvest,"* teaches that many tiny insects are faithful, industrious workers full of wisdom in catering, not only for the immediate needs of their colony, but for the uncertain future as well. They teach us that we too, imbued not with the instincts of insects, but with godly wisdom and strength, can pass on wisdom for living to our children. As parents do their part, none of their children will grow up saying, "Mummy, Daddy, you never taught me the value of living, working and thriving."

A 35 year-old man lives with his grandmother, and wakes up at noon. He finds food in a hot pot and hot milky tea in a flask. He eats, and walks into the town to "greet" his friends. He roams around visiting colleagues at their work locations, and then goes back home for dinner and television. He is also assured of out-of-pocket allowance to visit a few nightspots. The man, who barely made it through high school and dropped out of college, is too comfortable to look for work or get married.

Recently, in my clinic, I had a 24-year old who lives at home, has his clothes washed by his mother and his shirts ironed by his father. Discussing about his future, he declared:

"I cannot contemplate marriage. How can I look after another human being? I can't!"

"Precisely," I responded. "You need to grow up first, because it is not only a wife you'll soon be looking after, but a child or two as well."

"But I can't!" he insisted.

"And, why can't you?" I persisted."You are not sick. You are intelligent. You are not disabled. Let's begin with first things first. Can you at least wash your own clothes?"

We continued our sessions, breaking things down to small, manageable proportions. The journey towards change was beginning but it would take long. Would he have the tenacity to continue? This young man's "can't" was a long-term ingrained mindset that had been encouraged and reinforced by dependency, and his parents were the technicians in building and nursing this negative, destructive mentality. Now, the young adult was facing issues in his life that his parents could not help him with, and so his presence in my clinic.

In his book *Love Must Be Tough*, James Dobson insists that real love does not watch loved ones destroy themselves. If a parent lives with a child who will not work, then measures should be taken to ensure that difficult lessons of life are communicated surely, early, and consistently. We shall consider some suggestions in the chapter on "Parenting as Limit Setting." Keep reading.

Legacy of Integrity

A pretty face and fine clothes do not make character.
~ African (Congolese) Proverb

Bad friends will prevent you from having good friends.
~ African (Gabon) Proverb

A greedy man brings trouble to his family, but he who hates bribes will live.
~ Proverbs 15:27

The African proverb: "*A pretty face and fine clothes do not make character,*" teaches that character is more important than physical appearance. Many people, especially the young, may spend a lot of time and investment on makeup, gym, fashion and so on. These are good. However, balanced self-care involves taking care of a holistic me that begins with nurturing the heart and character through fostering integrity. This is the fulcrum of beauty from within that can then be followed by taking care of the body that houses the heart.

The second African proverb: "*Bad friends will prevent you from having good friends,*" is a reminder that one of the ways to ensure one's integrity is wisdom in choosing friends. No one can have good and bad friends at the same time. This implies that wise selection of the kind of friends a youth spends time with is critical.

The Biblical proverb: "*A greedy man brings trouble to his family, but he who hates bribes will live,*" underlines the importance of integrity as a value. Africans believe that the offender does not experience the outcomes of breaking the law of living in isolation. Just as Africans believe and the Bible reiterates: choices have consequences that reverberate not only across one's immediate and extended family but also into the future, affecting upcoming generations. This means that before one breaks any law of living, the question should be: Who will pay for this? This is because even a new born or unborn baby ends up paying for the sins of the parent.

The word integrity is derived from integral – the state of being whole or complete, unimpaired, of sound moral principles, upright, honest and sincere. Men and women of integrity do not pretend to be what they are not; they are solid inside, morally upright. The book of Proverbs states: "The integrity of the upright guides them, but the unfaithful are destroyed by their duplicity," (Proverbs 11:3). Duplicity refers to hypocritical cunning or deceptions, leading a double life, being one person in public and another in private, one person at home and another at the work place. People of integrity earn honest gain but unfaithful people cheat their way through life. Integrity denotes righteousness but duplicity leads to unfaithfulness.

Moral uprightness results in building others and doing them good while insincerity leads to gossip and betrayal. What do our children hear from their parents? Do they listen to us gossiping about others or blessing them in our utterances? Do they watch us cheat and tell lies or do they listen to truthfulness? Are our actions before our children kindness or do they see acts of cruelty? Do they witness us deceiving and mistreating our workers or do they observe us treating them fairly, caring for them in the same way as we do our family members?

In Africa and in some other parts of the world, some of the most mistreated persons in our society today are the domestic workers in our homes, especially house girls, who are often overworked and underpaid. Many are not even allowed to take a single day off work. They are on duty even on Sundays, a day when they should go to church to worship God, rest and reconnect with their friends and family. What legacy are we as parents passing on to our children regarding our care for house helps?

Parents also have the obligation to learn to model a combination of integrity and industry through making sure that children learn to clean up after themselves, to share housework with the house help and to model care for others right at home. Beyond moral uprightness, integrity also has to do with telling and living the truth.

A joke is told of a child handing in homework to the teacher who asks: "Did your dad help you with your homework?" "No," answers the young one. "He did it all by himself!" This child has begun to learn how to cheat very early. Integrity will carry a child far, and it is only the parent who lives it who can pass it on. Someone has said that children "hear" more what the parents do than what they say.

Legacy of Self-Discipline

One should punish a child the first time he comes home with a stolen egg. Otherwise, the day he returns home with a stolen ox, it will be too late.
~ African (Ethiopian) Proverb

He who ignores discipline comes to poverty and shame, but whoever heeds correction is honored.
~ Proverbs 13:18

The African proverb: *"One should punish a child the first time he comes home with a stolen egg. Otherwise, the day he returns home with a stolen ox, it will be too late,"* is a reminder that child training in integrity should start as early as possible, and that no wrongdoing is too small to confront. Bad behavior has a way of repeating itself. The child graduates from small misdemeanors to bigger ones. No thief started as a bank robber. There was learning from much earlier on, then teaching, training and reinforcement. Even jails and other correctional facilities are classrooms in wrongdoing.

The Biblical proverb: *"He who ignores discipline comes to poverty and shame, but whoever heeds correction is honored,"* reminds us that just as there is a reward for self-discipline, there is also a penalty for self-indulgence. As children grow up, they need to have both explained carefully with real life examples. The Bible uses many life examples of people who lived in obedience and were blessed, and those who threw all caution to the wind and suffered the consequences. The offspring too suffered alongside the defaulters. Africans also have stories of heroes and heroines who took the high road in ordering their lives while those who lived carelessly brought much sorrow to themselves and their families.

Self-discipline refers to self-moderation that develops self-control, character, orderliness and efficiency. The result of this self-regulation leads to orderly conduct, acceptance and submission to authority. Self-discipline does not come automatically nor does it happen overnight. Instead, it is a result of training, consistency and modeling. Training is the art of teaching new knowledge and thereafter coaching a child to internalize and practice it.

Consistency is the art of doing the same thing over and over again so that there is a logical connection from one action to another and firmness to impress the action. Discipline arises from principle-centered living where when behavior is wrong today, it will also be wrong tomorrow.

A parent may, for example, walk into her home to find her children watching an adult movie on television: "Switch off the TV right away! How many times have I told you that you're not supposed to be watching that program?" The children obey and switch off the TV or change channels. The following week, the same parent comes home in a happy mood. Maybe she has been promoted, or has received a long-awaited cheque. The same program is on and the children are watching avidly. "Hello everyone!" she greets them happily. "How was the day?" She then passes into the bedroom humming a little tune.

The children look at each other in confusion. They expected their mother to at least say: "What did we say last week? Switch it off right now!" She may even send them to their rooms and certainly, they will be denied any further watching of TV that night. This is consistency. Walking past in total blindness is inconsistency. Discipline results from consistent training.

Similarly and as far as possible, parents should clearly communicate expectations and allow children to develop understanding as to why those expectations exist. Clear limits should be set and adherence rewarded. Children who have learned the legacy of discipline clearly stand out in the way they speak, treat other people, in their attitude towards authority and in the manner in which they handle their private space. Their character and self-control speak of discipline. Disciplined children are controlled from within and are strong against negative peer pressure. They stand for what is right because they have learnt that doing right is rewarding.

The point in this chapter is that legacies are hidden values that make for longevity and riches that are lasting. We have also discussed the reality that legacies do not just happen. They are first owned by parents and then deliberately passed on to children and young people through consistent training and modeling.

Case Study on Passing Legacies

As I was writing this book, I talked to Prof. Jacob T. Kaimenyi, PhD. Prof. Kaimenyi was appointed by President Uhuru Kenyatta as Cabinet Secretary for Education on 25 April 2013. He is currently serving as Cabinet Secretary for Kenya's Ministry of Land, Housing and Urban Development. Before his appointment to the Cabinet, he served as Professor of Periodontology and Deputy Vice-Chancellor (Academic Affairs), University of Nairobi. He is a Fellow of the International College of Dentists and was honored by Kenya's President Kibaki with the title EBS –

Elder of the Burning Spear. He is a Trustee, Regina Pacis University College, Member of the Medical Practitioners and Dentists Board and immediate past Chairman of Meru Professionals Association.

I asked Professor Kaimenyi to share with me how his parents impacted his life, because someone must have instilled critical positive values in this man who continues to leave a legacy in his work and community. He highlighted specific values that his parents passed on to him. Indeed, he confirmed that his parents literally shaped his life. He emphasized: "A home is like a factory where the production of a future adult to serve his or her country is produced. This is achieved through good examples by parents on various aspects of life to their children. Examples are contagious: If a parent is a bad role model, history will repeat itself as the young ones' likelihood of developing unsatisfactory behavior and attitudes as adults increases. The opposite is also true, that good role models impact their children in ways that they too become examples to their own children, and so on."

Asked about specifically what legacies his parents imparted on him, he gave some examples:

The Legacy of Friendliness and Generosity: Prof. Kaimenyi remembers his late parents as very friendly and generous. He explains that although they were not one of the richest families by local standards, his father and mother were wealthy in many other ways. Their home was a place where the poor, the rich and the powerful were always welcome without any discrimination. For example, after every harvest season, young Kaimenyi's mother used to give various farm produce to some of their poor relatives to assist them to meet the nutritional needs of their children. His father also demonstrated the magnanimous spirit so evident in the Professor himself. The older man, who never went beyond primary school class six, was at home with the lowly and the mighty, including District Commissioners and District Officers.

Kaimenyi's father hosted these eminent individuals at his home and at the family's iron roofed "mabati" meeting point at the nearby market. In addition, the man used to pay school fees for children from very poor families. Kaimenyi adds that today, he finds himself modeling these same qualities of friendliness and generosity to all. In the spirit of his late parents, he regularly, pays fees for some children from very poor families.

The Legacy of Rewarding Industry and Appreciating Success: Prof. Kaimenyi explains that his late father, Musa M'Thuranira was good at rewarding success in his own children as well as in other young ones around him. The older man was liberal in his praise for any children who performed well in school and would often add a gift to affirm the verbal recognition. "Because of this upbringing," concludes the Professor, "I have always felt that those around me who have succeeded in their endeavors must be appreciated in word and deed the way my parents did. It is a joy to notice that as I repeat my parents' modeling in appreciating the success of others, I have found myself making and keeping many dependable friends."

The Legacy of Enterprise: Prof. Kaimenyi discussed the importance of hard work. "My late father believed that one should work hard and not be seen hanging around doing nothing, a common practice seen in some young men who just walk around "killing time." My father considered such behavior absolutely unproductive. Indeed, before Christmas, each one of us was given a certain area in our coffee farm to weed and clear before Christmas Day, 25th

December. Failure to complete the assigned work brought upon the culprit delayed purchase of Christmas clothes."

Let me explain that the gift of new clothes on Christmas Day was the annual great thing for every child to look forward to. Prof. Kaimenyi's father knew how to tie the reward of new clothes to desired training in industry. Professor Kaimenyi adds that in view of this modeling and training, he often finds it extremely difficult to hang out for long periods without doing something productive. "When I am not working, I make deliberate efforts to be doing something else which is worthwhile such as enjoying my hobbies or offering free community service. Those who know me well will attest to the fact that I participate a lot in community activities." Indeed, many people wonder when the Professor finds time to do his regular work considering how much he serves the community. Profitable time management was firmly wired in him from childhood.

The Legacy of Honesty: In discussing this legacy of truthfulness, Prof. Kaimenyi explains that his father and mother were honest almost to a fault. Both believed that a well brought up child must be honest and not lie if called upon to account for his or her actions. To do the contrary was seen as a disgrace to the family. Reflecting on his life today, Prof. Kaimenyi reiterates that to this day, he finds himself going out of his way to be honest and sincere in whatever he does, human failings notwithstanding. Honesty has its rewards. It is met with trust and confidence as his words attest: "I believe that because of this, I have had the trust and confidence of the young, my contemporaries and those who are senior to me and in authority."

The Legacy of Mentoring: Prof. Kaimenyi remembers that his late father was always concerned about his children's performance in examinations. Towards this end, the older man would hold a meeting with each child at the end of each school term so as to find out one's performance relative to the previous term. In those instances where one had declined in performance, the older man would demand for an explanation. He would even go further by asking the individual to outline an improvement plan. On one or two occasions, he repeated to all his children that people had the wrong notion that children from relatively wealthy families, like theirs was perceived to be, were foolish. "This is not true!" their father would declare. "You must all perform well and prove such stereotypes wrong." Professor Kaimenyi is an indication that these stereotypes were indeed proven wrong.

How did this coaching affect Professor's own parenting? He answers: "As a result of my father's encouragement and keenness to closely monitor our performance, I found myself doing the same when I was blessed with children of my own after marriage. This, I believe, has helped my children to do well in school, to the extent that by the end of 2013, my five children will have gone through the university, having performed well in their KCSE. Indeed, because of this family history, I am a firm believer that the best investment that one can make in a child is to assist that child attain the highest level of education, as long as the child is willing and has the ability to do so. This is my pride and I believe the pride of every parent."

The Legacy of Cleanliness: In discussing cleanliness and clothing, Prof. Kaimenyi remembers that his parents detested dirty and shabby clothes. Simply put, they detested poor hygiene. He explained: "My father could not entertain somebody walking around with a beard which was not shaved or a shirt that was not tucked in. As a result of this, I have tended to try and be smart and clean and set a good example to our children, so that they can behave similarly. This has also made me to be very sensitive about how our home looks like in terms of orderliness and cleanliness. My parents believed that it was not the size of the home that mattered, but having a very clean and orderly home. This is a legacy that I believe I should bequeath to my children, so that our grandchildren can follow suit."

The Legacy of Faith: Prof. Kaimenyi concludes the reflection regarding his parents with the legacy of faith. "My late mother, Mrs. Rebecca Tirindi Musa was a very staunch Catholic. She always attended the Sunday service and was one of those who pioneered the construction of our local Catholic church. She encouraged us to attend church services every Sunday without fail unless with good reasons." How has this legacy translated into Prof. Kaimenyi's life? He explains: "I have tried to religiously go to church every Sunday. If there is no Catholic church nearby, I visit any other Christian church without serious regard for denomination. To me, what matters is to worship. If I don't attend a church service on Sunday, I feel as if I have committed a very serious sin. I owe a lot to my late mother for instilling a sense of discipline in me. May the good Lord rest her soul in eternal peace."

It is clear that concluding with faith as a legacy, the Professor leaves us with no doubt that he is who he is because he is a man of faith, a fact he is not ashamed of as a scientist and as an academician. This life-sustaining, principled living is the fruit of "uneducated" parents who took time to deliberately, intentionally, consistently and lovingly pass on lasting legacies to this man. He in turn is working hard to pass the same life-changing values to his immediate family and to the nation as the current Cabinet Secretary for Land, Housing and Urban Development.

CHAPTER 5

PARENTING AS LIMIT SETTING

MEANING OF LIMIT SETTING

Tomorrow belongs to the people who prepare for it today.
~ *African Proverb*

He who spares the rod hates his son, but he who loves him is careful to discipline him.
~ *Proverbs 13:24*

The African proverb: "*Tomorrow belongs to the people who prepare for it today,*" teaches parents the importance of preparing our children for tomorrow as we prepare tomorrow for them. This preparation involves consistent goal setting, evaluation of those goals and training that goes hand in hand with motivation. Effective learning goes hand in hand with discipline that is also referred to as limit setting. This involves guiding the child to understand what he can and cannot do, starting all the way from birth. How many times have you heard a breastfeeding mother tell a baby: "Ouch! No! Stop! You may not bite my nipple!" And the baby understands.

As long as a child, youth or young adult is under the guidance of parents, limit setting will always go on, although in changing proportions. Telling someone else how far they can go may seem controlling and unfriendly, as if the parent is deliberately curtailing the spontaneous freedom and happiness of a child. However, limit setting with love and encouragement is possible, and is the parent's mandate. It is not the rod accompanied by an angry face that encourages limit setting. It is a soft, firm voice of respect that helps a child begin to love what he must do, appreciate the limits she must observe.

The Biblical proverb: *"He who spares the rod hates his son, but he who loves him is careful to discipline him,"* underlines that limit setting of any kind is an action of love for the child and no parent who does not control his child can claim that he loves him.

Limit setting refers to parental guidance that defines the area of free choice for the maturing child. This is how the child learns self-control and self-discipline and also internalizes knowledge about his world. Through limit setting, the child learns through teaching and training when to go and when to stop, as well as where to stop. Limit setting does not just say: "Don't," it also says "Do". From a psychological perspective, children learn better with dos than don'ts. This is because do's provide motivation and a sense of direction while don'ts discourage motivation and are likely to deter the child's natural curiosity and natural desire for exploration.

Limit setting demands parental planning and purpose. It requires principles that define the desired end product. It also calls for partnership between father and mother and in their absence, designated caregivers, so as to reinforce values that define those limits. Finally, parents cannot set limits by remote control but by presence and commitment. We shall discuss parental presence in a later chapter. Limit setting calls for consistency so as to enable the child to learn over and over the definition of expected boundaries.

Child's Age and Limit Setting

The moon moves slowly, but it crosses the town.
~ Ashanti Proverb

**Discipline your son, for in that here is hope;
do not be a willing party to his death.**
~ Proverbs 19:18

The African proverb: "*The moon moves slowly, but it crosses the town,*" comes from the Ashanti people of Southern Ghana. This wise saying reminds African parents that children will respond slowly to training, but just like the moon, they make progress through life, and hence the need for parental patience, tenacity, consistency, and focus.

The Biblical proverb: "*Discipline your son, for in that here is hope; do not be a willing party to his death,*" underlines that training and limit setting create hope for healthy maturation. Failure to guide the growing child means that parents will be contributors to any disasters that follow the lives of unruly youth.

Limits and boundaries change with the age of the child. Younger children have narrower limits as compared to older ones. In addition, how much freedom of expression is provided to the child depends on their ability and even willingness to manage that freedom. For example, since play is good, positive and necessary for holistic child development, a baby should have the play area clearly defined, that while you play, this is where and how.

As the child grows older, the play area is widened with understanding and negotiation. Research indicates that children who are given too much freedom without any limits experience anxiety and insecurity. Some parents do not communicate expectations of behavior to their children and many young ones are sadly left to navigate the chaos of life on their own. The assumptions by some parents is that children and young people do not like limits, that they are likely to rebel when pressured to fit into some expected code of behavior. However, this is not true.

I once questioned a group of high school adolescents regarding their attitudes on parental limit setting. In this case, we translated limit setting as discipline to enhance the youths' self-direction towards a desired outcome. The students were unanimous in their response. All of them agreed that parents should set limits and clearly communicate what the youth should and should not do, how they should behave and conduct themselves. "Why?" I pursued."Because if my parents really love me, they will guide me on how to live and discipline me if I don't behave as I should."

One young man added: "A parent who does not guide their child says: 'I don't care. You can turn out the way you want!' What kind of a parent is that?" We repeated this study across the four high school levels in several national high schools, and the outcomes were the same.

They indicated that for healthy child development, parental guidance is not a suggestion but an absolute requirement. We also learnt that parents should continue this guidance all through the youth's maturation. It is by no accident that the United Nation's Convention on the Rights of the Child states that the individual is still a child until the age of 18 years. This is irrespective of what human rights bodies and other 'freedom' agencies dictate. None of these organizations can replace the parent and only the father and mother can be held responsible for failing to build foundations for their child.

Negotiation and Limit Setting

The fool speaks, the wise man listens.
~ African (Ethiopian) Proverb

Better a patient man than a warrior, a man who controls his tempter than one who takes a city.
~ Proverbs 16:32

The African proverb: *"The fool speaks, the wise man listens,"* carries valued insight that wisdom does not abide in many words. Wise parents do not argue with their children or carry on shouting matches where no one hears what the other one is saying. They listen carefully and finally, in a few words, speak out and provide the sense of direction. They listen because they are not giving orders but including the child wisely in the final conclusion. This does not mean that a parent always gives in to the desires of the child. This is neither parenting nor is it wisdom and maturity. Listening makes the child feels heard and included, resulting in admiration rather than anger and contempt for one's parent.

The Biblical proverb: *"Better a patient man than a warrior, a man who controls his temper than one who takes a city,"* has much to say for patient parents and those who do not give in to anger while communicating limits or reinforcing the same to their children. It is easy for parents to lose their temper especially when dealing with teenagers who seem set to break every rule or answer back without much respect for their parents. These young ones seem more controlled by their peers than by parental expectations.

When parents remember the pull their children are going through - wanting to remain *dependent children* against desiring to become responsible, independent adults, this will remind them to remain the mature wise ones so as to ensure safety as the family travels through the adolescence crisis. Parental conquest with humility and firmness carries the day better than obedience acquired by force and violence.

We have mentioned negotiation as a way of adjusting parental limits for the maturing child. Limits shift but are not removed totally. And the shifting should be a shared parent-child process, involving consultation and child involvement in limit setting. Negotiation involves parental active listening. It stops the parent's propensity to lecture continuously with the expectation of absolute obedience no matter what the child feels about the demands made. Negotiation does away with mindless commands and parental dictatorship that usually contribute to child rebellion. Negotiation involves communication, and sets a pattern that is carried into the life of the maturing child.

Navigating life challenges typically causes anxiety, apprehension and fear. This is why no loving parent should ever desert their maturing youth at this critical time when encouragement is of utmost necessity for assurance and validation. It is true that young people may appear to rebel as they enter teenage years. This is a normal process called individuation. All parents desire that their children grow up to become independent, emotionally healthy adults. How will they learn to be independent except by acting independent? However, when young people begin to test life away from parental control, they seem to be pushing hard against parental limit setting as if to demand that the limits be removed.

Such a child is not asking for limitless freedom, but is longing for parental engagement to help define and clarify new limits. It is the same way that when a young person outgrows their pair of shoes and the fast growing foot is pushing hard against the leather, the child is not asking to do away with shoes, but is non-verbally requesting for a new pair. In limit setting, where there is healthy communication, the young person feels free to come back to the parent for clarification and encouragement to move on and face new experiences with courage.

Growing up is scary. More than ever before, our children have to deal with loads of difficult, often confusing information. Will your child be free to discuss those difficult matters with you or will he feel condemned when he brings up sensitive, thought-provoking matters?

Various studies indicate that many children are beginning to dabble in pornography very early in their lives. Availability of Internet at home, cyber cafes, school and on cell phones as well as unguided use of the same is ground for confusion and temptation for many children. Do you as a parent know how your child is using the Internet? Pornography can quickly lead to addiction to the images as well as early sex exploration, followed by sex addiction. Beyond images is actual early sex involvement. With the onset of HIV and AIDS has come the global pressure for the use of contraceptive devices for children and the license that the children have a right over their bodies.

This pressure for children to have a right over their bodies can translate in two ways: a right to say no to sex and a right to engage in sex. Let me quickly add that in their noble desire to lower AIDS and teen pregnancy, many sexuality education programs do not emphasize sexual abstinence. The emphasis is on child reproductive rights. However, abstinence assumes ability to control the sexual urge making the child a full participant in their own protection. Full participation includes training children in skills to develop self- control, the ability to use their minds over their bodies and so order behavior.

We know that God has given us faculties that if used, are enhanced, and what is not used is lost. We also know that as one of these abilities, self-control can be translated to other areas of life. Self-control in matters of sexuality will be evidenced in other matters of behavior because the child will be able to order the self to do the right thing when other alternatives present themselves. This is more so in areas of other types of indulgence and physical urges like diet, use of drugs and alcohol and other inclinations.

If sexual education curriculum writers do not include self-control in the children and youth training package and international bodies mostly leave it out of proposed guidelines, and if parents do not take action, who is to teach our children that acting on their sexual urges can be delayed? Concerned parents should worry about school curriculums that may soon tell your 8-year old that he should pack his math books and his condoms in the same school bag!

Secondly, there is also the pressure by human rights bodies agitating for legalization of alternative sexuality for lesbians, gays and trans-gendered, that if any child begins to explore an alternative lifestyle, that desire should be respected as a human right. I have nothing against people who choose alternative sexuality. My take is with leaving out the fact that as a child enters adolescence, when sexual feelings start in their life, attraction can sometimes feature as infatuation with the same gender. Maturing animals sometimes mount each other within the same gender! However, the animal soon learns that sexual expression is supposed to be between those of the opposite gender.

Now animals are guided by instinct. In the creation hierarchy, human beings are above animals. They have a God-given ability to choose and exercise boundaries in their sexual expression. However, no child is born with knowledge to make wise choices. It is only wise adult counsel and guidance that can empower children to make wise choices. Who will teach your child these limits and reinforce the same boundaries as the young one matures? Clearly, it is neither the classroom, nor their friends or the media. This responsibility is left to you as the parent, to a church mentor or whomever you have chosen to partner with you in parenting. The battle for your child is on, and you can make a choice as to who will win.

We have mentioned the fact that no one else except the child should have a right over her own body. This is a noble premise that is aimed at stopping or discouraging sexual abuse. However, someone else has a right over our bodies. This is our Creator. If you read the Bible, you will remember these words: "Do you not know that your body is a temple of the Holy Spirit who is in you, whom you have received from God? You are not of your own. You were bought with a price. Therefore honor God with your body" (1 Corinthians 6: 19-20).

Does your child know that she did not appear but was created, fearfully and wonderfully (Psalm 139:14)? Does your son know that he is answerable to the Creator as to how he uses his body or lets others use it? Do you, as a parent, model this stewardship over your body before your own children? In these days of free sex, immorality and infidelity, these are heavy questions. As a parent, you cannot ignore them, because you are a steward over the lives of your children.

Self-Control and Personal Limit Setting

As you bring up a child, so he will be.
~ African (Swahili) Proverb

Like a city whose walls are broken down is a man who lacks self-control.
~ Proverbs 25:28

The African proverb: *"As you bring up a child, so he will be,"* states an obvious truth that is not so obvious. African parents are reminded that no one can plant corn and expect to harvest wheat. We reap what we sow with consistency. And, whether we realize we are sowing or not does not stop seeds of whatever nature we scatter from falling to the ground and maturing. Mature they will, and we can only hope that we sowed in wisdom, doing the best we knew how and seeking to know what we did not know.

The Biblical proverb: *"Like a city whose walls are broken down is a man who lacks self-control,"* is a reminder that anyone, parent or child, who lacks self-restraint or personal limit setting is like a defenseless, disgraced city in whose broken walls enemies find gaps and walk in to cause havoc and destruction. Such people are surrounded by broken lives and broken hearts because their lack of restraint creates havoc and chaos in their lives and in the lives of their dearest and nearest.

Selwyn Hughes, a great counselor and Bible teacher speaks on the need for self-control and personal limit setting in his *Everyday with Jesus* devotional. He emphasizes that sex is one of the most important areas where we need to exercise this restraint. He states that controlled sex is creative while uncontrolled sex is chaotic; that sex outside marriage leads to disintegration of personality and not fulfillment.

When the God-given gift of sex is abused outside wedlock, whether for married or single people, disintegration may not come right away but given time, come it will (Selwyn Hughes, 1998). Parental stewardship that helps a child begin to internalize personal limits is critical. This guidance empowers the young one to avoid destructive chaos and use their God-given gifts and faculties to live a life of constructive creativity.

To prevent destructive chaos from the life of a maturing child, parenting should be in partnership with God as well as the child so as to eliminate the chaos of growing up. Parenting without limits easily allows chaos. Let us explain this type of parenting further by placing families on a line called a continuum. One extreme end of the continuum is the authoritarian parenting style while the chaotic style occupies the opposite extreme end of the line. In the middle is the authoritative parenting style. What do we mean by these terms?

The middle type, the authoritative parenting style refers to parenting that is validating and encouraging. Where the father is present, he is supposed to be the natural head of the family, present and engaged in the life of the whole household. He leads like a committee chairman: listening to each one and everyone, encouraging communication and dialogue. He notes the quiet members of the group and urges them to open up and to share. He identifies different gifts of family members and urges them to express and grow their talents. Such a leader models to his sons how to love and protect women by loving and protecting his wife and daughters.

Under such leadership, family members thrive. They identify, explore and develop their areas of gifting, and no child is forced to be like another or compared to the other. It is common knowledge that children born in one family can never be the same. Even identical children are different one from the other. Some grow up to become scientists while others are gifted artists. Some are intelligent while others are not so endowed. Some will get straight A's in exams while others will sweat their way to a C average.

The authoritative father allows each of his children to shine in their area of gifting by encouraging maximum performance to the ability of each child. Such a father does not make comparisons or favor the stronger child over the weaker. Now, we can see why we emphasize on the father's active engagement in the family, because none of this parenting can be done by remote control. In this family, the mother is also a leader. She encourages her husband to take the initiative of guiding the family by actively supporting him.

Such a couple talks and communicates a lot on the direction their family is going. They walk a shared path, thrash out differences of opinion and make decisions on the way that will provide the greater holistic advantage to each child. Such communication is deep and confidential. It belongs to the confines of a father-mother private space, away from the children. Should one of the parents disagree with the way the other is handling matters in the presence of the child, it is advisable to wait and communicate the dissent away from the child. Of course, these limitations can be extended as the children mature.

However, young children develop more confidence to face life when they do not have to deal with the anxiety of parental dissension. Once again, this supportive role of the mother's parenting and her fulfillment of maternal roles in child training presuppose her active engagement in the life of the child. She, too, cannot parent by delegating her role to someone else all the time. Authoritative parenting is also possible in single parent families. The parent who is present takes leadership with careful choice of parenting partners as discussed earlier.

Parental Responsibilities in Limit Setting

Having a good discussion is like having riches.
~ African (Kenyan) Proverb

The integrity of the upright guides them, but the unfaithful are destroyed by their duplicity.
~ Proverbs 11:3

The African proverb: "*Having a good discussion is like having riches,*" encourages people to value good communication and so make time for it. In a society that is filled with the stress of multitasking, parents may trivialize the need to talk with, not to, their children. Traditional Africans realized the need to communicate with others and feel heard as they, in turn, heard you. This is talking with. Talking to is giving a lecture or delivering a sermon. At the end, we say the Grace and go home. Most of the time, no one asks: "*But … what do you mean with that illustration?*" In our context, parents are reminded to take time to listen to and discuss matters with their children, and no question or comment should be considered childish or immature.

The Biblical proverb: "*The integrity of the upright guides them, but the unfaithful are destroyed by their duplicity,*" is a reminder that integrity is singleness of heart, single mindedness that helps parents keep the main thing as the main thing. If they are totally committed to God's call on them as a guide and mentor of their children, he will bless *whatever effort* they put in and the time they set apart to deliver this mandate. However, for those that take this role for granted and relegate their parenting duties to the bottom of their priorities, this disloyalty to their primary responsibility is labeled unfaithfulness and will destroy them and those they are supposed to mentor.

Parental responsibility is not a small challenge. Today's reality is that as life becomes more engaging, many parents have to juggle numerous responsibilities that constantly take them away from home. However, the choice to have children should be accompanied by the challenge to classify in order of priority what matters most and where children feature in terms of parental investment of time and energy.

How can parents rearrange their lives such that children receive the attention they need? Authoritative parents will usually discipline themselves and make choices to place God first, followed by the spouse and then the children. Work and other responsibilities should come after family in matters of apportioning time, resources and energy. Should we have children if our choices eventually cause us to lose them through chaotic parenting?

Habits that contribute to losing our children belong to the extreme left hand side of the continuum: the authoritarian parenting style. In this style, the father or mother as family leader is often emotionally absent. If the father is present, he is dominant and controlling. He allows no dissenting voice, demands respect but gives little of the same. He may be present, yes, but he is too present in the lives of the children since he smothers them with control.

I remember a controlling father whose daughter said: "I want to be free to enjoy my holiday, at least part of it."

"What do you mean?" I asked. "I thought your Dad said in your presence that he gives you freedom to do other things than study during the school holidays. What do you mean by wanting to enjoy your holiday?"

"Not quite," the 16 year-old replied. "What he does is that he tells us what he wants us to do other than study. For example, 'I want you to read one book each week of the school holidays. That will be from 2pm to 4pm daily. I want you to wake up at 8am, eat your breakfast then clean your rooms, and so on.' Of course we rebel against this kind of control, then, he gets very angry and punishes us."

"What would you rather have?" I pursued, "A dad who tells you what to do, or one who does not bother whether you study or not?"

"Why can't he just ask us instead of telling us?" she pursued. "He'll probably obtain the same results and we'll be more motivated to do what he wants us to do. He needs to involve us in decision-making. When he dictates, we rebel because we are not getting a chance to practice our freedom of choice."

This young woman just underlined the reality that authoritarian parenting is likely to negatively impact children for life. The strong-willed child may rebel against the parent's dictates, good as they might be, while the compliant child may become anxious and even depressed. Defiance and rebellion arise out of a *whatever*, don't-care attitude for the strong- willed child who finds that whatever he does cannot please the dictator parent.

The compliant child is likely to struggle with the same despondency. This sadness is often linked to the hopelessness of trying to please a parent who does not notice or seem to appreciate the child's desire to be good. This means that limits that are too strict from a dominant parent contribute to anxiety in children. They begin to lose the natural freedom to explore and learn about their environment within flexible limits.

The other end of our continuum is the chaotic parenting style. Here, both parents as well as guidance for the maturing are mainly absent. This absence may be physical, where the parent may be living at home but cannot be bothered to care for the child.

Take an imaginary couple, Rose and Henry Matoko. They are parents of young children, both under 10 years of age. The earliest they get home is after 9pm each day. They are too busy at work and run businesses in the evening and weekends. They have left all the care of their children to house girls. Due to the burden of running the house, cooking and cleaning and even sometimes overseeing children's homework, no house help lasts for long in the Matoko household.

There are no set times for meals. The family does not sit together to eat either. Each person eats whenever or wherever they want. There is no set time for play, homework or reading. The television is on most of the time sometimes playing PG movies – those that need parental guidance. Sometimes, the children play with their estate peers till late into the evening and may not even shower before they sleep. The children are unruly and perform poorly at school. The parents often quarrel in front of the children, blaming one another for the indiscipline and chaos in their home.

To mature in a healthy manner, children need a secure, safe and consistent environment to form the ability to attach emotionally to significant caregivers in their lives. This attachment takes place first in the early years of a baby's life, through childhood and then into pre-adolescent years just before high school. The Matokos' children are very young. They need quality time to connect with their parents. This best happens during periods of play and relaxation, family meal-times, story-telling and reading together, shared chores, and other times spent with parents or primary caregivers. Several things will affect the Matoko children negatively. First, there is chaos at home. This will impact on the children's security and self-worth. They may begin to feel that their parents do not care for them because if they did, they would spend more time with the young ones, ensuring structure.

Secondly, the absence of structure at meal times and play leads to lack of self-ordering and self-monitoring. This is because little training or learning can go on in such a chaotic environment. The third point is that the regular change of house girls affects the children's stability and ability to create healthy attachments. This is because as soon as they begin to attach to one house girl, there is a change. The negative effect multiplies if the mother is emotionally and/or physically absent as these changes take place.

Finally, the children are involved in un-moderated play and television watching. Family members use mobile telephones and tablets at meal times instead of communicating with each other. Young ones download Internet content with no control. Such children internalize many confusing values and there is no one mature enough first to know what exactly they are exposed to, to moderate it for them and to ensure that wrong values are not learned as well as practiced.

CONSISTENCY AND LIMIT SETTING

It is the habit that a child forms at home, that follows them to their marriage.
~ *African (Nigerian) Proverb*

Whoever loves discipline loves knowledge, but he who hates correction is stupid.
~ *Proverbs 12:1*

The African Proverb: "*It is the habit that a child forms at home, that follows them to their marriage,*" reminds parents that children do not change very much. What they are at home, they will continue to be in society, more so in the homes they go on to build later on. It follows that consistent training of children is an investment for their later lives. They will draw from the wisdom learnt in their parents' home to create their own families and pass on the same wisdom to their children.

The Biblical proverb: "*Whoever loves discipline loves knowledge, but he who hates correction is stupid,*" are strong words reminding us that true and sustainable learning can only happen within an atmosphere of consistent obedience and order. The proverb has strong language in stating that those who do not like correction are stupid. Proverbs 1:22 is a cross reference of Proverbs 12:1. It strengthens this case thus: "*How long will you simple ones love your simple ways? How long will mockers delight in mockery and fools hate knowledge?*"

Synonyms for mockers include people who are proud, arrogant, full of insults, hatred and strife. Parents should remain humble students who desire to learn more and more about parenting so that they can become better and better in limit setting. This way, they will maximize the gains of the time they are able to spend with their children. Those who are arrogant cannot learn and so find it difficult to teach or create time to train their little ones. Teaching and training demand presence and consistency.

Some parents may be away from home deliberately, not because they work away from their residence, but because they want nothing to do with their child. Other parents may be physically present but emotionally not connected to their child. Still others exhibit another kind of disengagement because they are inconsistent in limit setting. Elsewhere, we have emphasized the need for consistency in childrearing because children learn better when goal posts do not keep changing. Imagine the best footballer trying to score a goal for his team and each time he dribbles the ball to the goal area, he finds that the goal posts moved to another part of the field. The experience would cause the man immense anxiety and set him up for failure even if he is the best shooter.

A few years ago, a local newspaper, the Daily Nation carried a story of 12-year old Isaiah who was killed by his uncle. The older man pummeled the boy with a fork jembe, a several-pronged hoe, until his skull was crushed. The villagers came and managed to rescue the child. Being a remote, rural area without transport access, they took over one hour to get him to the nearest health center. By the time they got there, he was already dead.

What happened to young Isaiah? The newspapers reported that the uncle killed the boy for being HIV+. His HIV status notwithstanding, the boy actually died due to the chaos in his life. He was born to a young HIV+ mother who was kicked out of wedlock by her husband. Mother, Isaiah and his baby brother moved in with their grandmother. Isaiah was then barely three years old. Soon after, the baby, who was also HIV+, died of AIDS-related illnesses. Isaiah's mother soon followed, leaving the boy alone with his aging, ailing grandmother.

There is no telling the chaos, grief and want the boy suffered. He went to school and struggled with poverty, hunger and his own illness. Eventually, grandmother also passed away. The child was passed on to an aunt and later ended up with his uncle who isolated him from the rest of the family because of his status. Isaiah was now a maturing, young boy determined to get an education against all odds. His uncle made him sleep in a chicken pen, marked all the plates the boy ate from and engaged a neighboring woman to come and cook for him.

One sad, fateful morning, Isaiah was sent by this woman to borrow a matchbox from his uncle so that she could light the fire and make him his breakfast before his long walk to school. No one knows what triggered the man's violence, but he is said to have picked the jembe and clobbered the child in the head. Isaiah did not succumb to the HIV virus, but to the chaos in his life, chaos created by adults who should have been his protectors.

Isaiah's case is rather severe. He lacked an adult who could love him, parent him and create a safe place for him. Many children suffer for lack of love, caring, order, discipline, and example. A connected parent will be physically and emotionally at hand in the lives of his children. This creates the security the child needs to grow in body, mind and spirit. A caring mother will teach and train the child to live right. This way, values for rightful living can be consistently emphasized into the child's life.

In Deuteronomy 6:4-9 on, God admonishes parents to love God with all their hearts, with all their soul and with all their strength. Then, they are to internalize God's commands and then impress the same on their children all the time and everywhere: when they walk, talk, lie down and get up. They are required to have God's commands written where all can see them and even on door frames and house gates. This means that training of children has to be an integral part of any home, and that teaching should not be information-based but life-oriented. Parents need to use the context of each day to teach values and should be part of the child's daily life experiences, helping children to know what God expects of his people as part of daily living.

Such engagement means that if parents who are present, loving and caring set clear limits, their children will not get lost in the chaos of life. For example, parents may desire to communicate the importance of honesty as a life value. They let the children know right from birth that the family, whether adults or children, tell the truth. Then, they all tell the truth all the time. Beyond telling, they live the truth at home, work, in society, while doing exams, spending money that is not theirs, or playing a game.

They do not cheat on their spouses and expect children to return all the change after doing some shopping for the family. Parents communicate that they do not apply one set of rules for their children and another set for the adult in the family. Principles are principles and they become codes by which the family lives. This emphasis will create security for the child because young ones learn that they do not have to recall what they told the parent last week because truth is consistent. No one has anything to hide, so they do not have to work hard at hiding anything.

Parent-Child Attachment and Limit Setting

A child brought up where there is always dancing cannot fail to dance.
~ African (Nyanja) Proverb

She watches after the affairs of her household ... Her children arise and call her blessed.
~ Proverbs 31:27-28

The African (Nyanja) proverb: *"A child brought up where there is always dancing cannot fail to dance,"* comes from the Nyanja, also known as Chewa, people of Malawi. It describes the power of attachment in child development. Attachment refers to the bond of love, affection, and emotional connection that a maturing child develops with the primary caretaker - parent or guardian. This bond enhances learning. It is like glue that attaches the lessons a parent teaches to the heart of the child. The child learns not only by direct imparting of knowledge but by watching the parent model behavior. It is like an absorption of good things that causes the child to blossom wanting to model the way the parent does them.

The Biblical proverb: *"She watches after the affairs of her household ... Her children arise and call her blessed,"* describes such a parent who takes good care of the needs of her family and of course the father who also watches lovingly over his home by supplying their holistic needs. The children live to bless such parents through working hard, living responsibly, and doing all they can to make their parents proud. Such an impact cannot happen by remote control when children are removed from their parents during their formative years.

In this final part of this Chapter, we shall examine the

ever-growing tendency especially in Africa to send children away to boarding school at a very early stage of development. Until the young one gets to teenage years, they are not ready to leave home yet. Even in adolescence, the teen still needs parental guidance. However, the closer young people get to adulthood, the more parents need to learn to release them so that in time they can become their own persons. Boarding school for young children denies them constant parental guidance that no amount of academic education can replace. Every parent will remember that we are living at a time and age where so many things are battling to shape the life of the child.

We need to emphasize that there are special cases where young children end up in boarding school because there is no alternative. This is the case, for example, where a family relocates very often because of the parents' career. Armed forces personnel, navy families, certain government jobs and even missionary or church work might require that parents are transferred often and the family has to relocate each time. Parents may choose to have the child in boarding school if home schooling is not an option. Whatever the family situation is, boarding school before teenage years does not always yield good results because it limits the parent-child proximity for life skills training and attachment building.

Life foundations for holistic living are laid between birth and age 12 or 13. If a parent does not train children in values, attitudes, work ethics, faithfulness, purity, selflessness, sharing, respect, morality, etiquette, tidiness, cleanliness, self-care, and so on, someone else will. There is no lack of alternative teachers. We have the media, music, Internet, books, magazines, wrong peer relationships, warped adults, and wrong role models.

This is not to say that these teachers are not in the home environment or that we can insulate our children from society. We cannot ban the Internet or the television from our children, nor can we keep them from socializing with their friends. However, when we are physically and emotionally close to our children, impressing the right values with boldness can happen more consistently. This is because guidance can be closely administered in small, consistent doses.

Doctors advise patients: "Take one tablet three times a day, as prescribed." With education curricula fast changing to allow all sorts of things at school, parents will want to track closely what their children are learning. For example, caring, listening parents may already be hearing a voice that is arguing that children and youth have the right to choose their sexual orientation as well as partners with whom to practice their choices. This encouragement by rights activists adds that children should be empowered to negotiate whether or not to have sex with a partner. Does negotiation work with bullies? Does it work with rapists – individual or groups of them?

One hears horror stories of children forced into sex, even between similar genders, by other children who are expressing their right to choose their sexual orientation. This reality suggests that parents need to ensure that the large amounts of money many of them pay for their children's education away from home are a wise investment. Wisdom evaporates if destruction is introduced into a child's life.

With reduced adult supervision in both boarding and day schools, we have increasing reports of school bullying. I have had cases of suicidal adolescents who suffered bullying from early years in school and others who experience the same even in university. One young woman was not only bullied but also sexually molested by a group of boys while in an exclusive, private school. Through the years, she lived with self-reproach, low self-worth and self-loathing, believing that there was something in her that made her peers bully and mistreat her. She wished to die. She went ahead and tried many ways of taking her own life, but somehow, she did not succeed.

In therapy, she said: "I hate myself that I am a failure even at taking my own life!" Sadly, the young lady's parents were too engrossed in their careers to notice the struggle going on in their daughter's life. Thankfully, between professional help and a lot of support and understanding from the parents, the youth was soon on her way to health and wholeness.

This argument is not an attempt to condemn boarding or private schools. Our appeal to parents is to take responsibility to parent their children with physical, emotional and spiritual commitment, until the time when the young one has matured well enough to leave home. In cases where the parent has to send a child away to school because of situations that cannot be avoided, then the obligation to create as much presence with the child as possible still applies.

Delegated parenting often fails. Where it succeeds, the child is likely to attach more to the surrogate parent than the biological one. How many young mothers bemoan the fact that their child feels closer to a nanny or house girl than to the one who gave birth to them?

Attachment includes emotional and cognitive connection that the child so much needs for stable development. This kind of closeness helps establish the young one's identity: Who am I? What is my purpose in the world? Where am I headed? Identity ensures stability that crystallizes the child's perception of the world as a safe place. A recognized and negative psychological impact on children is the challenge of adjustment when there is too much disturbance and change in the child's environment. A stable environment makes for stable identity.

To understand this need for stability better, let us take the example of a plant. We grow seeds in the seedbed. When they are mature enough, we prepare the recipient ground with lots of manure and adequate water. Then, we transplant the young shoot. We leave the sapling in the new location so that roots can develop. We regularly water that plant and watch out for pests. We are happy when new leaves and branches form and joy comes when the flowers and buds develop. We do not keep transplanting the young plant from one spot to another. Such a plant, disturbed over and over again, finally withers and dries away because its roots were disturbed too many times.

The same applies to a child: one year at home with mother, then a year at grandmas, two years in boarding school, another year with an auntie, then back to mom with boarding school in between. Because of innate fear of detachment, such a child stops trying to get emotionally attached to anyone. Roots were not allowed to grow long enough to emotionally attach to significant others.

This young one is likely to remain aloof and seemingly emotionally cold. The youth also suffers the inner emptiness of a poor sense of belonging. Energy is spent trying to adjust to a new environment each time change happens. This uncertainty erodes identity leaving a vacuum that can easily become a doorway for destructive tendencies in later life. In some extreme cases, such children suffer from fear of abandonment and are likely to struggle with various mental health and behavioral issues in adulthood where detachment may have included neglect and/or abuse. Parent-child attachment is a critical element in healthy maturation and should never be compromised.

Case Study on Limit Setting

Parents struggle with challenges on how to limit the amount of time children spend watching television. This is not a light concern considering that according to Dr Aric Sigman, by age seven, a child with a television at home and allowed to it will have spent a full year glued to the screen. Indeed, some parents have been known to use the devices as "electronic baby sitters." Why so much concern?

What are the negative outcomes of too much television on children? Watching television reduces the time a child spends in active play and so encourages immobility. Negative outcomes are indicated as obesity, Type 2 diabetes, attention problems and psychological difficulties. Why do parents find it so difficult to reinforce limits? Do limits hurt?And how do children turn out living with parents who are able to reinforce limits when there is so much to do, be it on the family front, in business, at work and so on?

Rev. David Oginde is the Bishop of Christ is The Answer Ministries (CITAM), one of the largest and most influential ministries in Nairobi, Kenya. He is reported to be a highly educated and well-traveled man, and a favorite speaker and teacher. As the head of the ministry in Kenya, he is a very busy man and would therefore not be easily available to give an interview. However, I ran into him in Bangalore, India, where we were both attending a Global Leadership Forum. I requested for a brief interview with him one day, wanting to know what his parents did to help turn out such a disciplined leader. Was there any limit setting? If there was, what nature did the discipline take?

Bishop told me that he came from a polygamous family, and that they all lived in a large home in the same compound. Indeed, there was such an age variance that his oldest brother was old enough to be his dad! In the same compound, there were also two uncles on his father's side with their own wives and many children. All in all, there were 60 members of this large family in one large compound.

Bishop pointed out that with such a large number of adults and children, there was obviously need for order. His father was the head of the whole household. He provided clear boundaries on what everyone could and could not do, and went ahead to reinforce these boundaries seriously. The family lived and played by these rules, and the older man literally held the family members all together.

David's father made sure that the family studied and internalized the Ten Commandments and these were reinforced "without mercy," he added. Anyone doing what was wrong had the act spelt out clearly with a warning. Each family member was expected to attend church and no witchcraft or superstition was ever allowed in the family. David's father taught the family to live above fear of evil and emphasized God's protection over the household.

Bishop Oginde gave an example where one of his older brothers tried to get involved in witchcraft by going to see a traditional healer who was known for the practice. When the family head learnt about it, the man involved was disciplined "like a small boy," and told categorically that he could not "bring those things into this home."

Was the punishment meted in private or public? David responded that his father never called anyone aside but disciplined the offending person right in front of everyone. I asked the Bishop if, in his perception, this was an acceptable way of dealing with indiscipline. His response was that in retrospect, although it seems like "open-air" discipline might have humiliated a child, it, instead created mutual accountability, with children warning one another to behave well to avoid their father's rod.

Rev. Oginde was also of the view that his father's consistency and no-compromise attitude towards limit setting enabled the older man to communicate unwavering standards that created stability in the family.

As he reminisced regarding his past, the Bishop could now identify some of his father's qualities in his own life: personal discipline, wisdom, mentorship, integrity, order, respect and role modeling.

CHAPTER 6

PARENTING AS ROLE MODELING

The Meaning of Role Modeling

When you follow in the path of your father, you learn to walk like him.
~ African (Ashanti) Proverb

Do not set foot on the path of the wicked or walk in the way of evil men.
~ Proverbs 4:14

The African proverb: *"When you follow in the path of your father, you learn to walk like him,"* is a reminder that parents are role models by the simple fact that they are fathers. Children will most likely become like them. Parents should always remember therefore that children become like them slowly and shape their lives against what they see, hear, touch and smell.

The Biblical proverb: *"Do not set foot on the path of the wicked or walk in the way of evil men,"* is a regular reminder that one should be wise not to keep the company of immoral people. If this person is a parent, then that same immorality is transported home to the children.

In this context of parenting, roles are functions or activities of a parent that can be passed on through imitation or copying. Roles can be good or bad but they have the capacity to flow from parent to child either to build or to destroy. This is the meaning of role modeling, in that whether parents purpose it or not, children still copy them, and they do so quite closely.

Someone has said that what we hate most in our children are their qualities that so closely mirror our own. We quickly recognize unsatisfactory behavior and even get scared that our children are becoming too much like us. It is then that we lash out in anger. What we often forget is that we did not just bear the children but shaped them to become who they are, often living out models before them, intentionally or not.

CHILDREN 'R US!

Children will hate all those who give all things to them.
~ African Proverb

Wisdom is supreme; therefore get wisdom.
Though it cost all you have, get understanding.
~ Proverbs 4:7

The African proverb: "*Children will hate all those who give all things to them,*" is a reminder that spoilt children end up despising the very parents who spoilt them. As they grow up, they may throw tantrums and make demands, but inside, they are craving for love that demands restraint.

The Biblical proverb: *"Wisdom is supreme; therefore get wisdom. Though it cost all you have, get understanding,"* is a cry urging parents, in our context, not to spare anything to learn parenting skills. No one goes to school or college to earn a degree in parenting, so competence in childrearing is left to each of us to acquire. And, for each child, there is no second chance. None of them can be born once again for second-chance parenting. If we blow it once, we have blown it, but for the grace of God. The proverb urges us therefore to leave no stone unturned in asking God for wisdom which he liberally supplies when we seek to know. Our role is to do the best then leave the rest to him as Creator.

A common advert reads "Toys 'R Us." I thought about this advert when I considered the reality that our children are really like us! Once, I had a very angry mother in our clinic. She had brought a rebellious 15 year old whom she claimed was rude and spoilt. She narrated how the young woman became very angry when she was crossed.

"You can't believe it, Doctor," narrated the mother. "The other day, my daughter became so mad that she kicked a hole through the door of her wardrobe! How can I control her?"

"What methods have you tried to deal with Achieng's anger?" I asked.

"Well, I take away privileges, but it doesn't help."

"Give me an example of a recent attempt," I pursued.

The mother looked at the child who sat there with a smug look on her beautiful face. "Remember last Wednesday Achieng? I found you playing with your phone instead of doing your homework. What did I do?" She asked.

"Mom, you grabbed my phone and smashed it against the wall!" wailed the adolescent. "Yes Doctor. Exactly!" confirmed the mother. "I decided to break the phone! And now, maybe without it, you can settle down and do your homework in peace."

"Did it work?" I pursued.

"Of course not," answered the mother. "That's why we are here!"

What was the difference between Achieng's angry outburst and her mother's behavior? None, really. The child was just mirroring the parent. The adolescent had learnt that instead of talking about issues, the way out was to lash out in anger and violent outbursts. Temper tantrums are not the preserve of young children. Many parents are probably still emotionally adolescents in their ways especially when angry, stressed or distressed.

Sigmund Freud discusses a psychological process called fixation. He argues that during our psychological development, we graduate from stage to stage beginning from childhood, via adolescence to adulthood, then late adulthood to old age. Very much like African initiation stages, it is only after navigating one stage that we can legitimately move on to the next one.

Sometimes, an adult is admonished to stop acting or talking like a child if there is display of immature behavior or attitude. Psychology indicates that if, for some reason, we get stuck in any area of our lives at some stage, we may mature physically or even progress academically but we remain childish at the stage where we got fixated. If threatened at any point in our lives, we are likely to revert to our childish ways. In our adult bodies, even dressed in a suit, we might actually behave very much like the child we are trying to discipline.

Meme, not his real name, somehow missed the role modeling that would have taught him skills in problem solving. His father expected him to be a faultless person. Indeed, the older man had no patience for mistakes or weakness in his son. As a young man, Meme worked hard in school and at home, pushing himself to perform. In university, he studied engineering and as a worker, did all he could to perform. He would consider it weakness to ask for help. The engineer would not allow anyone to think for a moment that he did not understand or know how to deal with ambiguous situations.

Life, however, is full of ambiguity. As an example, his wife became depressed. Meme wondered why the woman would torture herself with tears and cries of: "All you care for is your work. You come home late! You don't love me because if you did, you would touch me. You no longer do!" Meme did not seek for help or try to understand what was happening. One day he came to our clinic with his 16-year old son in tow.

"Doctor, you help young people such as these. Please help my son," he explained. "How long will you take?" Then, he turned to his son: "Jimmy, I'll pick you up after one hour."

After these brief introductory remarks, the man got into his new car and drove away. I turned to the slender, sad-looking youth seated before me.

Normally we get the parent of a youth below 18 to cosign the therapy Consent Form and complete the intake together with the parent. It is through the eyes of the parent that we first see the child as well as understand how he navigated his developmental milestones. We also ask the youth to help us understand the situation at hand using the child's perception of his family life. This father was, however, in a big hurry to hand over his son to me, promising to come and pick him up after he had been "sorted out." I noticed the man's speed of packaging the problem and got curious to find out what was really happening. I soon found out.

"So, Jimmy. What's up? What can we do for you?" I asked the young man as I closed the door and sat facing him in the counseling room.

His response: "He didn't tell you why he dragged me here?"

"No," I answered. "He seemed to be in a hurry to go somewhere."

"He's always in a hurry," replied the young man with a sad, quiet smile. "I wish he'd stop sometimes to listen to others as well as to himself!"

"Anyway, let's not talk about him since he is not here. Shall we? Let's talk about you instead." I responded.

Jimmy started talking and the more I listened and encouraged him, the freer he became. He described himself and his home. He narrated his parents' relationship with him, and life at school. Thirty minutes into the session, I realized that my real client had already driven away in his new car. The young man sitting with me in my clinic could be referred to only as the identified patient. Whatever the father saw as the problem was only a mirror image of a dysfunctional father and an equally wanting marriage and family life. The challenge was how to bring the man into the clinic. He was the one that really needed help.

Triangulation – The Enemy of Role Modeling

When there is peace in the country, the chief does not carry a shield.
~ African (Ugandan) Proverb

Better a dry crust with peace and quiet than a house full of feasting with strife.
~ Proverbs 17:1

The African proverb: *"When there is peace in the country, the chief does not carry a shield,"* points to the fact that where there is harmony, there is security. People, even leaders, are watchful if there is discord. When there is strife and discord in the family, children use mental and emotional energy worrying. Worry leads to anxiety that begins to affect their maturation, relationships, freedom to explore, spontaneity, learning, relationships, and so on. It is for this reason that parents should ensure marital and family harmony as much as possible not only for their own happiness but also to ensure that home is a safe place where there is happiness and joy.

The Biblical proverb: "*Better a dry crust with peace and quiet than a house full of feasting with strife,*" underlines the critical need for peace in the family. The main parental focus should therefore be on ensuring quiet and peace at home rather than emphasizing prosperity as the main thing at the expense of harmony. It is better if prosperity and peace can co-exist because poverty can also threaten harmony. The fragile nature of peace and harmony in relationships suggests that constant watchfulness is necessary lest we lose what we need for transient material gain.

The Systemic Therapy of Family Systems Theory of Psychology describes the situation in Jimmy's family (discussed in the last section) as triangulation. Derived from the word triangle, the term means that two parents having a problem between them, just like the engineer, get into an avoidance mode. They suppress negative feelings and move on as if everything is all right. For a person living in active denial of problems, the tendency is to blame someone else when things go wrong. Clearly, things were not right in Jimmy's home and his mother's response was depression while his father was busy looking for someone to take up the role of scapegoat. The older man may have been nursing the fear that Jimmy might become depressed like his mother.

Whatever the motivation or reasoning, Jimmy's parents were the first people that should have been in our clinic that day. I did not send the child away. I kept on seeing Jimmy, offering support for anxiety and other needs. Through his presence in therapy, I was able to request for his parents' presence and eventually, the whole family came for help.

However, the father came last, and only when I said: "Please, come because I need your help to work with your family." In his projection, he had always blamed others for problems in his marriage and family, but now, he finally began to self-examine and to understand the connection between his upbringing and the stubbornness in his relationships with his family members.

Parental Engagement and Role Modeling

Do not let what you cannot do tear from your hands what you can.
~ African (Ashanti) Proverb

The wise in heart are called discerning, and pleasant words promote instruction.
~ Proverbs 16:21

The African proverb: "*Do not let what you cannot do tear from your hands what you can,*" is a reminder that no parent should ever despise their ability to mentor their children and role model positive attributes to them. Single mothers often despise their ability to raise emotionally healthy children. A poor parent may also wonder how their child will turn out when he does not have all the good things that well-endowed parents can purchase for their children. Doing the best with what we have in our hands is what the Creator requires of parents.

The Biblical proverb: "*The wise in heart are called discerning, and pleasant words promote instruction,*" underlines that there are precious things in life that any parent can share with their child. There is wisdom that is above all riches, and pleasant words that enable children to learn what their parents teach them. A child whose parent is able to discern his needs - be they physical, emotional, mental or other, provides what the young one needs at whatever phase of development he is at. Riches, position, gender, or any other attributes do not determine who possesses this wisdom. Rather, God provides it to parents who are willing to raise their children right. Such wisdom begins with positive role modeling.

Negative role modeling needs no effort, planning or self-discipline. However, what are the ingredients for positive role modeling? Becoming role models to our children does not happen through parental lectures. It happens when parents are engaged in the life of their children. Children love to watch their parents, read their facial expressions, listen to the tone of their voices, watch them dealing with difficult situations, listen as they respond to criticism and so on. They therefore desire role modeling of values that are obviously visible and not ambiguous.

While in the USA and Germany, we noticed that many homes have a garage workshop with all sorts of hand and electric tools. After work and school, fathers and sons spend lots of time in the workshop. Most home repairs and even construction are never outsourced. Fathers work with sons shoulder to shoulder putting up sheds, painting a house over weekends, repairing the roofs, laying a new floor and even opening and repairing a car engine. These men - fathers and young adults or the father and a younger son, may not say much to one another as they work together, but values of hard work, integrity, diligence, self-control, thrift and so on, are passed on through a garage workshop.

We also noticed that mothers will be training young women, even toddlers, how to bake, cook, do a pot roast, and even pick and arrange some flowers or greenery as part of setting up the dinner table. Soon, the table is set and the men are called to wash up and sit at the table for dinner.

The family bows their heads and the father says grace. The family eats together and afterwards, men clean up the kitchen as other family members read, or play musical instruments. Mothers may even knit or crotchet before retiring to bed. In many families, especially Christian ones, the television was not in the shared living room. In some homes, the set was absent. The family had decided that they did not need it.

Later on in Australia, we were amazed to find that in several families, men were excellent cooks and prided themselves in shopping for food items and then preparing and serving three-course meals to their families. They chose to be present and to make family life fun.

We in Africa often think that the western world and their values are exactly what we watch off Hollywood movies and TV comedies. However, let me emphasize here that the average western family is solid. Values of industry, self-discipline, integrity and hospitality are modeled purposefully. No wonder America produces men and women, who can create a craft that can soar from the earth, reach the moon, collect data and bring it back!

While some of our men boast that they can handle several women as wives at the same time and also father children right, left and center; and while some women may struggle with who really fathered their son; while our governments spend millions supplying billions of condoms to men and their sons who must act out their sexuality; while we struggle and debate on the rights of adolescents to contraceptives, and the need to legalize abortion; the rest of the world matches on to greatness. They have purposed to model positive values to their offspring.

Discipline and Role Modeling

Train a child the way he should go and make sure you also go the same way.
~ African Proverb

The path of the righteous is like the first gleam of dawn, shining ever brighter till the full light of day. But the way of the wicked is like deep darkness; they do not know what makes them stumble.
~ Proverbs 4:18-19

The African proverb: "*Train a child the way he should go and make sure you also go the same way,*" is a polite remember that a parent cannot live wrong and expect the child to live right. Ensuring child adherence to parental training in right living depends on whether the parent is living what he is teaching. Therefore the model is train and don't just tell the child, then model what you train. Training is a process that takes time and energy; checking and confirming that the child understands, and even disciplining the one that errs. However, if this effort is to bear fruit, living by example is mandatory.

The Biblical proverb: "*The path of the righteous is like the first gleam of dawn, shining ever brighter till the full light of day. But the way of the wicked is like deep darkness; they do not know what makes them stumble,*" implies that living right provides safety and clarity that enables one to walk correctly and avoid the pitfalls of life. The contrary is true, that deliberately living wrong can be likened to walking in deep shadows where stumbling is a norm. How can a parent stumbling in darkness point the way for an insecure youth who longs to know how to live right?

Someone has observed that often, before we have undisciplined children, we start with undisciplined parents. I thought of these words recently as I walked and drove through Seoul, Korea, admiring a city where you hardly see a speck of dust. I traveled on the underground train which had clean public toilets where ladies would sit and touch up their make-up and children play as they waited for their mothers. The walls around the underground railway were clean mosaic, with no graffiti and no trash visible anywhere. I watched disciplined, hardworking masses walking on the streets or manning their businesses. I admired the training of children in schools, and the industry of a nation that seems to be like a kingdom of organized ants at work.

Sitting in a train in the underground railway in Seoul, a four year-old child accompanied by her dad looked at me, the only black person in the packed cabin. She must have been examining possibly the first black face she had ever seen. She pointed her little finger at me and said something to her father. The father slapped her little hand and said something reprimanding. The child obviously apologized and tearfully turned away. I guessed that she must have said something derogatory to get such a scolding. The father gave a firm little lecture in their language and all the adults looked at the pair with approval. As a training model, discipline has to be purposed by each parent as it does not happen automatically.

Thoughts on Fathers of Honor

Rev. Prof. Peter Mageto is a Methodist church minister, Professor of Ethics, and Deputy Vice Chancellor, Academic Affairs, Kenya Methodist University. He is an intelligent, ethical, married man and father of two adolescents. Recently, he spoke at Lavington United Church on a topic titled *Fathers of Honor*. I asked him if I could share his thoughts in this book, and he straightaway said: "Of course. Feel free to do so."

Prof. Mageto noted that responsible parents are missing in action! Fathers of honor are in short supply. There is lots of reference to mothers but not enough on fathers of honor. In Exodus 18:13-27, Jethro counsels his son-in-law Moses on recruiting men who would be his administrative support in judging over Israel: "Look for godly men," he advised Moses.

Godly men are also needed in parenting. Men may be successful in business, leadership and other enterprise, yet if they fail in fatherhood, they have little to show for the continuity of their names. For example, Jacob failed in his paternal leadership when he favored Joseph over his other children. That coat of many colors that he gave the young man caused divisions, envy, plotting evil and murderous intent.

Eli, Israel's priest failed to instruct his sons. The young men became rebellious, arrogant and wicked, totally disregarding the expected norms of priestly fatherhood and behavior. David, a king who was described as successful in many ways failed in being a model to his sons. One of his most glaring failures was his adultery with Bathsheba and the subsequent plan to murder her husband. His son Absalom killed his brother and the family was beset with rebellion. Prof. Mageto added that many fathers have become the witchcraft within their families by absconding from their duties and responsibilities.

Other young people have missed a father. They have never been *fathered.* Others do not know who their fathers are. What are the qualities of fathers of honor? Men of truth, those who fear and honor God, who do not just do church or religion but also live out the values therein. They hate dishonest gain, and seek a firm foundation through a personal relationship with God because only the Almighty knows what makes our children tick.

These men must love their children unconditionally, with compassion and an invitation for reconciliation for the wayward. The father of the prodigal son moved towards his son and embraced him in a welcoming hug. Fathers cannot allow gaps and distance to grow between them and their children. Instead, as the mature family leaders they should be, fathers should take the initiative to close relational gaps between them and the children.

This closeness implies ongoing training of children. In Hebrew, explained Prof. Mageto, train means dedicate or give the child back to God as a gift by recognizing his interest and sovereignty over the child's life; instruct – meaning teach with clarity of content; and then motivate them towards hope for life and living. Prof. Mageto noted that society has many depressed and unmotivated young people, and that motivation is not provision of activities but provision of connection that makes for rich living that is independent of money and position.

Some parents have given "fat" checks to their children to start a business and are surprised when the establishment soon collapses. "What am I missing?" Some fathers wonder. Prof. Mageto noted that many women take courses in counseling and invest in relationships. However, many men lack communication skills especially with their children and do not seek to learn them. If they study anything, they invest in entrepreneurship courses or those that enhance their careers.

With regard to the family, instead of staying with the challenge and seeking to learn how to navigate it, many fathers become absentee dads, who chase after the wind, meaning that they invest their time in other pursuits outside parenting, leaving the seemingly less important enterprise to mothers. Women struggle to fit both roles, and stress mounts up in the marriage with the blame game as an escape whenever parenting crises appear.

Later on, with surprise, the fathers wonder why their children have not turned out with focus and confidence like others. Prof. Mageto concluded that fathers can come home at any time and that their coming home will begin to bring prodigal sons and daughters home. After the wayward youth came home, the father of the lost son declared: "He was lost, but now is found." The profession of fatherhood is a *now* vocation. *Now* fathers who love, train and motivate the gifts of their children can be described as fathers of honor.

Case Study on Role Modeling

H.E. Judge Joyce Aluoch sits at the International Criminal Court at The Hague. How do women like these emerge from rural Kenya to sit at one of the most powerful international courts? There must be someone or some individuals who left a strong mark in Judge Aluoch's life. In the book *Life Journeys* (Susan Wakhungu-Githuku, 2010), Judge Joyce shares that since her father worked away from home as was common in colonial and post-colonial Kenya, she was raised mainly by her mother among 10 siblings, seeing her father only over the school holidays. She writes that her mother was her greatest role model, working hard to raise her 10 children without grumbling or whining.

Judge Aluoch left home early to go to boarding school but she adds that although her father lived mainly at his place of work as District Commissioner, he keenly followed her progress, ensuring that he guided her to join the legal career. Here, she lived out the values impacted in her by her parents in the way she handled the Nairobi Children's Court, later establishing the Family Division of the High Court. This determination was to ensure that children were raised by their parents and not allowed to roam the streets alone. She was also instrumental in institutionalizing the rights of children and child protection against child abuse. The values internalized in her growing up years are repeated in her life through the unwavering support of her husband as she carries on her duties.

Matters of faith and family continue to be clearly important as she is a practicing Christian to this day, observing the disciplines of family connectedness, prayer and Bible reading. She models to her children and to other young people the need for focused living as well as determination to succeed in spite of life's challenges. She also reminds leaders, be they parents or other, that value-based living is not an option. Role modeling is therefore a critical commitment for Judge Aluoch. From The Hague, she continues to live out character traits that were implanted into her life all the way from the village as she carried water from the river, collected firewood in the bush, and followed after her mother, the greatest influence in her life.

CHAPTER 7

PARENTING AS PRESENCE

MEANING OF PARENTAL PRESENCE

If your cornfield is far from your house, the birds will eat your corn.
~ African (Congolese) Proverb

He who fears the Lord has a secure fortress and for his children it will be a refuge.
~ Proverbs 14:26

The African proverb: *"If your cornfield is far from your house, the birds will eat your corn,"* has its background in a common African practice to watch over crops such as corn and millet so that birds do not destroy the crop. Indeed, my husband, Dr. Gershon Mwiti, often uses a version of this proverb that is common among the Meru people of Kenya. In the Meru language, the proverb is sung as poetry: *"Rware rwaba-Kamami iru tukwingiria mirugu ii."* The literal translation of the song is: "I will chase off birds from my crop and push them towards the range of those who sleep [and hence do not watch over their crop]." These two sayings emphasize that parents need to be holistically present and in close proximity in the lives of their children, otherwise the birds or factors that destroy children will take root in their lives.

The Biblical proverb: *"He who fears the Lord has a secure fortress and for his children it will be a refuge,"* underlines that the parent's proximity to God through listening and obedience is a sure way for parents to receive the courage and resources they need to positively impact their children. Closeness to the young ones and godliness create a safe place of protection, peace and resources necessary for the child's holistic maturation.

A young college student in a private Christian university was misbehaving. He was turning up in class with a hangover and was also caught smoking. He had been apprehended before and sternly warned. His father worked for an international organization in West Africa and his mother had been appointed to serve in a foreign mission abroad. She had already left the country after placing his two younger siblings in boarding school. The college counselor decided to call the father and warn that his son was on the verge of suspension. After the counselor explained the problem, the father retorted: "What's the matter? Do you people need money? I can wire some tomorrow!"

The school referred the student for therapy. When he came, the young man, a sensitive soul, narrated that as he grew up, he hardly ever saw his parents. "Money has never been a problem in my family," he explained. "The problem is that none of us have gotten to know each other well. My parents were never there. They made sure that we had house helps and other workers, but they were too busy to spend time with us. Throughout primary school, while other children did homework with parents, we had tutors even during the school holidays. We've grown up in boarding school. I left home when I turned 12, sent away to a boarding primary school. Dad has always done what he did today – simplified all our needs to money. Money is not everything!" the young man sadly concluded.

Kenya is a nation that is living counter to many other nations where education and the role of parents is concerned. I am yet to learn of a country with so many boarding schools. No one seems concerned that many children, at the age when they need parental presence most, are torn away for the sake of acquiring what is often described as *a good* education. The result is over-emphasis on academics at the expense of character, values, discipline, patience, morality, self-confidence, and so on. These qualities are gained in an atmosphere of love, consistency and modeling, the kind that can only be obtained in a close family setting, with consistent family presence.

Throughout this book, we shall continue to emphasize that parenting means child guidance and shaping towards responsible living, and that this modeling cannot be done by remote control. We have likened parental input into the life of a child to taking a doctor's medication as prescribed – dose-by-dose, once a week, twice daily, morning only, or even just before retiring to bed. Parental presence assumes constancy, consistency and presence that nothing else can replace. Doctors prescribe medication after they have assessed the patient's age, living patterns, past illnesses and health, and current complaints.

A more positive perspective is comparing consistency of parenting to the feeding of a child. We ensure a balanced diet and respect the body's demands for regular, nutritional food. We ensure that all the body's needs are supplied – carbohydrates, proteins, fruits, vegetables, and nuts and so on. A responsible mother will take time to go to the market or delegate the same but with clear guidance regarding the needs of the family. So should parenting be planned with equal care: that the ingredients that make for holistic child maturation and character are present and administered in a timely, consistent manner.

Following Through as Presence in Parenting

By crawling, a child learns to stand.
~ *West African Proverb*

Those who plan what is good find love and faithfulness.
~ *Proverbs 14:22*

The African proverb: *"By crawling, a child learns to stand,"* reminds us that child development is additive from one level of maturation to the other. Remembering that their duty is to facilitate this maturation, parents should seek to do all possible to create a favorable environment that fosters healthy child development. In this regard, responsible parents do not leave the education of their children to chance. They provide school fees, guide them in the choice of schools, and follow through on academic performance. Following through refers to attending to detail with consistency as the child moves from one education level to the other.

The Biblical proverb: *"Those who plan what is good find love and faithfulness,"* is a reminder that, in our context, when parents take time to map out the developmental steps of their children and adequately determine how to provide for these needs, the outcomes are a blessing and relationships are enriched.

This constancy that often demands patience, wisdom and maturity cannot happen when the fathers and mothers are always absent. Another word for successful parenting is presence, presence and more presence; engaged presence and present presence. Even when they have to be physically away, present parents are emotionally present.

This is the essence of this chapter. We are living at a time and age of parental absence, most of it for no reason at all.

Recently while visiting Accra, one of the major, bustling cities in Africa, I picked up a newspaper and read an article on men and their responsibilities at home. Unfortunately, the point made in the article would have applied to any other African city, for the same disease stalks our fathers, whether in Accra, Lagos, Nairobi or Johannesburg. The writer, a man, bemoaned the carelessness, irresponsibility and naivety of some African fathers who are never seen in their matrimonial homes. They will be either at work, in the girl friend's apartment, in the local nightclub or just roaming around.

Such men come home only to change clothes, eat a ready meal that they did not provide for and demand sex from their dutiful wives if their girlfriends have kicked them out for whatever reason. This kind of absent, philandering fatherhood will not do for a continent that hopes to compete with the rest of the world. True fatherhood is the ingredient for building a tenacious generation that has the capacity to raise Africa to the next level. Transformation of Africa to become a leading continent will be possible only if our fathers provide consistent, engaged presence to their children.

Responsible 'Present' Fathers in Africa

What the child says, he has heard at home.
~ African (Nigerian) Proverb

All hard work brings a profit, but mere talk leads only to poverty.
~ Proverbs 14:23

The African proverb: *"What the child says, he has heard at home,"* states that children pick, absorb, internalize and then repeat what goes on at home. With such intelligent imitators, parents should ensure that the content of communication at home is above board because children are watching and listening, shaping their thinking, behavior and values from what they hear.

The Biblical proverb: *"All hard work brings a profit, but mere talk leads only to poverty,"* speaks into parenting in that what impacts children is not mere talk but consistent training and input into the child's life. There is promise of gain and profit in committed parenting, the kind that is evident in responsible fatherhood.

Let us be quick to point out that Africa has some responsible fathers. These proud men do not have to riot around the city or village to prove to anyone that they are men. They come home from work and keep busy doing what every father is supposed to do - engaging with his wife and children, following up on with their lives, listening, encouraging and affirming. Such a parent cares about and plans the family's future. He invests wisely, builds the family home, ensures that food is available to feed the family for another season and trades as he can to increase the family's resources.

Beyond his immediate family, this man cares for aging parents and relatives who need his care, brothers, sisters and cousins who value his mentoring and so on. Then he has the community that, for churchgoers, includes responsibilities of worship and service. Beyond the church and family, the man attends to the communal call to care for the bereaved, the poor and sick.

Can such a man have nothing to do after a busy day's work or during weekends? Does such a man have to spend weekends in sleazy bars, making out with the bar girls and prostitutes? I do not think so. The choice to have children and to be a father presupposes the choice to be present to bring them up. Someone has said that fatherhood is more than making a woman pregnant. It requires investing time and energy to bring that child up to responsible adulthood. Only then can a man claim to be a father.

There are several types of presence and all these deliberate engagements make demands on the parent. Sometimes we assume that physical presence is the main thing that matters. However, many parents come home and sit in front of the television set, eat dinner watching the action, news, football or soap operas without engaging the family.

Physical presence has to set itself up in such a way that it allows other types of presence. For example, each family needs to eat together, at least one meal a day. They should make a decision to sit together around a meal, put off the television or other distractions, and eat while engaging one another, not by interrogation or attacking, but through relaxed conversation. Communication around a meal should not be forced but relaxed, happy, jocular and accommodating.

Challenges to Parental Presence

It is not hard to nurse a pregnancy, but it is hard to bring up a child.
~ African (Swahili) Proverb

Stop listening to instruction, my son, and you will stray from the words of knowledge.
~ Proverbs 19:27

The African proverb: "*It is not hard to nurse a pregnancy, but it is hard to bring up a child,*" underlines the fact that parenting is no easy task. Conceiving a baby and giving birth are much easier when compared to the task of bringing up a holistically balanced child. The word *hard* here is not a negative concept but a reminder that parenting is more than the desire to have a baby. The greater job will be the task of raising that little one to become a responsible adult.

The Biblical proverb: "*Stop listening to instruction, my son, and you will stray from the words of knowledge,*" is caution that underlines the need for parents to adopt a learning posture. There is no time ever when they can say that they have attained complete learning as far as parenting is concerned. At each developmental phase, each child will need unique parenting skills. The parents learn and practice, learn and practice some more, and this repetition ensures that they gain the skills to bring up their child with understanding and wisdom.

As much as we are pointing out the critical need for parental presence in child rearing, many factors will fight against this commitment. African economies are fast becoming 24-hour financial systems. Downtown Nairobi or Lagos, one will find shops, hair salons, and eating spots open till late at night. Many universities and colleges have evening programs. Streets bustle with activity into the late hours of the night.

Living in such an environment, parents will have to make a choice: "As a father or mother, where is my presence really needed at any given time of day? What takes priority in my planning and why?" When we distance ourselves from our children, we lose them by inches through the years until finally, they are gone. In later years, we shall look for these children and they will be emotionally and even physically absent.

Today in the West, there are increasing cases of elder abuse, not only by helpers but also by one's own adult children. These children wait until their absent or abusive parent is old and helpless, and then get their revenge by mistreating the aged, helpless parents who once neglected their parenting roles. Now, these same mothers and fathers need the care of their adult children, but instead get slapped, denied food and even abandoned in old people's homes. Unless Africans wake up to some of these realities, it could be where we too are going when we fail to prioritize parenting and childrearing.

Parental neglect leaves vacuums in the hearts of the maturing children. Someone has noted that most young women who go out with older men are not usually looking for sex. They are seeking for a father figure to notice and affirm them, if their fathers do not meet this need. The older man wants sex with the young lady but all that she is looking for is a present father who can value her and make her feel good about herself. Since sugar daddies can never replace fathers, the child keeps looking and repeats one abusive relationship after the other, with her seeking eventually becoming like searching for water in a desert.

It has been said that if a father consistently fails to appreciate his daughter as only a young woman needs, when another man drools over her, she will follow the stranger even if he is a hyena! Her actions may seem foolish to an observer but she is asking for and seeking paternal presence - love and caring that is consistently present.

Emotional Intelligence in Parental Presence

Haste and hurry can only bear children with many regrets along the way.
~ African (Senegalese) Proverb

When pride comes, then comes disgrace, but with humility comes wisdom.
~ Proverbs 11:2

The African proverb: "*Haste and hurry can only bear children with many regrets along the way,*" underlines the need to walk slowly and with patience along the road of parenting. Sometimes, children may seem to have learned how to reason, behave and live. However, as they navigate a life stage, it seems that all they knew disappears. It is only a wise, understanding parent who can have the capacity to repeat the teaching at this new life phase and then wait patiently for change to take place.

The Biblical proverb: "*When pride comes, then comes disgrace, but with humility comes wisdom,*" can be applied to parenting in that humbleness is wisdom while arrogance can bring one down. Humble people ask many questions because they acknowledge that they do not know everything. Since each child has a unique personality, the opportunity for parents to learn is always fresh for every child and for each child's developmental phase as well as unique experiences. This learning assumes that parents are in close proximity to their children.

Parental physical presence in the lives of their children is reinforced by emotional presence that is portrayed through emotional intelligence. Emotional intelligence is becoming of great demand in our world. Many people value academic knowledge above intelligence, and intelligence quotient or IQ above emotional intelligence. A purposeful parent will use all three: emotional intelligence, emotional presence and cognitive presence to enhance the child's academic performance.

Physical attending and emotional presence need to be reinforced by cognitive presence. This has to do with informed parenting that works from two positions: that of knowledge and wisdom. Obtaining knowledge arises from a deliberate proactive attempt to acquire information about a particular perspective, for example, the current challenges of growing up in our contemporary society. Does the parent know and understand the struggles that their child is facing? What struggles is the child experiencing in school? How does he get along with his teachers?

A young child may come home and say: "I don't like teacher Mwangi." The parent can respond in several ways. For example: "Don't be stupid. Teacher Mwangi is such a nice young man. He is the son of my friend Waititu. Go off now and play and let me not hear you say bad things about your teachers." However, such a parent is oblivious to the fact that his son was trying to communicate something important. Maybe teacher Mwangi picks on him in class. A wise father would have responded: "Son, what's up with teacher Mwangi? Come, sit on my lap and tell me." The child may then have said, "Daddy, teacher tells others that I have bat ears. I feel embarrassed because all the boys in my class now tease me. They whisper 'bat ears' in the playground. Now even some bully girls have joined in."

School bullying is increasing and some children are scared of school. Knowing that so many of our children are struggling with many issues, a wise parent will listen to his son and even want to know more. Another positive response to this child would have been: "You don't like teacher Mwangi? Tell me more." A parent who has cultivated a knowledgeable, secure presence with the child will most probably be told the whole story and the truth.

Cognitive Understanding and Parental Presence

If there is character, ugliness becomes beauty; if there is none, beauty becomes ugliness.
~ *African (Nigerian) Proverb*

A wife of noble character is her husband's crown, but a disgraceful wife is like decay in his bones.
~ *Proverbs 12:4*

The African proverb: "*If there is character, ugliness becomes beauty; if there is none, beauty becomes ugliness,*" underlines the importance of character development in stressing that quality is of more value than beauty. It is a reminder for parents that investing time in inculcating integrity in children builds lasting foundations for the young ones. These fundamentals will never wear away. People age and beauty is lost. People lose riches and become poor. However, character is a trait that abides for a lifetime.

The Biblical proverb: "*A wife of noble character is her husband's crown, but a disgraceful wife is like decay in his bones,*" underscores the reality that character is precious. It becomes a tiara on the head of the people in the individual's life. Family members and even friends love to be associated with a person of good repute. However, people of poor reputation bring shame. These are the realities that parents need to bear in mind as they prepare their children for right living.

Children do not only struggle with things happening at school. The world around them can also be overwhelming. What message do media programs carry for our children? What of the entertainment industry? A parent may be teaching integrity to her children, for example in the usage of money: "Do not take what is not yours. Do not use people to make money, for example, in gambling or in blackmail. Do not sell yourself for money, for example, by exchanging favors or doing something wrong and then being paid for it. Never sell drugs or act as a conduit for them."

On the other hand, some daily papers and other media carry stories glorifying thieves, corrupt people and drug lords. These people drive several limos, own private jets, live in posh estates and give lots of money to charity. Our children are aware of these differing messages. A wise parent will want to know how the youth is processing this information and so encourage the young one's resolve to choose to live right and honorably.

A parent who runs a kindergarten recently told me that when some children are asked the common question: "*What do you want to become when you grow old?*" the answer is: "*I want to become a policeman so that I can be given money.*" How do children know that some policemen receive money? Could they possibly have watched a parent hand over a bribe to a traffic policeman? How much of the parent's behavior do the children watch, internalize and quietly adopt?

In our society, there is pressure to separate morality and character but the two are tied together since the former informs the latter. Indeed, character is defined as an individual's pattern of behavior or personality that is informed by moral constitution, ethical strength and fortitude.

This definition of character as integrity implies that a good reputation is determined by moral behavior. In other words, moral strength determines character. Aware of this link, the parent will guide the young person from a position of awareness on two fronts. First is the task of standing for morality against the pressure to conform. Secondly, the parent will understand the issues that constitute the young person's struggle to remain firm and courageous in the face of the temptation to give up the struggle to be different so as to fit into the popular culture. All this knowing and actively relating with maturing children constitutes cognitive presence.

Besides knowledge, cognitive presence also involves wisdom. Wisdom is defined as the power of judging rightly and following the best course of action based on knowledge, experience and understanding. Many of us are familiar with the story of the prodigal son. Many parents reading this book will be bearing the pain of a child who has turned out wrong, and so may closely identify with this old biblical story. Jesus told this story about a young man, possibly a young adult, whom the Lord regarded as prodigal.

Prodigal Sons and Parental Presence

It is those ugly caterpillars that turn into beautiful butterflies after seasons.
~ African Proverb

Do not withhold good from those who deserve it, when it is in your power to act.
~ Proverbs 3:27

The African proverb: *"It is those ugly caterpillars that turn into beautiful butterflies after seasons,"* is a reminder that the process of metamorphosis is a natural reality. In our context, some children take long to change and mature into responsible adults. Who can ever guess that an ugly, sometimes hairy caterpillar will ever emerge one day as a beautiful, iridescent butterfly! This knowledge informs parents that waiting patiently and continuing to parent unsightly children will one day be rewarded when those young ones become transformed into responsible, caring adults. The prodigal will one day come home!

The Biblical proverb: *"Do not withhold good from those who deserve it, when it is in your power to act,"* thus encourages parents to continue blessing their children whatever the response to their parenting is. It is in the parents' power to care for children and all offspring deserve to be cared for just because they belong to the family. This is the challenge. Can parents continue to love and care for wayward children? How long will it take before the prodigal *comes home*?

Prodigal means that the youth was exceedingly or recklessly wasteful. In the story that Jesus told, the young man was wasteful of possessions and wasteful of life. The young man woke up one morning and told his father something like: "Dad, I want to go away on my own. Give me my share of your inheritance." The father may have tried to dissuade his son, telling him possibly to wait until he was more mature, or to complete his studies first, or even to do a course in business management and investment. However, the youth would hear none of it. Eventually, the father must have said, "Alright son, have it your way."

We are not told if the demand took some time to fulfill, but we can assume that the father would have tried to talk the young man out of the decision to go away from home without a plan. The way the story ends clearly indicates that the youth did not have a life plan or even a business strategy. However, he had his way and took off with his life share of everything his father could give him. Many children have left home without a life plan. Some even drop out of school or college and rebel against their parents' wish and desire for them. Leaving home without a plan, with no education or training, and taking off in rebellion can easily set the young person on a road to destruction and waywardness. This is what happened to the biblical youth.

The Bible continues that the young man "set off for a distant country where he squandered his wealth in wild living," (Luke 15:13). He did not lack friends who were ready to help him consume his inheritance. Eventually, money did what it does when handled carelessly in lavish living: it ran out. After all his money was gone, there was a famine in the land. The penniless youth faced double tragedy. On one hand, he had no money. On the other, there was famine such that even well-wishers had little to offer the hungry, despondent young man.

The youth was so hopeless that finally he had to look for work. The only employment he could get was to feed pigs for a farmer. There, his need continued and hunger was ever present because "no one gave him anything," (Luke 15:16). This need led him to the level of desiring to eat the food fed to the swine. One day, having fallen to the lowest level of his being, he finally came to his senses and asked himself: "What am I doing here? The servants who work for my father have enough to eat and spare, and here I am starving to death! I will get up and return home!"

As the young man set on his way back home, attention shifts from the figure of a dejected, bedraggled, once-too proud and overconfident, cocky young man trudging homewards to an ever-loving father who is waiting for his son to come home. For this reason, it is said that this story is more about the father than the son, and rightly so. The father seems to have been looking out for his son, because when the young man was still "a long way off, his father saw him and was filled with compassion for him. He ran towards his son, threw his arms around him and kissed him," (verse 20). The father's actions basically signified the unspoken words: "Child, welcome home!" This welcome went beyond words.

The whole house was involved in receiving the lost child. There was a party complete with slaughtering a fattened calf that the father may have kept aside deliberately waiting for the day he believed the youth would eventually come home. The father also had a robe ready and there was music, dancing and a great celebration, because "this son of mine was dead and is alive again; he was lost and is found," (verse 24).

The father's behavior signifies a discussion I often have with parents struggling with the reality of a prodigal child. As the father waited for his prayers to be answered he must have practiced present presence. He waited for his child without giving up. He never locked the door of his heart against the young man. Indeed, in a sense, he kept a light burning at the window of his home and his heart, and the child must have sensed this love from afar.

Deep down, the youth knew that his prodigal actions merited judgment, punishment, a long, hard lecture about his wayward ways and even rejection. However, upon his return, stinking like the pigs he had fed for so long, he did not receive a negative response but instead, got a warm welcome.

The father's love and forgiveness led the youth's older brother to complain. "Alas!" he said. "All these years, I have been slaving for you, father, and never disobeyed your orders. Then, this son of yours who has squandered your property with prostitutes comes home, and you kill a fattened calf for him!"

This father acted from a position of wisdom. Accepting the return of his child and opening his heart unconditionally to the youth was wisdom derived from cognitive presence. The older man knew that he was wiser than his son. He was certain that his love that had been severely tested would win the day. He was convinced that he had made his home a safe place. This safety gives the children freedom to make mistakes and yet come back to the stability that home provides.

Child Rebellion and Parental Presence

A child who has no mother will not have scars to show on his back.
~*African (Nigerian) Proverb*

Do not say, "I'll pay you back for this wrong!" Wait for the Lord, and he will deliver you.
~ *Proverbs 20:22*

The African proverb: *"A child who has no mother will not have scars to show on his back,"* indicates that in parenting, child discipline is normal. It is only children with no parents who receive no discipline. In traditional Africa, there were no orphans. Children who lost biological parents were quickly absorbed into and cared for within the wider family. In addition, adults generally cared for and disciplined more children than their biological ones, because no child could dare do wrong in the presence of an adult. The older person would provide discipline and instruction. Of course currently, challenged by numbers of AIDS orphans, this resiliency of care has been shaken but many communities still uphold the practice as far as they are able.

The Biblical proverb: *"Do not say, 'I'll pay you back for this wrong!' Wait for the Lord, and he will deliver you,"* is a reminder that it is easy for wronged parents to desire for retribution for children who have caused them suffering. Turning back from evil is enough payback. It is God who repays the parent for the wasted years of child rebellion.

What is the point of discussing child rebellion? We are not trivializing the fact that parents need to guide their children, insist on rightful behavior by their young adults, and discipline their wayward ways. The emphasis is that even after the parents do their best, some children still rebel. At such times, parental love holds the ground steady and communicates the reality: "Child, I'll always be here for you."

I watched a documentary of an Australian young man who was raised right but fell into wrong company. He made a series of foolish decisions. Desiring the thrill that comes with trying new, dangerous behaviors, he was wooed into drug trafficking. The plan was to carry drugs from his country to some East Asian destination without getting caught. The traffickers would partner him with a young woman from the country of destination. The two would travel as a newly married couple going on honeymoon. On arrival, the traffickers picked up the drugs at the airport and then the two would separate and go their way.

The young man succeeded in the delivery several times, each time changing partners as well as his name, and using fake passports. However, one day, in Hong Kong, his luck ran out and he was arrested. He spent several years in jail, experiencing horrible conditions and every day regretting the stupidity that led him into drug trafficking.

The young man told this story as a free person. During imprisonment, he spent a lot of time talking of his mother who never gave up on him. She hired lawyers, had many appeals sent to the authorities of the nation holding custody over him, as well as requesting support from her government. Finally, he was released. As he walked out of prison, there was his aging mother, waiting. He fell into her arms weeping and asking for forgiveness.

When he finally got home he had to go through rehabilitation to recover from drug addiction, a habit he had picked up in jail to be able to survive the mental torment he experienced. After some years, he got married. In concluding his story, the middle-aged man deeply regretted his many wasted years and the pain he had caused his single mother.

The wisdom that causes a parent to receive a wayward child home, and sometimes not once but over and over again, can only be God-given. It is insight that is given to a parent who has chosen physical, emotional and cognitive presence. These three attributes lift a parent to a level of maturity that provides stability to engage and survive difficult experiences that children and youth face as they mature, experiences that the parent also goes through in full measure.

Children and parents are complete interdependent systems. Whatever happens to one affects the other. Africans believe that a connected family is like a spider's web. You touch one section and the whole trembles. This is the reason why connected mothers stay up the whole night praying for a wayward child. And, we believe that the prayers of a loving mother, like arms of love, draw the prodigal home, sometimes sadly after the mother's death.

Case Study on Parental Presence

An online magazine, *Science and Tech* carries a research report by Laura Clark, (October 2012): **http://dailym.ai/RmS0tk,** that presents findings titled "Good parenting is more important than good schooling in determining your child's academic results." Basically, the article underlines the critical importance of parental presence and involvement in the life of the child. Marked by "trust, good communication and active involvement in a child's academic life," good parenting contributes more to the child's success than education in a first-class school.

Examining facts gathered from a study on parenting, researchers analyzed information on 10,585 adolescents from 1,000 randomly selected secondary schools in the United States. Findings indicated that young people do best with parental presence: assistance with homework, communication on the need for education, attendance at school occasions and generally engaging in the child's life. These children tend to perform better even if they are studying in poor quality schools.

The bottom line is that it is not the quality of schools that produces performing, balanced children but the parents' holistic investment referred to in this chapter as parental presence. Several times, we have underlined the reality that parenting is not like operating a television set by remote control. Children and young people flourish with close and positive parental presence.

Another study considered children's academic performance as it related to the quality of their schools, a quantity referred to as school social capital. This was compared to the quality of parental involvement in their lives also referred to as family social capital.

Parents with high levels of social capital were classified as those who engaged in their children's life, for example: regularly checking homework, talking about school with their children, attending parents' evenings and so on. This kind of involvement creates an opportunity for parents to pass on knowledge and values to their children. Schools with high social capital were classified as those who created conducive learning environment ensuring little disruption and lowering levels of truancy. Such schools provided rich extra-curricular activities and kept close contact with parents. They also reported high morale among teachers and students.

Outcomes indicated that while schools with high school capital indicated increased levels of achievement, the influence of family social capital was the stronger variable in determining high levels of achievement. More specifically, according to the study, published in the journal *Research and Social Stratification and Mobility*, "young people with high levels of family capital but low school capital tended to do better in exams than pupils with high school capital but low family capital."

Dr Toby Parcel who led the study added, "While both school and family involvement are important, the role of family involvement is stronger when it comes to academic success." The doctor added that many parents do not recognize the critical role their presence with their children and the investment of time plays in the young ones' progress. More information on this topic can be obtained from **http://dailym.ai/1jIHDsX**

CHAPTER 8

PARENTING AS MENTORING AND LIFE COACHING

THE MEANING OF MENTORING AND COACHING

Wisdom is wealth.
~ *African (Swahili) Proverb*

Whoever gives heed to instruction prospers, and blessed is he who trusts in the Lord.
~ *Proverbs 16:20*

The African proverb: "*Wisdom is wealth,*" is a profound reminder for parents that wisdom precedes true wealth and should be sought after at any expense. This is because we have many stories of wealthy people whose families were scattered and wealth destroyed as soon as the parents passed on. Vicious fights broke out among siblings creating life-long rivalries, murders, plots and court cases, and fighting over the estate of bereaved parents. If only these children had wisdom as a legacy, a lot of this pain would have been avoided.

The Biblical proverb: "*Whoever gives heed to instruction prospers, and blessed is he who trusts in the Lord,*" underlines the treasures of godly wisdom that result from listening and learning from God, wise parents and mentors. Prosperity and God's blessing will follow such. Instruction comes from faithfully seeking out and listening to godly mentors, some of who may be parents or other adults of integrity.

In previous chapters, we spent a lot of time discussing the critical importance of the presence of a parent if children are to be empowered and equipped for life. Parental presence ensures balanced maturation, where all faculties develop adequately. In this principle of parenting, let us now consider two terms: mentoring and coaching.

Derived from a Geek legend, a mentor is defined as a loyal friend and wise advisor. Spelt as a proper noun, *Mentor* was an individual who was a teacher and guardian of Odysseus, son of Telemadius. This person exemplified the qualities of loyalty, guardianship and wise advising that are synonymous with mentoring. These activities assume parental commitment and engagement in the child's life.

The second term, coach, refers to a person who instructs or trains athletes or actors, and stretches to include preparing a person for an examination. In our present day, coaching has been developed into a profession where a qualified individual walks with and instructs another on how to navigate special challenges at the work place. As a profession, coaching has grown to include help for those preparing for an interview, job changes, promotion or just people interested in improving a specific area of their lives. This kind of helper is referred to as a life coach.

Mentoring and Coaching in Traditional Africa

When a child knows how to wash his hands well, he eats with the elders.
~ African (Tshi) Proverb

Train a child in the way he should go, and when he is old he will not turn from it.
~ Proverbs 22:6

The African (Tshi) proverb: *"When a child knows how to wash his hands well, he eats with the elders,"* comes from the Tshi, Tchwi, or Oji, a group of people living in Ghana. The wise saying underlines the outcomes of mentoring and coaching. Traditional African communities attached a lot of importance to rites of passage that included specific rituals that would be carried out after years of training. Many parts of current Africa still emphasize the practice, the only sure way of teaching the behaviors and expectations of each developmental phase.

Some of the practices in traditional society are bolstered by Church discipleship and training and others emphasized through value-based training in school. This maturation leads not only to learning of the responsibilities of growing up but also attainment of the privileges that accompany the achievement of each phase.

The Biblical proverb: *"Train a child in the way he should go, and when he is old he will not turn from it,"* is a reminder that instruction of children has its benefits. The outcome is the child's life-long consistency if trained right. However, there is a negative implication as well, in that there is a kind of training where the parent repeatedly does wrong in the child's presence. A thieving father or an immoral mother indirectly trains the child through wrong role modeling because the child learns that this is the *right* way to live. After all, their parents live that way.

These two definitions of mentoring and coaching summarize the practice of parenting. In traditional Africa, these practices were part and parcel of parenting. From my tribe, the Meru of Kenya, mothers and close female relatives took an active role in mentoring their female children. These women walked closely with their children, teaching them proper deportment for women, child care, farming, food preparation and respect for elders – both male and female.

I remember that if one met an older person while walking on a path, the child or young woman was expected to pass on quietly, keeping a respectful distance. Sometimes, if the trail was narrow, the youth would stop by the side of the path and allow the older person to pass them and then proceed on after a respectful responsive greeting. The young person would wait to be greeted first by the elder and then respond appropriately.

In traditional Africa, young people did not talk or chatter away carelessly in front of older women. This training was not taken for granted but was delivered intentionally and deliberately just like school learning is intentional. One might argue that this was unfair to children as they were denied their rights; that they should have been trained to speak out for their rights, argue back and so on.

Except in abusive situations, this demand does not hold much water. Respect for anyone older than the child cuts across all societies. Even in America, a nation lifted as the home of free speech, many homes exist where children's respect for older people is expected, given and received.

The Meru people of Kenya live on the eastern slopes of Mt. Kenya, right at the Equator. Among the traditional Ameru, mentoring existed for the boys as well. Men took the boy child under their wing and watched them fit into the clearly laid out patterns of behavior. The young ones learned courage by herding animals away from home and returning them safely in the evening.

The youth trained themselves in the self-discipline required to wait until evening to eat because far away in the wilderness, there would be no hot meal. The only food might be millet pouches brought from home or wild fruit gathered in the bush. Boys and young men could not complain to their peers: "You guys, I'm so bored. I'm out of here!" They were expected to self-manage through discipline and self-taught survival mechanisms. While in the wilderness herding the flocks, they learned the art of war using sticks and so on, all the while, protecting the animals from marauding animals or thieves. Young men exhibited respect for older people and were quick to obey when called.

Later on as the child matured to adolescence, there was specific coaching aimed at preparing the young people for adulthood. Carefully selected men and women were given the specific responsibility of coaching the young men and women respectively and helping the young ones cross over from boys to men and girls to women.

The whole training of young women was referred to as taking place in the *Kiuru* - the abode of women within the family home. That of young men took place in the *Gaaru* - the male part of the homestead. Mention the words *Kiuru* and *Gaaru* – and Meru people would recognize it as figurative representation of mentoring and life coaching for young women and young men respectively.

The Meru people were agricultural and known for excellent farm work – planting and harvesting, as well as basketry, pottery, making nutritious traditional porridge, and so on. All these presented coaching opportunities for young women. The tribe was also known for the art of war, protecting their property from raiders. The Merus were famous for environmental stewardship, trade through bartering, animal husbandry, bee keeping and so on, activities that provided training opportunities for young men.

These examples from the Meru people represent similar other African communities. This account is not an attempt to glorify African tradition but to point out that parents had a plan to fulfill as they trained their children for life. Such commitment to mentoring assumed protection of the child's self-worth such as safeguarding the young one from shame, abuse, defeatist attitudes and discouragement. "You can do it," urged the mentor. "I am here for you. Come and visit if things are too tough at home."

Many aunts could tell the story of creating a safe haven for their sisters' or brothers' children in times of difficulty for the other family. Indeed some individuals moved permanently to live with their uncle and became absorbed and mentored alongside the other children with no mention of the fact that that they did not belong to this particular family. In addition, life coaches spent a lot of time with their protégés: "Bring that arrow. This is how you fit it into the bow. Here, I'll show you how," and so on.

CURRENT NEGLECT OF MENTORING THE BOY CHILD IN AFRICA

If your child is dancing clumsily, tell him: "You are dancing clumsily"; do not tell him: "Darling, do as you please."
~ African (Twi) Proverb

Listen, my son, to a father's instruction; pay attention and gain understanding.
~ Proverbs 4:1

The African (Twi) proverb: *"If your child is dancing clumsily, tell him: 'You are dancing clumsily'; do not tell him: 'Darling, do as you please,'"* comes from the Twi language or Ashanti Twi, spoken by over nine million ethnic Ashanti people of Ghana. The wise saying indicates that mentoring young people is a serious assignment that should never be neglected or left to chance. Parents dare not pretend that a child is doing well when he is not. Instead, they need to speak truthfully into the lives of maturing youth whether they listen, obey, change immediately, or not.

The Biblical proverb: *"Listen, my son, to a father's instruction; pay attention and gain understanding,"* is a plea to children to take parental mentoring seriously. In Africa, father-son relationship does not refer to biological links only. It also includes any instructional relationship where an older or more experienced person guides a learner. This relationship should be sought after, valued, appreciated and exploited. There is much concern that since mentorship is often informal and does not have direct results like school or college learning, it can be regarded as being of no consequence.

Today in Africa, there is hue and cry regarding the mentorship neglect of the boy child. "Whatever happened to boys? Many of them never became men!" the nations cry. While women seem to carry on their roles as wives and mothers, many men seem to be missing in action, except in the action of biologically begetting children. After the child is born, some daddies do not seem to want to know what Junior eats or how Pauline will make it through high school.

Africa has many loving responsible fathers but single parenting is also on the increase where it is the mother that takes up the sole responsibility of childrearing. In addition, the AIDS pandemic has left many orphaned children who need responsible caregivers. In times like these, the continent is in need of more male mentors, proud fathers, caring uncles and doting grandpas.

The most amazing thing, as one will find mothers discussing and comparing notes in regular women group meetings, is the observation that most fathers do not seem bothered by their absence from matters of childrearing and youth training. It seems that many men have lost the sense of shame and guilt. It is as though they are saying – "Whatever!"

"Ai!" the women wonder. "The man comes home and eats a balanced meal. But he has no clue how the food got there! He doesn't even ask how the family is getting on, and few say 'thank you for dinner!'" Another woman chips in: "In my case, the kids were supposed to report back to school yesterday. Throughout the holidays, their father never said a thing when we reminded him that school was about to begin. Finally, when the day came, John said, 'Dad, we're going back to school today. Where is our school fee?' My husband retorted, 'Do you think money grows on trees? Go and ask your mother for money. I have nothing!' You know what? I had to keep the children home for an extra day, while I hustled to get a SACCO loan. Up to now, the term is almost over and he hasn't as much as asked: 'How did the children go back to school?' Whatever happened to the African man?" she wonders. SACCO here refers to a Savings and Credit Cooperative Organization, a membership society where members pool their savings and borrow from the same as necessary.

"Ladies, do not give up," counters one with a more positive experience. "Let me tell you about my brother. You remember I lost my older brother who died leaving a young wife and two sons in high school. My younger brother, who is a hardworking businessman with three children of his own, has taken over the responsibility of my older brother's family. He set up a business for my sister-in-law and took over school fees for my nephews. His wife describes him as a faithful husband, loving father, and doting uncle."

As much as Africa cries for men to care for their families, we know that just as not all women are faithful wives and loving mothers, many men are committed husbands, responsible fathers and devoted uncles. These men do not while away their time in drinking dens or chasing skirts in sleazy lodgings, but instead are faithful husbands who take up their position as leaders and can be depended upon at home, in the community and within society.

AFRICA: THE LAND IN-BETWEEN THE MISSING GAARU

It is the duty of children to wait on elders, and not the elders on children.

~ African (Kenyan) Proverb

To have a fool for a son brings grief; there is no joy for the father of a fool.

~ Proverbs 17:21

The African proverb: *"It is the duty of children to wait on elders, and not the elders on children,"* underlines what happens when mentorship is missing. Roles are confused and chaos reigns. For example, when young adults expect fathers and mothers to take care of them, or the elderly to give precedence to the younger in any relationship, then something is very wrong. If by any chance this behavior becomes the norm in society, then the older have failed in passing on the baton of respect and maturity to their sons and daughters.

The Biblical proverb: *"To have a fool for a son brings grief; there is no joy for the father of a fool,"* emphasizes the plight of those who lack wisdom in their actions or relationships. Lack of mentoring or ignoring the wisdom of listening and adhering to instruction for life creates foolish sons and daughters. *"There is no joy for the father of a fool,"* indicates that this stupidity may last a lifetime and cause continuous heavy grief to parents and others associated with the individual.

Africa is a land in-between, we hang between the old and the new, suffering disconnect from our resilient African traditions and reaching out to an illusion created by a classroom education that does not equip us for life. Parents assume that the classroom teacher has answers, when all this individual knows is Geography and Mathematics, not answers to what real living is all about. Whatever happened?

Dr. Gershon Mwiti, a Meru man of character and integrity, leadership consultant and mentor is also CEO and founder of Leadership Institute of Kenya. He has an explanation that sheds light on this dilemma. He came to this conclusion after years of observing and working with his community. As a lover of the legacy that traditional Meru should pass onto the younger generation, Dr. Mwiti explains that in many ways, the coming of western education disconnected the tribe from its moorings.

In traditional Africa, boys were socialized in the *Gaaru,* the dwelling of the men of the tribe that was represented by the father in every home. This means that a boy's education and training was done at home by the father, corporately reinforced by his peers through corporate socialization and undergirded by tribal mores, practices and values.

However, as Dr. Mwiti observes, the school system emptied the traditional calabash of life training systems and instead emphasized teaching foreign subjects that were delinked from the peoples' culture. Book learning took the place of Meru wisdom of the ages and the schoolteacher replaced the village elder. Geography and Math were just that - subjects about topography and numbers. School learning went ahead to exalt academic learning and label Meru traditions as primitive. These life subjects were discarded for book learning and passing academic tests. Meanwhile, the book learners consistently failed to receive teaching on subjects about relationships and values.

Students proceeded to pass examinations to go to excellent universities and graduated with professional degrees, yet many who did not have mentoring and coaching did not have any idea what was required of them as men. Eventually, the *Gaaru* for growing men disappeared, leaving a vacuum. Men who were not coached closely by their fathers and uncles had nothing to pass on to their sons.

Where the school system failed, the church did not succeed very well either. The gospel often disconnected believers from their cultures, labeling traditions as ungodly. Basically, neither the school system nor the Christian church took over the training of their sons. The training of boys to men, formerly a corporate tribal enterprise reinforced by the men in the family, was now left to individual families.

Here, many fathers were either absent, or if present had no clue what to do.

Now when the men become disconnected from age-old tradition and values, when the older cannot mentor or coach the younger, then the *Gaaru* can be described as empty, with no activity therein. There are few men busy mentoring and coaching young people, and the result is that fewer and fewer boys are becoming men.

While the *Gaaru* stands near empty, an enterprising present father does his best to mentor and coach his sons. If he is wise and chooses other wise men from the church, family or community with whom to partner in his enterprise, then his sons receive the reinforcing they need to become men. These are the present day fathers who are trying to recapture the *Gaaru* for their sons.

Gaaru Disconnected, Kiuru Persisted

The good mother knows what her children will eat.

~ African (Akan) Proverb

The tongue has the power of life and death, and those who love it will eat its fruit.

~ Proverbs 18:21

The African (Akan) proverb: *"The good mother knows what her children will eat,"* comes from the Akan people group residing on the Gulf of Guinea in the southern regions of the former Gold Coast region that today covers Ghana and Ivory Coast. The saying acknowledges that responsible mothers take care of their children. They plan ahead of time on how to meet their needs and persistently hang on no matter the odds. Many stories of these mothers exist in

Africa, complete with the sacrifices these women make. They take care of both daughters and sons and are there especially as their daughters mature into adulthood, enter the world of work, marry and start families. Mothers are always there.

The Biblical proverb: "T*he tongue has the power of life and death, and those who love it will eat its fruit,*" underlines the fact that instruction is often verbal. In our context, parents have the choice to instruct and so bless their children, or neglect and abuse, and so pass curses to their children. Africans believe that the *tongue* of a parent has the capacity to bless or curse, and so parents should use their words wisely.

There is also the *love of the tongue,* indicating that many words have their consequences, good or bad. The underlying message here is the wisdom when to speak and when to keep quiet. There are times when a parent should hold their peace even if the temptation to burst out is very strong. Maturity, patience and wisdom guide the timing of speaking. All these are elements of mentoring.

Dr. Gershon Mwiti continues to observe that while the *Gaaru* has generally been shaken, the *Kiuru* for the women remains largely intact. *Kiuru* refers to the ever-persistent role of women in mentoring their daughters at the individual family level, corporately through mothers' *chamas* - small women cohorts that meet on a regular basis, and through the undergirding of traditional mores and values on role expectations.

Indeed, most mothers are present to mentor and coach their daughters. Girls learn work ethics and self-discipline, and are trained on the job on how to run a household. Many mothers will look for their sisters, friends or fellow church members to help reinforce to their daughters the things they have been trained to do. All the way to the wedding, many young women are reminded how to run their homes.

Watch a group of women conduct a bridal shower, the modern way that is adequately replacing the traditional bridal preparation for marriage. The women, friends and relatives of the bride's mother, who have already shared in the child upbringing, meet on the given day, bringing items to use as examples to strengthen the lessons they have been giving the young lady. The women come in carrying sweeping brooms, hot flasks, dusters, dishcloths, towels, even a Bible or two. Each woman takes her turn to coach the bride on how to succeed as a married woman.

During the bridal shower, the bridesmaids are often present, and they too listen in. They learn the details of running a home, and having a successful marriage. For the bridal shower, men are usually absent. This fun-filled, all-women's day is followed in some communities by what the Kikuyus call the *itara*, the day when the parties from both families meet at the bridegroom's home for the bride to be shown the granary, the kitchen, the place where her mother-in-law to be keeps the firewood and so on.

Once again, women take time to underline to the bride what makes for success in running her home. As women are busy coaching the bride, the men often sit around and eat, waiting for the women to finish their thing and so end a successful *itara*. Something is obviously missing here. One would wonder: What is the equivalent of a bridal shower for the bridegroom? Is there ever a bridegroom shower? All is, however, not lost.

Restoration of the Gaaru – Where are the Men?

A child who is to be successful is not to be reared exclusively on a bed of down.

~ *African (Akan) Proverb*

A foolish son brings grief to his father and bitterness to the one who bore him.

~ *Proverbs 17:25*

The African (Akan) proverb: "*A child who is to be successful is not to be reared exclusively on a bed of down,*" reminds us that although mentoring and child training is a painful process, no child should be spared the pain. No wisdoms are learned in a state of luxury and leisure. This is one of the reasons why for many communities in Africa, rites of passage for boys had to be accompanied by instilling of some pain. Changing boys to men is not a ride of comfort where the young ones are placated and pampered. It is a tough journey of making soldiers from fledglings, leaders from followers.

The Biblical proverb: "*A foolish son brings grief to his father and bitterness to the one who bore him,*" summarizes what happens when mentoring of sons is ignored. Society ends up with foolish sons who cause much grief and sorrow by behaving and living imprudently and thoughtlessly. It follows that the neglect of fathers is capable of unleashing a great deal of sorrow that affects future families, institutions and even nations.

Aware that Meru men have lost a critical part of mentoring, some men are beginning to restore the lost time by gathering to hold a bridegroom shower while the women are busy with their bridal shower. I have witnessed one extremely successful bridegroom shower where there was no more room to fit in men, both young and old, who craved to hear what the older men were telling the bridegroom. Some of them noted: "No one ever told me this!" Such efforts will reduce the number of neglected youth who enter marriage in a vacuum, expected to succeed in areas where they have no clue what to do. Indeed, many young husbands are expected to pass exams in subjects that no one taught them.

The call for Africa today is for a multiplication of responsible men, fathers who are present, pay up school fees in time, are thoroughly engaged in the lives of their young ones and love their wives like Jesus Christ loved the church. Men in Africa should raise their sons to consistently counter the reality of the growing number of men who have prolonged their boyhood and live carefree, bachelor lifestyles within wedlock, complete with womanizing, playing around, lacking commitment to their marital vows, taking the institution of marriage for granted, exhibiting blatant infidelity, passing laws to legalize polygamy, and imbibing too much alcohol.

Some have exchanged mothers for wives, continue to be dependent, and live a rogue, careless existence. Their umbilical cords switch from mother to wife, and they have no qualms about it. African men will be created by other African men just like African women will be shaped by other African women, those that value the gift of nurturing and passing on legacies that last.

Many pray that each parent, mother or father, will take the mentoring and coaching of their children seriously, that parenting becomes an intentional plan. Deliberate parenting is both vertical as well as horizontal: vertical to obtain an education from kindergarten to college or university, preparing them for a good job or business;

and then horizontal to live holistically, equipped to live with integrity and balance. Parents need to mentor and coach their children to know how to handle money, how to make and keep friends, how to respect the opposite sex, how to relate with authority, how to walk and live as people of honor, to refuse negative peer influence, and to be disciplined at work, at home and in society.

Mentoring presupposes that each parent will remember that each child is different: uniquely created and uniquely gifted. Some of our children and young people are easy to mentor because they listen and obey quickly. Others will test the patience of the parents because they do not seem to hear, let alone understand, what the father and mother are saying. Mentoring will call for maturity and patience in the parent as well as noting the young one's progress and rewarding any step each takes in the chosen direction.

Mentoring as Releasing and Letting Go

A child does not fear treading on dangerous ground until he or she gets hurt.

~ African (Bukusu) Proverb

How much better to get wisdom than gold, to choose understanding rather than silver!

~ Proverbs 16:16

The African (Bukusu) proverb: "*A child does not fear treading on dangerous ground until he or she gets hurt,*" comes from the Bukusu who belong to the larger ethnic group of the Luyha people of Kenya. The saying is a reminder that children are normally curious, with a hungry and healthy gift of exploration. They want to taste everything and touch anything. However, sometimes, they get hurt in the process of discovery. Should parents prevent children from exploring and learning? Yes, and No! Yes, when there are serious dangers of exposure and No where the child is safe to explore. Striking this balance is the role of parents in parenting: protect the child from harm and yet, offer enough leeway for them to learn on their own depending on developmental stage.

The Biblical proverb: "*How much better to get wisdom than gold, to choose understanding rather than silver,*" is a reminder that children who are trained and mentored on how to navigate life's way are provided with wisdom whose value surpasses education, money and great riches. What use is there to be an educated man but a fool when it comes to principles and rules of holistic living? What use is there to be an influential person in society and yet fail to make wise life decisions?

While parents mentor their children and train them in wisdom needed for living, whose responsibility is it to choose the direction children take? Is it the parent or the child, or is the choice a corporate affair? When children are young, the parents may make unilateral decisions in matters that affect their lives: what school to attend, what to wear, when to do assignments, go to sleep, and so on. However, as children grow older, parents are advised to include them in decision-making by teaching them how to weigh options and arrive at a wise choice. If parents do not listen to children as they mature, anger and rebellion may result, especially during their teenage and young adult years.

Many years ago, I had in my clinic a young man who was very angry. He was becoming rebellious and was full of resentment because his father was determined that the he should study medicine at university. After high school, the older man demanded that the young man, his only son, should study sciences at A Level through the International Baccalaureate (IB) two-year pre-college program. He registered his son for this course in a school in a different country, purchased a ticket and sent the young man there. However, once he got to school, the youth decided to fulfill his personal desire and registered to pursue the study of languages since he eventually wanted to register for Linguistics in university.

This young man never came home for holidays, and sent reports that he was doing well in school. The father religiously sent school fees and other support. After two years, the young man performed very well and joined university graduating a few years later with a BA in Linguistics. When the father discovered that he had been disobeyed, angry as he was, it was too late to force his hand any more. In our sessions with the parents, we had to objectively ask the father: "Did your son really disrespect you by choosing to remain in school and pursue what he was really motivated to study?"

Eventually the father realized that he was trying to create his son after his own image. Later on, he confided in me that while growing up, he had really desired to become a doctor. However his own father had died early leaving the man, the first-born son, to care for his siblings. He had to drop out of school to take on casual work so as to assist his mother. His siblings had studied while he himself had to be satisfied with a minimal two years high school education. The older man's unfulfilled longing came alive in his desire for his son. "What I didn't become, my son must." In the family session, the older man was humble enough to ask for his son's forgiveness. Fellowship was restored.

The father was finally willing to let his son become who God had made him to be through developing his unique gifting. He was able to give thanks to God that his son had worked faithfully and diligently to complete university and graduate successfully. Mentoring and coaching considers the unique gifts of each individual child, and listens to the children's personal and individual dreams. Loving parents count themselves blessed and privileged when they have children who are willing to open their hearts to parental coaching and mentoring.

Mentors are not perfect because they are human and prone to failure. Fathers and mothers may have made mistakes in their youth or even within their marriage. In this regard, guilt can play a big role in making parents elusive and absent in as far as coaching and mentoring their children is concerned.

Mr. Mondo, a father of two adolescent sons knew that he needed to get actively engaged in the lives of his boys. He provided for them and fulfilled his financial obligations as a father. The family lived in a good home and never lacked for anything. Yet, they never ate together, never met as a family, and everyone minded their own business. Mr. Mondo was scared of ever getting emotionally close to his sons.

What right did he have to tell them how to live when his own wild past shouted loud in his ears? He had several children out of wedlock, all with different women. Even after marriage, he had carried on an affair with his secretary, one that began long before he met his wife. For sometime, he had also given in to a fling in strip clubs and sex dens. A few years later, he had decided to turn around and go to church. The decision had not been easy but he had seen many of his colleagues die of AIDS, leaving behind them secrets that the whole world became aware of sooner or later.

Mr. Mondo was a believer now and attended Bible Study Fellowship (BSF). BSF is an international, interdenominational, highly organized Bible study program where men, women, children and young adults meet to study the Bible together.

In spite of his changed life, he had never disclosed his past to anyone, least of all, his sons. However, he knew that his sons were aware of his past, especially the years when he had lived as a bachelor although married to their mother. How could he hope to gain their confidence, their respect, and the right, or was it privilege, of mentoring them?

One day, he was so burdened that he poured his heart to an older man, Mr. Msamai, whom he met at BSF. They met for lunch, ate together, and sat in deep conversation in a secluded room in a restaurant. Their discussion stretched after lunch to 4 pm in the afternoon. The older man listened and finally helped Mr. Mondo understand that opening himself to the scrutiny of his sons was not weakness but strength. Only strong men dared accept their weaknesses and vulnerabilities.

The most important thing, Mr. Msamai added, was to dare start the conversation and sit there answering any of the questions the young men might ask, and do so truthfully. Msamai pointed out that the boys might be repressing a lot of anger regarding their father's infidelity with his secretary, although as Mr. Mondo explained, his wife had forgiven him. Due to their anger, they might be vengeful and resentful, a reality that the father needed to appreciate and live with.

Mr. Msamai pointed out that the fear Mr. Mondo had in sitting with his sons was possibly interpreted as rejection by the boys, and rejection was ripe ground for low-self esteem in any adolescent, who just by virtue of their age, desired closeness with their father. Love, closeness, and attention communicate value and value helps them to develop their self-esteem.

Msamai cited psychologist Scott Peck, who in his book *The Road Less Traveled*, explains that when children know they are valued, they develop self-value, a main pillar of self-discipline and self-care. Peck believes that the earlier children learn these lessons, the better, because the rest of their lives depend upon this critical reality that interweaves into all they are developing to become.

Msamai ended the conversation by urging Mr. Mondo to pray for courage and begin moving emotionally close to his sons because no one else could take the place of the father in mentoring them. "Mondo, it is not to us we point our children. We are not perfect examples. We point the right way to the young ones especially because it is spelt out in God's word and then stress that God is their enabler. Our children pretty well may succeed where we failed, so for their sake, the voices of our weaknesses should never be allowed to become louder than our call to responsible mentoring and coaching of our children," concluded Msamai. "And, time does not wait for any man. Or does it?" "Certainly not," agreed Mr. Mondo. This was the beginning of change in Mr. Mondo's relationship with his sons.

Kenya's *Daily Nation* of May 14, 2012 carried an article on Mothers' Day, a date that is gaining more and more global attention as fitting to celebrate the gift of mothers. The article by Joy Wanja Muraya noted that in many languages, the word "mother" begins with the letter M. Quite interesting when we realize that in all languages, a baby's first word is Mama.

Ms Muraya provides the word mother in various languages, for example: English - mother; Kikuyu ~ maitu; Kikamba ~ mwaitu; French ~ mere; Danish ~ mor; German ~ mutter; Kiswahili ~ mama; Latin - mater; Spanish ~ madre; Swedish ~ moder; Dutch ~ moeder. She went along to offer quotes by some significant men who in one sentence summarize the impact their mothers had on their lives:

Industrialist Dr. Manu Chandaria: "*My mother passed away many years ago, but I once wrote a tribute poem to express my appreciation to her for bringing me up to be a hard worker."*

Musician Stevie Wonder: *"Mama was my greatest teacher, a teacher of compassion, love and fearlessness. If love is sweet as a flower, then my mother is that sweet flower of love."*

US Evangelist Billy Graham: *"Only God himself fully appreciates the influence of a Christian mother in the molding of a character in their children."*

Author/Poet Maya Angelou: *"To describe my mother would be to write about a hurricane in its perfect power."*

Case Study on Mentoring

Reverend Linda Ochola-Adolwa, Executive Pastor of Mavuno Church in Nairobi, Kenya, graduated from the University of Nairobi with a BA Honors and a Masters in Divinity from Nairobi Evangelical Graduate School of Theology, now Africa International University. She was part of the team sent by Church on the Hill, formerly Nairobi Chapel, to initiate Mavuno Church. She is a popular preacher, mentor and author. Asked what kind of mentoring saw her become a role model to many women in Kenya today, Pastor Linda talked about a mother and father who guided her along her way to become who she is today.

She describes her mother as a warm, energetic and generous woman, creative and always brimming with ideas about what to do next. "When I was growing up she seemed to always bounce back from any setback. I think my determination comes from her. I am not as social as she was but she taught me to value people. She taught us to be generous and industrious. She also introduced me to faith in God. We prayed as a family in the evenings and sang together and she made sure that we went to church. In this way she opened the way for me to come to faith in Jesus."

Pastor Linda describes her father as a responsible man who always made sure that the basics like food and school fees were provided. "My father worked as a civil servant in the Ministry of Health and later as the Member of Parliament for his rural constituency. I think my passion for social transformation comes from him. Without professing to be a Christian, he demonstrated a sense of social responsibility seldom found even among Christians."

Pastor Linda adds that her father understood that as a leader, he had a role in providing for the widow and the orphan, a reality that was underlined for Pastor Linda during her theological studies. She adds that this mentoring in the social responsibility component of faith has become an organising principle in her own life.

Pastor Linda's eyes sparkle whenever she communicates. She has an underlying sense of humor that makes her a great teacher and preacher. Clearly, this is a quality she picked from her father whom she describes as having a great sense of humor and as a great orator. She is sure that these qualities have also shaped her life. "I see humor in many ordinary circumstances and have grown to be a good communicator."

This is the essence of mentoring. Dr. Gershon Mwiti's doctoral supervisor at Fuller Seminary's School on Intercultural Studies used to tell his students: "My commitment to mentoring you is a wish that you all become better than me, and accomplish more than I've ever accomplished." Children should carry on after the parents to pass on to their own children deep values that they have received and those that have positively shaped them for life.

CHAPTER 9

PRAISE IN PARENTING

THE MEANING OF PRAISE IN PARENTING

What you help a child to love can be more important than what you help him to learn.
~ *African Proverb*

Be wise, my son, and bring joy to my heart; then I can answer anyone who treats me with contempt.
~ *Proverbs 27:11*

The African proverb: "*What you help a child to love can be more important than what you help him to learn,*" underlines the fact that in learning, emotion is important because it drives attention, which in turn makes learning and memory easier. This is why if a child hates the teacher, hatred blocks the learning process. On the other hand, if there is respect and appreciation between teacher and student, the learner enjoys the process and so learning and memory are facilitated. The proverb then underlines the fact that if a child loves and enjoys any subject, faster learning is facilitated. This is the basis of motivation in learning.

The Biblical proverb: "*Be wise, my son, and bring joy to my heart; then I can answer anyone who treats me with contempt,*" implies that if the son or learner does not show wisdom and morality in his conduct, the trainer: parent, mentor or teacher will be blamed for it. This is because the youth's behavior will be the judge of the efficacy of the mentor's training, while wisdom, as indicated in the youth's maturity, will be proof of the merit of the mentor's instruction. Motivation is a factor in life-transformative learning.

In this discussion, praise generally means the way parents encourage and motivate their children to learn and keep learning. Our actions are linked to the manner in which other people respond towards our attempts to perform well. When we hear: "Well done! Keep it up!" we run faster, hold on longer against discouragement and believe that whatever we are doing is making a difference. We also learn to appreciate our abilities because other people's praise affirms and validates our gifting.

Another way to define praise is cheerleading. In many countries, sport teams often hire a professional group whose only responsibility is to cheer their team as they play. Cheerleaders will often be seen, young beautiful women in uniform, wearing the colors of the team and singing the groups' winning song. Why is praise necessary? We are creatures who become empowered by appreciation. Some of us seek it out while others need it less, but all of us appreciate appreciation.

Psychologists and human resource specialists emphasize the role of motivation in the workplace. The question is often asked: "How do you appreciate your staff?" The advice given is that the appreciation needs to be linked to the action so that the praise is specific. Many reward schedules are suggested, but the bottom line is that praise and appreciation are necessary for all of us, and more so for the developing child. Approval reinforces positive behavior, making it possible for the child to repeat the same action in the future.

Psychology teaches that before adolescence, the child is emotionally very close to the parent and quickly responds to positive praise. A young one who knows that the parent is watching to commend rather than criticize his achievements will most probably repeat the same action due to encouragement received. If more parents remembered these facts, even recalling their own pleasure when commended for doing well, they would appreciate their children's success more often.

The Power of Praise

A child brought up where there is always dancing cannot fail to dance.
~ African (Nyanja) Proverb

Perfume and incense bring joy to the heart, and the pleasantness of one's friend springs from his earnest counsel.
~ Proverbs 27:9

The African proverb: "*A child brought up where there is always dancing cannot fail to dance,*" emphasizes the power of the environment in which young ones learn. Where there is joy, the child learns with joy. However, where there is sarcasm, abuse and neglect, the child's learning is negatively affected. The implication is that parents need to be aware of this factor in their children's capability to learn and then develop the ability to set the tone of the learning environment. Let there be appreciation and joy in the home as the primary atmosphere where child mentorship begins.

The Biblical proverb: "*Perfume and incense bring joy to the heart, and the pleasantness of one's friend springs from his earnest counsel,*" refers to the preciousness of a faithful mentor. As fragrant perfumes refresh and comfort tired, drooping spirits, so does the presence of a true, faithful mentor. The learner's soul is encouraged and empowered even when he is drooping from the uncertainty of life's challenges. Such is the joy that fills the heart of a young person, for example, when she knows that she is going home to meet a loving parent, a cheer leader, an encourager and a faithful mentor who offers praise and encouragement when all seems lost.

Some parents do not commend their children, believing that praise will *get into their heads* making them haughty and proud. However, can the parent over-praise the child? In other words, can too much praise spoil a child? Shouldn't the parent correct the child again and again incase the young one becomes vaunted up with too much "Well done?" No, a parent cannot genuinely over-praise a child. Research indicates that if parental praise is authentic, we can never over-praise a child at whatever age. Psychology teaches us that criticism is so destructive that for every condemnation we voice, we need over ten positive commendations to wipe away the memory of the single, negative comment. This is how deeply hurtful words cut.

We have already mentioned that before teenage years, children do not hide how much they long for the parent to notice their attempt to do well. Many parents know that even a simple drawing will be waved before their face. Little Tim runs to his parents with the words: "Mummy! Daddy! Look at my picture. I drew it all by myself." His parents turn away from watching television and respond: "Wow Tim! That's clever. You can draw so well. Now go and shade inside the lines!" and Tim runs off to shade inside the lines, and so on.

With encouragement, appreciation and commendation, the child blossoms. This blossoming begins to touch other areas of the child's life. Confidence in Mathematics becomes confidence in drama and public speaking. The child believes that he is good at everything he does. He senses that the parents are emotionally present and interested in his performance. This is the essence of parental cheerleading.

Older children may not run to Daddy or Mummy with their A Grade in English, but they hand in a high school report or a college project paper with a wide smile where encouragement and praise have been present in the past. The youth is motivated to excel because the cheerleader is watching from life's grand stands. So far, we have assumed that the child or youth's parent or parents are present physically and emotionally, and that they are engaged in the young person's life.

We have taken for granted that parents know what tasks need completion and how challenging the child is finding the assignments. We have therefore assumed that the parent is encouraging the young one to stay focused on the task at hand and that support and praise will be forthcoming as the task proceeds and is completed.

We have already explained that one cannot over-praise a child. This is because where and when the child receives a deliberate negative comment or is ignored by the would-be cheerleader, the impact is vicious and wounds to the core.

Let us explore once again what may happen when young Tim runs to his parents with the words: "Mummy! Daddy! Look at my picture. I drew it all by myself!" Daddy does not look up. He continues watching television. Mummy looks up briefly: "Go away and play Timmy. We are busy! Can't you see Daddy is watching football? Stop bugging him!" and they turn back to watch their program. Tim stops in his steps as if knocked by a locomotive. He lowers his head and tears well up in his eyes.

Disappointment and anger may cause him to tear up the picture and throw it on the floor. Other children with a different temperament might go away, shoulders slumped, arms flailing, and vow: "Never again will I draw another picture!" The pain is deep. They may transfer the pain to school and hate their Art class, resulting in poor performance or misbehavior. The parents, who missed opportunity to praise their child, may be the same ones who discipline him later on for performing poorly or misbehaving.

Reading this, you may ask: "Why do some parents do such stupid things?" Yet, this negative reaction by Tim's parents is all too common. We may react in the same way when we are busy, tired or stressed or when we want the child to concentrate on serious things like science homework instead of drawing useless pictures, and so on. It follows that parents need to exercise care that they do no trivialize any activity the child or youth is involved in, and so praise should be deliberate, specific, intentional and genuine.

Can Parents Be Unwise?

When a man curses his own child, it is a terrible thing.
~ African Proverb

Better is open rebuke than hidden love.
~ Proverbs 27:5

The African proverb: "*When a man curses his own child it is a terrible thing,*" is a scary truth that cautions parents on the things they speak or wish over the lives of their children. There is power in the parent's tongue, the verbal things they speak with regard to their children. They can bless or curse, and any parent who has the audacity to curse his own offspring is self-defeating because children are their parents not only genetically but also as life that continues parents' heritage.

The Biblical proverb: "*Better is open rebuke than hidden love,*" reminds parents that freely taking the honest liberty to correct the faults of their children is more valuable than having passion in the heart and then not communicating the same to the children. Love and appreciation that is not communicated has no effect. Children will not live with us forever, and no opportunity should be lost to appreciate and encourage them.

Deliberate praise and appreciation imply that a parent is emotionally and physically present as well as engaged in the child's or young person's life. For example, a parent who is aware that his son is acting in a play will plan to be present to watch the child.

For many years at my church, we held annual musicals which were written, produced, choreographed, and acted by the youth group. We made sure that every child took part whether in acting, dancing, playing a musical instrument, painting the props, singing, costume design, back-stage management, ushering and so on. The month of preparation and rehearsals attracted many of the children's friends, even those that did not normally attend church and many from the neighborhood. We made sure that the team was well fed and supervised. Every adult knows how much young people value good food and adult attention. Most parents supported the process by dropping and picking up the children, sending food and snacks, and attending rehearsals where possible.

One surprising observation is that while we gainfully occupied their children, there were parents who never showed up or cared where their children spent the days, right through the month that it took us to produce and put up the musicals. We had to request other adults to drop these children after late-night rehearsals and final performance week. Some of these children with absent parents were immensely gifted and took lead parts in acting, singing and so on. However, whereas other parents and siblings were present to cheer their own, some of these gifted youth had no family members present as they shone on stage, although we knew that the child lived with both parents and some of these families were in the neighborhood.

Maybe, some of these children with absent parents reported that they were in a major acting role at church and actually received an award for best actor and so on. We do not know. Perhaps the parent might have said "Good job!" However, this praise is misplaced. It indicates no active interest and no deliberate intent to identify, encourage, nurture, and appreciate the youth's gifting. For praise to work, it needs to be deliberate and planned, not disconnected and fake. Specific praise is physically and emotionally engaged. It focuses on what the child has accomplished that is necessitating the compliment.

Is there a Right and Wrong Way to Praise?

Dine with a stranger but save your love for your family.
~ African (Ethiopian) Proverb

The crucible for silver and the furnace for gold, but a man is tested by the praise he receives.
~ Proverbs 27:21

The African proverb: "*Dine with a stranger but save your love for your family,*" underlines ties that bind family members. These are the links that remind parents that if they fail in the responsibility of mentoring their children, it will be very difficult for someone else to do the work on their behalf. This is why motivation for learning as well as the content of child mentoring should be deliberate for each parent.

The Biblical proverb: "*The crucible for silver and the furnace for gold, but a man is tested by the praise he receives,*" is a reminder that praise needs to be specific. Specific, intentional praise concentrates on the here and now: what the child is doing and has accomplished. It avoids generalities and takes the focus away from what the parent feels about the achievement. For example, a mother discovers that her 14 year old daughter cleaned up the house, washed the dishes, and started dinner. The mother might say: "Monica, you are a good girl." Wrong! No one is a good girl all the time, and chores do not necessarily make one good. Monica might wonder: "Am I really good? What of the day you punished me for breaking your favorite bowl?"

The mother might also say: "Monica, you make me happy! You cleaned the house" Not good enough! The statement focuses on the mother's feelings and needs, not on Monica's character. This selfish statement does not do the child any good. Indeed, such sentiments sometimes create people pleasers, children who behave well to purchase parent's good feelings. The better way for the mother to praise Monica is to say: "Monica, thank you. I noticed that you cleaned up the house, washed all the dirty clothes and have even started dinner. Now we can all eat early!" Monica recognizes that her selfless actions have positively impacted the lives of the other family members. She also learns to appreciate actions that other people do for her and to say thank you for the same.

Psychologists recommend that the mother go further and engage Monica in discussing how she managed the day all by herself. Something like: "Monica I notice that you cleaned up the house, washed all the dirty clothes, and have even started dinner. How did you manage to do all that by yourself? How did you plan your time so well?"

Monica's ability to plan her duties is reinforced through her mother's specific approval.

Besides being specific, praise should also be intentional and not vague and accidental. A parent who follows a child's life with interest and is emotionally engaged in the youth's progress will remember that praise is an important part of maturation. Intentional praise is aware of motives and avoids responses that are self-centered and manipulative.

Still on specifics of praise, a child may walk into a room wearing muddy shoes. The mother shouts: "You are naughty. Who do you think will clean the house after you?" The following day, he removes his shoes before entering the house. "You are a good boy. You remembered to remove your shoes."

The first comment is obviously wrong because instead of specifically talking about dirty shoes, it attacks the character of the child and points out the reason for cleanliness as the convenience of the cleaner without explaining the benefits of cleanliness. The second comment is no good either, because it takes the focus away from the action to the child and therefore does not reinforce cleanliness. Praise that is not intentional, focusing on the intended outcomes, may err in the ways indicated above.

In this regard, intentional praise would be something like: "Thank you for taking off your shoes. Do you know why we do not walk around the house in muddy shoes?" The parent now engages the child in a brief question and answer session to explain the benefits of cleanliness, the need to be considerate of others who may have to clean up after us after we mess up, and so on. This way, the child's behavior is intentionally reinforced with understanding. The child may even become a trainer of others, reminding them of the worth of cleanliness and consideration of others who work to help us. Intentional praise desires specific outcomes and uses opportunities to train the child, create understanding and shape behavior.

Need for Genuineness in Praise

Peace is costly but it is worth the expense.
~ African (Kenyan) proverb

A lying tongue hates those it hurts, and a flattering mouth works ruin.
~ Proverbs 26:28

The African (Kenyan) proverb: "*Peace is costly but it is worth the expense,*" emphasizes the preciousness of peace and harmony in a family. Peace creates an atmosphere of trust and security where genuineness thrives. Parents are not afraid of misinterpretation when they speak into the lives of their children because there is no hidden agenda. Similarly, children are confident that since parents love them and have created a peaceful learning environment, they are expected to thrive, and so concentrate on doing exactly that.

The Biblical proverb: "*A lying tongue hates those it hurts, and a flattering mouth works ruin,*" underlines the destructive power of lies and flattery. Fake praise has the capacity to spoil a child because it is out of context, unreal, and divorced from the actions of the young one. Children know the truth about their own behavior. If they do wrong, they know. If they obey, their conscience does not judge them.

Flattery, however, destroys because it constantly blurs the lines between truth and lie. Flattery is blind to faults and is selfish and other-centered, not child-centered. Why would a parent praise a child endlessly without balancing commendation and correction? Studies indicate that a child treated as a special, precious, fragile element and naturally deserving praise is more likely to become a narcissist: self-centered, self-obsessed and insensitive to the needs of others.

Besides being intentional and specific, praise should, therefore, be genuine. Although some parents are afraid of over-praising their children, genuine praise does not spoil a child. Genuine praise is real, attached to specific actions, intentional and deliberate. Genuine praise asks questions to understand details. Genuine praise is unconditional, meaning that the child knows that she does not have to fake action to receive appreciation.

In these days when academic performance is often taken as the only measure of success, young people may be tempted to cheat in an examination for the sake of seeking parental approval. However, a child who knows that the parent communicates genuine praise that is warm and loving knows that he does not need to fake success to be loved and appreciated. Genuine parents do not refuse to commend a child who messed up yesterday because there is always a chance of performing better tomorrow. Hope for improvement gives life whereas parental condemnation locks the young one into hopelessness.

Take the case of Maina who borrows his father's car and is involved in a minor accident. Insurance will take care of the damage but the father is very angry believing that the young man should have been more careful. Maina apologizes but his father is still very angry. The following day, Maina receives a letter telling him that he has passed the interview to go to the USA as an exchange student. With excitement, he runs into the house to tell his family the good news. Can his father separate the two incidents and genuinely congratulate his son?

The older man may use synthetic praise and say sarcastically: "Oh! I see. Now you've got your wish!" Here, there is no praise, and no appreciation. Another type of praise is referred to as a sting in the tail. Maina's father might say: "Congratulations Maina, but I wonder how many other cars you will crash in America!" Ouch! That hurt, didn't it?

Genuine unconditional praise, however, will say: "Well son, congratulations! You prepared hard for that interview. We all watched you study ardently every evening. You deserve it! And, by the way, forgive me for my harsh tone about the car yesterday. I know you didn't mean to have the accident. You'll be more careful next time, won't you? Now, as for this trip ..." The father has genuinely congratulated his son and used the opportunity to deal with the car incident. He also took the opportunity to express part of the reason he had been angry. It was not totally about Maina, but a result of the fear that something worse might have happened during the accident.

Genuine praise is not self-centered. It does not seek to deflect the attention from the child to the parent. For example, a parent with selfish praise would have said: "That's my boy! I always said that my genes are not that bad after all! Do you hear that dear wife? My son is going to America!" he concludes, pointing proudly towards Maina's mother. By taking the focus away from Maina, his father fails to reinforce the hard work and commitment that earned the young man the recognition. Genuine praise yields the fruit of encouragement and has the capacity to reinforce positive behavior.

Not Abilities but Achievements

An ugly child of your own is more to you than a beautiful one belonging to your neighbor.
~ African (Baganda) Proverb

He who works his land will have abundant food, but the one who chases fantasies will have his fill of poverty.
~ Proverbs 28:19

The African proverb: "*An ugly child of your own is more to you than a beautiful one belonging to your neighbor,*" reminds parents to appreciate their own offspring no matter what their abilities or frailties may be. This attitude overcomes the temptation to compare one's children to others. Some parents are tempted to ask their children: "Why can't you be like Paul? Look how hard he works on his father's farm. All you do is read all the day!" Children are differently gifted and none of them, even twins, are totally identical. It follows that each child should be appreciated for who they are and trained to live out their particular strengths fully.

The Biblical proverb: "*He who works his land will have abundant food, but the one who chases fantasies will have his fill of poverty,*" underlines the fact that even God takes an interest in what we achieve with the abilities he has given us. Two people, equally gifted, could have different outcomes depending on how they exploit their strengths. Both could be academically endowed but one of them wastes time and does not study and so fails his exams, while the other carefully attends to his learning and listens to his lecturers and so excels in his grades. The first one receives disapproval from his parents while the other reaps appreciation for hard work.

When parents praise children, they need to direct the appreciation at the results of the child's achievements and not on the young one's ability to achieve. Achievements are outcomes while abilities are possibilities that offer room for change. For example, we know that some children are more intelligent than others. However, not all intelligent children perform well in every subject. They may be excellent in some classes and perform poorly in others.

Similarly, academic excellence does not necessarily translate to excellence in sports or other pursuits. If praise is directed at the child's intelligence instead of on the outcomes of intelligence, the child may be afraid to try an activity in the areas where they do not have natural gifting. This is because she is afraid of being labeled stupid because, after all, the parent always describes his daughter as the cleverest girl in her class.

Let's give an example. Katia is an intelligent young woman who excels in Sciences. However, she is very poor in languages, especially Kiswahili. If her Science teacher said: "Katia, you are so intelligent," describing the girl's A-grade in Chemistry, in the Kiswahili class, Katia will not answer any questions so as to avoid sounding stupid. Instead the Science teacher should say: "Katia, your Chemistry performance is above average," while the language teacher might say: "You have tried hard in your language exam," describing the girl's C grade in Kiswahili. "Why don't we meet tomorrow so that we can discuss areas that you find a bit challenging in this subject?"

Katia will soon learn that her challenge to understand languages does not make her a failure. It simply means that she is not gifted in languages as she is in Chemistry. Similarly the Kiswahili teacher is ready to help Katia to understand her weaknesses instead of simply telling her where she is weak. Both teachers are helping the student to own the fact that she is good in Chemistry and that she finds Kiswahili challenging. This way, Katia can begin to develop a balanced view of self.

Rewards of Genuine Praise

A united family eats from the same plate.
~ African (Baganda) Proverb

When I was a boy in my father's house, still tender, ... he taught me and said,"Lay hold of my words with all your heart; keep my commands and you will live."
~ Proverbs 4:3-4

The African proverb: *"A united family eats from the same plate,"* teaches that unity in family creates bonds that make learning possible. Eating from the same plate could refer to shared ideals, common purpose, care for one another, encouragement of the weak and rejoicing with the strong. The reverse is true, that a disjointed family has the capacity for evil competition, malice, a don't-care attitude regarding the welfare of others and malicious joy – the delight one feels when his competitor fails. This kind of family cannot eat from the same plate.

The Biblical proverb: *"When I was a boy in my father's house, still tender, ... he taught me and said, 'Lay hold of my words with all your heart; keep my commands and you will live,'"* is a reminder that the source of genuine praise is a loving father and parent who has taken time and with knowledge imparted the truths of his life to the child. Flourishing for the maturing youth will depend on how well she is able to remember and adhere to the parent's instructions. This training begins in the child's tender years and continues to adulthood. All this learning is accompanied by parental engagement in the youth's life and the encouragement that goes with it.

Psychologists agree that praising a child creates the opportunity to educate and train him. It increases competence, self-confidence and truthfulness that aid child development and positive maturation. Intentional praise focuses on specific values that the parent desires to develop in the child and specifies behaviors that the parent desires to reinforce.

Who should reinforce behavior, a parent or the child? Behavior reinforcement refers to actions that make the identified behavior likely to be repeated and so strengthened with a likelihood of becoming part of the individual's character. In our context, we are discussing how positive behaviors can be strengthened, so shaping the child's character.

Lasting change happens when parents encourage children and youth to reinforce their own behavior. Young people who depend on external reinforcement of behavior may turn into people pleasers who do good things for the sake of a reward, and not because the action is of itself positive. Continually dishing out praise for the sake of praise creates an everlasting hunger for approval, making the child dependent on the parent, and not on her own efforts and accomplishments.

Such young people may develop an external locus of control where their behavior is shaped by what others think of them, versus an internal locus of control that is based on personal values and convictions. Children with an external locus of control are likely to suffer damaging effects of peer pressure as they mature because they are always worried what other people, especially their peers, think of them. They will quickly conform for fear of displeasing other people.

Self-Reinforcement and Character Consistency

A child is what you put into him.
~ African (Nigerian) Proverb

Hold on to instruction. Do not let it go; guard it well, for it is your life.
~ Proverbs 4:13

The African proverb: *"A child is what you put into him,"* reminds us that children end up reflecting our parenting styles. Of course, not all children turn out the way the parent intended and not all situations have the promise of things turning out the way we wish. Situations change. Families face illness, loss and bereavement, and the capacity to parent is challenged. However, the persistence of doing the best and then leaving the results to God is a good focus for parents.

The Biblical proverb: *"Hold on to instruction. Do not let it go; guard it well, for it is your life,"* suggests that consistency is a critical value in completing what we set out to do. Parents continue to learn from God and other mentors with consistency and commitment. They then teach their children with the same passion, so reinforcing character change and personal responsibility. This desire to grow in wisdom ushers in holistic wellness for themselves and their children. This life enriches society impacting others whom the family touches. Life is continuous, like a river that refreshes wherever it goes.

Self-reinforcement refers to the child's internalized ability to self-evaluate and self-monitor so as to develop consistent character. To this end, parents should encourage children and young people to reinforce their own behavior. For example, Lucy's friend Tabs was so angry with her parents that she wanted to punish them. She decided to disobey them by sleeping out at her friend's place without her parents' knowledge and permission. She shared her plan with Lucy as they walked home from school. Lucy managed to talk Tabs out of the plan and Tabs agreed to go back home and discuss with her parents about the incident that had made her so angry. It was not an easy decision but she gave up the idea of sleeping out.

Back home, Lucy narrated the case to her mother. Her mother could have said: "Well done! You just saved the day!" However, the older woman said: "How do you feel about what you just did?" Lucy responded "I'm happy Mom because I think that this incident will help Tabs build better communication with her parents. She will learn that acting out of her anger would not have improved their communication. Running away from issues does not help, does it?" Through this kind of conversation, Lucy's mother is helping her daughter to reinforce the listening and counseling quality the young woman is already practicing with her friend Tabs. She allows Lucy herself to analyze and acknowledge her action and its outcomes.

Praise is a key pillar in parenting and needs to be handled with care. It can be used to shape behavior, teach values, and help young people reinforce positive behavior. Parental praise and approval should be unconditional and genuine, able to evaluate each action by its own merit and so shape the child's positive behavior. Such praise is possible when a parent is present, physically, emotionally, cognitively and relationally, as well as engaged in the life of their child all the way through maturation – from birth to childhood and adolescence through young adulthood. Praise, appreciation, commendation, "well done" and "I'm proud of you" will matter for as long as the parent-child relationship remains, and that is through life, for as long as the two shall remain.

No child, youth or young adult should ever have to live in a desert devoid of parental praise and encouragement, if that parent is alive. The world has enough discouragement without having to live with parental disapproval and condemnation.

Case Study on Praise in Parenting

Dr. Gershon Mwiti remembers that his parents lived as a couple and worked as a team. They also actively participated in community activities. As a child and young man, Gershon says that he was not embarrassed by the way his parents lived although they were not the richest or best endowed in the village. They were joyful people who talked a lot together, joked, and teased one another. In particular, they praised one another, his father even composing love songs in poetic, idiomatic and figurative language for his wife. The effect was that growing up, Gershon felt loved, secure and cared for. This imparted courage and confidence to grow up, explore and extend his abilities.

In particular, Gershon remembers his parents' overt praise. The young man was a gifted athlete, winning many awards and filling his home with the trophies of the day: cups, plates and bowls. His mother emotionally and graciously received every award Gershon brought home, an attitude that motivated the athlete to do better.

Gershon remembers a particular day when he was afraid to go traditional dancing among older boys, so he asked his mother to take him. She agreed and went with him, behavior that was not common. At the dancing floor, his fear disappeared. Since his parents loved him and spent time with him, he was a well-behaved child and grew up to become the village favorite child, and a ritual boy, performing special assignments for them.

As an example, Gershon reminded me that a few years ago, we constructed a river bridge for our village. Between our village and the neighboring range, there is a deep river that brings water down the valley from the melting snows of Mt. Kenya, 17,000 feet upstream. Many years ago, to cross the river, the village constructed a bridge with two huge dugout logs. As it was very scary to walk across the old swinging bridge, many old people and children crawled across. Over the years, one of the logs wore out and fell off.

Gershon decided to do something about the bridge. With the partnership of Rotary Club, he designed and constructed a brand new footbridge using local labor and local materials that included the innovation of utilizing two 14-foot lorry chassis to reach across the river. It was such excitement, as the whole village turned up each day for many weeks in the spirit of the common Kenyan motto of *Harambee* – pulling together - to build the bridge. The older men carried the stones and sand, the younger men hauled the chassis across the river, the masons mixed cement, the women cooked the food to feed the army of workers, and the children sat at a distance watching.

When the bridge was complete, we had to observe a consecration ritual – a boy and girl specially selected by the village had to be the ones to cross the beautiful bridge as the first people to ever use it. This was the kind of thing Gershon used to do as a child. His confidence and good character was motivated by his parents and he became confident, a fast runner, obedient and willing to be a blessing to other people.

In particular, he remembers that he was selected to *gwikia nduma*. This meant that he was the one to ascertain if an initiate was healed after circumcision. Just before the coming-out ceremony, the initiate would be given a sheath with a bunch of arrows and a bow. He would shoot the arrows and young Mwiti would run and pick them up. The shooting and picking would continue over some distance, covering as far as the arrows went and shooting all the arrows in the sheath.

When the last arrow was shot and gathered, Gershon and the initiate would race back home as fast as they could. If Gershon got there ahead of the initiate, then the young man would have to spend more days in the house to heal. If he arrived ahead of Mwiti, the initiate would be declared healed.

On such occasions, Gershon explains that the village hosting him would treat him as an honored guest, cook for him and look after him well. All this special regard was before he was 10 years old, and he was honored because of the motivation, encouragement and modeling his parents accorded him.

The honor was a reflection of the way the village also honored his parents. He demonstrates this by relating an occasion where going to school once, he picked a long, red, cloth rope on the road and used it to hold up his shorts because as a young child, he did not have a waist belt. One just improvised and used ropes or banana fiber. A few days later, he met a man who grabbed him and took him to the village court claiming that Gershon was a thief!

The man explained that a few days earlier, thieves had broken into his house and stolen clothes, among other items. "The red tie that the boy claims he picked up from the road and has been using as a belt is not a cloth rope but my neck tie," screamed the man. Gershon was flabbergasted. He apologized again to the elders, exclaiming that he did not know what a tie looked like: "I thought it was just a piece of cloth!"

One of the elders said, "People, this boy IS NOT lying. He cannot be a liar. He is the son of Baituuru and the son of Baituuru cannot lie." Baituuru was Gershon's father. So, the character of the parents had become that of the son: purposeful parenting, praise, training and role modeling helped transfer the parents' good qualities to their son.

CHAPTER 10

PARENTING AS PROTECTION

Definition of Protection

Advice is a stranger; if he's welcome he stays for the night; if not, he leaves the same day.
~ *African (Malagasy) Proverb*

For the Lord gives wisdom ... He holds victory in store for the upright, he is a shield to those whose walk is blameless.
~ *Proverbs 2: 6-7*

The African proverb: *"Advice is a stranger; if he's welcome he stays for the night; if not, he leaves the same day,"* underlines the need to be open to learning as a life posture. As children grow up, the change is sometimes too fast and parents find it difficult to understand what is happening to their young ones. The learning posture and openness to what one does not know and yet maintaining parental authority and maturation is like welcoming a stranger called wisdom. Blessing shall follow parents who seek wisdom for themselves and their children.

The Biblical proverb: *"For the Lord gives wisdom ... He holds victory in store for the upright, he is a shield to those whose walk is blameless,"* states the rewards of those who seek God's wisdom and who grow in his fear and obedience. *Holding victory in store* is a promise for parents who faithfully keep on loving and training their children even when there is little evidence that these parents' effort is making a difference. For such, the pledge is that one day, the change will come. Meanwhile, God is the one who protects the mind and spirit of waiting parents.

Protection can be assumed to mean guarding, shielding and providing security for both parents and their children. In this regard, we assume that from the moment of conception, children are vulnerable. They are the weak ones while the parents are the strong ones. This is the assumption that informs doctors' urge to mothers to make sure that they have a healthy pregnancy. Mothers are reminded that the fetus cannot feed itself. For this reason, the pregnant mother is reminded to take care of her diet by including healthy foods and excluding harmful substances.

I remember watching a recent documentary on street children. The journalist interviewed a young, pregnant street girl who had a bottle in her hands. She admitted sniffing substances, but she was quick to add: "I don't sniff glue. I sniff petrol." Street children have a street name for petrol. They consider petrol purer than glue. However, they do not know that any substance that alters the mood of the parent has lethal effects especially on the brain of the fetus. In her own warped way, this young woman, nevertheless, seemed to differentiate substances she should and should not take when pregnant.

In our world, more and more babies are born with fetal alcohol syndrome or horrible symptoms of drug withdrawal. Such children struggle not only with life but also with healthy child development, which increases chances for brain retardation. With stress increasing in our society, stressed mothers also pass stress to the fetus. Studies indicate that when a pregnant woman is distressed, the fetus is also stressed. Some of the damaging stress comes from increasing cases of domestic violence, abuse and insecurity.

All these examples underline the need for parents to

extend child protection to pregnancy, realizing that unborn babies are as much aware of their environment as other children. Stress in pregnancy has been linked to baby distress with symptoms such as colic, crying too much, lowered baby immunity, and so on. Peace and tranquility during pregnancy have also been linked with peaceful babies, better immunity and healthier child development. From birth, protection includes early holistic care for the maturing baby, issues of safety, the need to create emotionally stable environments and protection from moral pollution.

Physical safety includes careful selection of caregivers when the parent has to be away from the child. Parents cannot afford to be careless with child protection. I once heard a story of a mother of two boys aged six and three years respectively. She had a houseboy and assumed that the boys were safe with a man taking care of them. Although she was often at home at the boys' bath time, she would leave their bathing to the houseboy.

This mother noticed that each time bath time came, the children would cry, cling to her and refuse to go to the bathroom. She assumed that they were just being naughty and would threaten to beat them. The houseboy would drag the crying boys to the bathroom and shut the door. The little ones screamed throughout their shower time while their mother sat and watched television. As naïve as this mother may seem, she was blinded for several years until the older boy summoned the courage to disclose what went on in the shower.

Many parents reading this story will obviously be horrified that the ignorant mother did not read the signs of the times. By the time she learnt the truth, she had allowed the little ones in her hands to be damaged for life. These children had lived with the threat: "If you tell your mother anything, I shall slit your throats with my kitchen knife."

Is it possible that child abuse can happen right "under the parent's nose?" Yes, it can. Often, parents have failed to educate themselves on the signs and symptoms of child abuse. In case you feel incompetent in this regard, my book *Child Abuse. Detection, Prevention and Counseling* (Evangel Publishers, Nairobi, Kenya, 2005) may be useful.

We now know that most child molesters were molested as children themselves. Researchers generally agree that abuse tends to be intergenerational with those who were abused as children being more likely to repeat the act when they themselves become parents and caregivers. The intergenerational pain is passed on as hurt people end up hurting other people.

As a result of this, parents who were abused as children need to utilize extra caution. We discuss sexual abuse first in this chapter because it is the most devastating form of abuse. Sexual abuse has the capacity to negatively impact the totality of human functioning beginning from the onset of maltreatment on to maturation. The severity of the impact depends on the seriousness of the abuse, the identity of the abuser, the duration of the abuse as well as the age of the victim.

Signs and Symptoms of Sexual Abuse

However long the night, the dawn will break.
~ African Proverb

Reckless words pierce like a sword, but the tongue of the wise brings healing.
~ Proverbs 12:18

The African proverb: *"However long the night, the dawn will break,"* reminds us that the journey of parenting can be filled with sorrow and long nights of waiting for periods of pain to pass and calm to be restored. Families face alcoholism, drug abuse, domestic violence, illness and even child abuse. When one is navigating around such a challenge, it is not easy to believe that things will ever get better again. However, *dawning* eventually comes. It may leave people shaken and their perspectives and status changed, but calm is eventually restored as the healing process is engaged.

The Biblical proverb: "*Reckless words pierce like a sword, but the tongue of the wise brings healing,*" underlines the destructive nature of abuse: emotional, sexual, physical, spiritual or harm caused by neglect. Recklessness or carelessness in childrearing can expose a child to abuse. Protecting a child or youth from any type of abuse from close relatives or any other predator is a key responsibility of every parent. This is because the damage so incurred impacts the whole personality, takes long to heal and sometimes persists for a lifetime.

There are telltale signs that may help a parent identify the likely presence of child sexual abuse although symptoms alone are not conclusive evidence. More investigation is necessary so as to make a conclusive decision but the impact affects the totality of human functioning. Psychologically the child or youth will be fearful, have sleeping problems, panic attacks, nightmares, irritability, outbursts of anger and low self-confidence.

To manage the inner pain, resulting from abuse, some young people may abuse drugs and/or alcohol, become depressed, self-destructive and suicidal and even engage in careless sexual behaviors. Socially, because of poor self-confidence or fear of loss of control when relating with others, social withdrawal may be evident. Physical complaints may include abdominal pain, nausea, headaches, back pain, and all manner of chronic complaints that do not have a physical cause or illness.

Eating disorders may occur among sexually abused children. Some seem to hate and detest their bodies. One beautiful young woman, sexually molested in childhood by her older brother for a number of years consistently refused to look at her face in the mirror, convinced that she was ugly and fat.

Once again, depending on the seriousness of the abuse, some abused children and youth have been known to develop symptoms of posttraumatic stress disorder (PTSD), a psychological clinical condition marked by a cluster of symptoms such as unconscious denial and repression of the memory of abuse. The young may refuse to talk about the abuse and to acknowledge that it ever happened. Another cluster of PTSD symptoms involves re-experiencing the abuse if any sensory experience or even dreams and nightmares trigger a remembrance of the abuse. An 11-year old child experienced stomachaches and diarrhea every time her abusive cousin came home to visit. Finally abused children may be jumpy, irritable and angry and find it difficult to fall asleep.

Protecting Children from Abuse

It is the fool's sheep that break loose twice.
~ African (Ashanti) Proverb

Through love and faithfulness, sin is atoned for.
~ Proverbs 16:6a

The African proverb: *"It is the fool's sheep that break loose twice,"* points to the fact that it is only a fool or unwise individual who would allow their charge to be abused twice. The first time, the parent may not have been aware or may have failed to keep close watch over the child. However, the second reveals that the parent is acting like a fool who is totally unaware of the danger the child or youth is in. This is foolishness. How can we describe the parent's behavior if child abuse takes place a third time?

The Biblical proverb: "*Through love and faithfulness, sin is atoned for,*" provides the way out for neglect, wrong doing and disobedience. When a parent fails to protect her child from abuse, she can ask God and the child for forgiveness and then practice obeying God through loving the child and faithfully facilitating the healing process.

Parents are called parents, a word that means caregivers, guardians and protectors. They look after, care for, protect, nurse and tend, and fulfill their God-given responsibility that ensures their children's safety. Psychologists suggest that parents need to protect the child through close supervision, especially in prudent selection of caretakers. Older relatives and siblings can also be abusive, so caution is advised without unduly suspecting family members of ulterior motives.

Parents also have an obligation to set appropriate boundaries especially in sleeping arrangements and privacy. Parental perceptions of sex should also be appropriate because abuse increases where the parents' own morality is in question. Child and youth abuse have been known to increase if a parent is having an affair that is likely to lead to family disintegration. In families where parents are unhappy and marriage disintegrates, children have been known to turn to each other for nurture, raising probability of abuse through incest. Parents may also turn to children in unhealthy ways to have their own needs met.

Finally, parents have the obligation to ensure that care of

children is entrusted to responsible adults, especially where there is divorce, bereavement, illness or whatever other factors that may take the parents away from the home. Where mothers are sick and bedridden or hospitalized for long periods, some fathers have been known to turn to their daughters for sexual satisfaction, especially where the older daughter takes her mother's position as the family's caregiver. Burdening an underage daughter with family care is called *parentification* and is already a form of child abuse. Adding incest to this status is a heavy burden that scars the young woman for life.

Besides protection from sexual abuse, there is also protection from wrong value systems. We have emphasized the need for role modeling and principled living in earlier chapters. However, in the context of this chapter, we shall underline the need for parents to ensure healthy socialization of their children. It is in the interest of every parent to know their children's friends. Who are they? What values do they adhere to? Are these children supervised or are they left to run wild, to watch any television program, play any video game or watch any type of movie? Are these children given cell phones? Do parents guide in the use of these phones?

This caution does not mean that parents need to limit the child's contact with the environment. It means greater care in choosing schools, selecting the child's social networks, and investing in deeper, involved and knowledgeable guidance to the maturing young ones. The bottom line is that parents can no longer make assumptions that "my child's school is safe, my neighbors' house is safe or my relative is safe."

We have allowed our society to become secular and have fought hard for the freedom to do whatever we want and live the way we want. Proof of this desire for freedom can be seen in newspaper pages as individuals write about their limitless lives and doing what they want and with whoever they choose.

It reminds one of the nation of Israel as narrated in 1 Samuel 8, where the elders went to Prophet Samuel and demanded a king. "We want to be like other nations," they cried. The idea of having a God they could not touch or see made them feel strange. God told the prophet: "Obey the voice of the people… for they have not rejected you, but have rejected me from being king over them," (1 Samuel 8:7). Israel got their king, and the very freedom they chose began making them slaves.

This analogy means that child protection cannot happen if parents do not know what safety looks like. Similarly, protection cannot happen if parents do not understand the impact of child violation. Violation and abuse can be physical, where the child is hurt physically; or spiritual though abuse of their divine connection with forces beyond their understanding like in the case of witchcraft, the demonic and evil rituals. In relational abuse, the child's healthy link with others is tainted or broken, for example, when one spouse poisons their child against the other. Psychological abuse involves calling the child names and "beating them" with the tongue through degrading, discouraging and breaking the child's spirit.

A young woman, Mimi, struggling with the devastating effect of witnessing domestic violence between her parents for many years was so sick that she had to be cared for by professionals to help her recover from depression. Her mother, who had contributed to this condition, kept telling Mimi: "You'll never get well. Look at you!"

These critical human systems: physical, relational, psychological and spiritual systems can run amok when an alien damaging force enters the child's schemata. As much as child abuse can be experienced through various systems of the child's functioning, the impact affects the holism of the young one's being. For example, sexual abuse, a practice that is increasing in our society in alarming proportions has a devastating impact on the child. Besides violating the very essence of the child's being, helplessness and hopelessness increase since the abuse is usually shrouded in silence and so its damaging effect continues to live in the child's psyche.

A woman who knew that her husband was taking their adolescent daughter to bed most nights was heard quipping: "How can I talk about it when he is the one who pays their fees in private schools and makes sure we live in this estate? If I tell, what will happen to us? He'll throw us out!"

When Physical Abuse is Confused with Discipline

A man who uses force is afraid of reasoning.
~ Kenyan Proverb

A gentle answer turns away wrath, but a harsh word stirs up anger.
~ Proverbs 15:1

The African proverb: "*A man who uses force is afraid of reasoning,*" is a self-explanatory statement that an individual who wants to understand and be understood does not need to use physical violence. Speaking out and discussing matters communicates volumes and brings people closer by enhancing awareness, whereas force generates anger and resentment. Using force, especially physical violence, opens doorways to much more than the pain inflicted.

The abused person starts asking: "Why me?" The unspoken answers can be colossal, most of them probably far-fetched and untrue. The child may say: "I am sure he hates me, that's why!" "May be I am not her child. I was adopted. That's why she hates me so." A child who is regularly beaten without discussing the reasons for the punishment experiences physical pain, emotional perplexity and thought confusion. As already stipulated, punishment is not discipline. The first communicates pain, anger and rejection while the second conveys love and desire for the wellbeing of the child.

The Biblical proverb: *"A gentle answer turns away wrath, but a harsh word stirs up anger,"* cautions that our words should be kind, gentle and tender. This is very difficult especially when a parent is angered by a child's deliberate intent to hurt and harm. However, speaking and lashing out in anger is always counterproductive because it sends out messages that the communicator did not intend. This is one of the reasons given for parents never to discipline a child when angry. Anger has the capacity to dissolve listening and reasoning.

Uncontrolled physical beating is violation of the child's safety in the pretext of administering discipline. We have earlier emphasized that punishment and discipline are two different things. Punishment inflicts pain while discipline lovingly trains the child through reinforcing parental limits. In the chapter of limit setting, we discussed three types of families: authoritarian, authoritative and chaotic. These types are defined by parenting styles.

A case is told of an authoritarian father. You may remember this type as dominant, too present in the child's life, often angry and demanding and seeming to derive pleasure in making other people suffer. This parent demanded that each child present to him the report card on the final day of the school term. Although he hardly attended Parents Days at the children's school, and barely participated in monitoring the children's academic progress, the man believed that his role was that of a policeman - to force good grades by punishing poor performance.

Knowing fully their father's sadistic inclinations, the children were scared of two days: the final day of the school term when they would have to hand in the report card to their father, and the last day of the school holidays. The first day was very scary because it pre-empted the second day. In the clinic, John, now a struggling young adult described one of the meetings with his father: "John, I see you've brought your report card," said his father, looking up from the newspaper he was reading. "Yes, Dad," answered the 12 year old, as he passed the card to his father.

Dad did not say another word as he looked at the document. John's grades were: English A. Other subjects were A-, B+ and so on. The worst was Math, where the young man had scored a D flat. The older man gave back the card to John with the words: "I see." John knew his father. He was sure that the man had noticed the D grade, but remained silent. The whole reporting system followed a pattern. The first day of the school holidays pre-empted a scary, anxiety-filled school holiday. The children were supposed to work on the farm and obey their father with unquestioning commitment. John was not scared of hard work. He was used to it. He did wish, however, that his Dad would treat his loving, quiet and long-suffering mother more gently.

What scared Johnny the most was that the school holiday weeks would pass in dread of the final day. His father had a whip reserved for any child, boy or girl, who would ever bring home any Grade below a C. That final evening, with schools opening the following day, Dad would wait for nightfall when everybody was ready for bed. He would then call each child that was targeted for punishment and say something like: "Come here Johnny. Last term you brought a D home. I will teach you how never to play with my hard earned money. Or do you think that your school fees fall from the sky like rain?"

At that point the man would set on the child with the whip. Not even his mother could rescue Johnny. She knew not to intervene. This behavior by John's father can be described as punishment not discipline. It did not help the boy to improve in Math. Instead, the older man's cruelty succeeded in planting hatred for both the subject and the punishing parent. This kind of authoritarian parenting inflicts pain and is a violation to the child's safety.

Where a parent cannot protect a child from harm from the other parent, this may be the time for another person to intervene to ensure that the vulnerable child is protected. The African saying: "It takes a village to raise a child" is relevant here and provides a way of intervention for child protection. In traditional Africa, a fast disappearing status, relatives and neighbors would be up in arms against a parent who deliberately abused a child like in the case of Johnny's father.

Abusive families, however, often succeed in isolating themselves, especially if the family lives far away from relatives. In addition, urban living, where a family is embedded in a suburb with strangers on either side, may encourage silence and harboring of parental abusive practices. This is where the school system and child protection agencies need to undertake closer monitoring of the status of children's safety in schools and communities as well as foster homes. It may be necessary for Parent Teacher Associations or children rights groups to lobby more for child protection especially in homes where parents are absent or too weak to protect the children.

THE LASTING IMPACT OF EMOTIONAL ABUSE

A fight between grasshoppers is a joy to the crow.
~ African (Lesotho) Proverb

The lips of the wise spread knowledge; not so the hearts of fools.
~ Proverbs 15:7

The African proverb: "*A fight between grasshoppers is a joy to the crow,*" emphasizes the foolishness of those who belong together fighting and destroying one another. The only one who gains from this in-house conflict is the crow, which waits for death to have a feast. Crowds really do not care what happens to our families. If we cannot value and protect what is our own, no one else has the deep commitment to do so. Prophesying on the restoration of Israel, Prophet Obadiah declared: "… and the household of Judah shall take possession of their possessions," (Obadiah 1:17), meaning that there would not only be freedom from their oppressors and restoration and but also that the people of Judah would once again value and jealously protect what belonged to them. They would not destroy or trivialize what was theirs.

The Biblical proverb: "*The lips of the wise spread knowledge; not so the hearts of fools,*" summarizes what happens when we set out to use our lips to bless. Wisdom leads to imparting of knowledge but the hearts of fools cannot produce insight. They are likely to generate abuse and destruction that has the capacity to destructively reverberate in a child's life for many years.

Child protection goes beyond the physical to shielding them from emotional abuse. Emotional wounds hurt deeper than physical ones. This is because emotional abuse has the capacity to demean and destroy the young one's identity and self-image as well as threaten the child's sense of security. Emotional and psychological abuse communicate to the child that she is not wanted and that try as she might, she will never be able to make a meaningful life space for herself. This type of abuse can lead to other types of maltreatment such as neglect and denial of basic necessities to the maturing youth.

Emotional and physical abusers use bad, demeaning language towards the child:

"You are stupid! You can never do anything right! You break everything you touch. You're just like your clumsy mother!" These words can easily be found on the lips of a stepmother talking to, say, an eight year-old little girl whose mother passed away and father remarried. The stepmother acts sweetly towards the child's father and pretends to care for the children when he is around. However, as soon as the man leaves, all hell breaks loose as the stepmother unleashes a barrage of demeaning, hurtful language on the children. Let me hasten to add here that many stepmothers are wonderful people, but just like some biological parents, some of them can be cruel and abusive.

These words can also be found on the lips of a woman who has taken a young child as house help. The older woman may have traveled and visited a home in her rural area looking for house help. Someone has told her about a young girl who has completed Primary 8 and could not join high school for whatever reason. She humbly asks for the child from the mother, promising: "I'll be your daughter's mother in the city. I'll take care of her as my very own." However, back at work, the young one is mistreated, overworked and even starved. She is called names whenever she fails to do something right, and generally lives a life of fear and helplessness.

Such children, who live with constant emotional and psychological abuse, do not answer back. They are unnaturally quiet, do not have any initiative, lose spontaneity and generally fail to thrive. These are symptoms for the other parent to look out for. If the children are changing from happy, carefree, spontaneous little ones to quiet, scared, accident-prone individuals, these behaviors should act as red flags. Are the children safe?

Relational Abuse and Parentification

When two elephants fight, it is the grass that gets trampled.
~ African (Swahili) Proverb

A man of wrath stirs up strife, and one given to anger causes much transgression.
~ Proverbs 29:22

The African proverb: "*When two elephants fight, it is the grass that gets trampled,*" is a reminder that when two people fight, it is the weaker ones in the vicinity that are bruised, torn and wounded. This wisdom cautions parents that their conflict directly hurts children. It makes them helpless, angry, confused, anxious, and threatens their identity and integrity.

The Biblical proverb: "*A man of wrath stirs up strife, and one given to anger causes much transgression,*" cautions a parent that uncontrolled anger has the capacity to hurt and cause more hurt. There is truth in the statement that *hurt people hurt people*. Anger leads to disobedience and bitterness, factors that can lead to lashing out against others. Indeed, research indicates that abusers were once abused themselves. Parents who may be carrying memories of pain from their own past need to seek help and so break the cycle of pain so that they do not end up abusing their own children.

One other form of child violation is relational abuse, for example when an individual is so angry and unforgiving towards a spouse who has hurt her that she poisons a youngster against him. Commonly found in unhappy homes, one parent plays a child against the other parent. No child should ever be involved in parental differences and conflict. Some parents take out their differences on the child in a practice we have already referred to as triangulation. Instead of approaching the other parent directly, they access one another through the child.

For example, the mother needs money for food. She sends the child: "Go and tell your father there is no food in the house." The father is actually sitting down inside the house at the time, maybe reading a newspaper, watching television or listening to the radio. "Dad," says the child. "Ma says to tell you that there's no food in the house." Her father looks up and responds: "Go and tell her I have no money. Does she think bank notes grow on trees?" Upon returning to the mother, the child cannot say directly: "Ma, Dad says he has no money. He also asked you, 'Do you think bank notes grow on trees?'" The young one knows that such a remark may earn her a slap for being naughty! So she sieves out the negative information through repressing it and filtering off the toxins into herself so as to protect her mother. She paraphrases the answer thus: "Ma, Pa says he doesn't have money now."

In placating the mother and protecting the father, the child has swallowed emotional bitterness and taken over the role of parenting the parents. This is the source of the psychological term: the *parentified* child. *Parentified* children are abused children. You will find them siding with one parent against the other. Caring for alcoholic or drug abusing parents, dropping out of school to take care of siblings after the parent dies of AIDS, begging on the streets with a blind parent, pushed into the streets by a healthy parent to ask for alms, and even forced into prostitution to earn money for parent upkeep are all forms of parentification.

Some young children frolicking as teen prostitutes at night have been sent out to bring money from the streets and if they do not come home with a specific sum, they are beaten. This is relational abuse where roles are reversed and the child takes a position to which they do not belong because the parent has failed in the role of parenting.

Some parents abuse their children relationally by telling tales about the other parent to the child. They poison the minds of the children against the perceived irresponsible spouse or against the opposite sex in general. Some young women growing up in single parent homes may have been fed with derisive speech against men in general along with their daily meal.

"Eat my child," the mother may say. "I wonder what your father is doing right now, just enjoying himself with his women while I toil alone to bring you up. Anyway, who says that men will not do what they always do! Just father the children and then disappear. That's all they're capable of!"

The child may respond: "Don't worry Ma. When I grow up, I'll look after you. I'll never leave you." And some never do.

Do not light a fire under a fruit-bearing tree.
~ *African (Ghanaian) Proverb*

Life is a gift of nature but beautiful living is a gift of wisdom.
~ *African (Malawian) Proverb*

The tongue of the wise commends knowledge, but the mouths of fools pour out folly.
~ *Proverbs 15:2*

The African (Ghanaian) proverb: *"Do not light a fire under a fruit-bearing tree,"* cautions parents not to destroy their children through abuse and neglect. Children are younger than their parents and they also embody a lot of promise for the future. Someone has labeled children the *emerging majority*, while parents are the *diminishing minority.* This is very true for Africa if one was to look at numbers. Children, however, carry the promise of a better tomorrow even without a physical head count, and so they need parental protection.

The second African (Malawian) proverb underlines this wisdom: *"Life is a gift of nature but beautiful living is a gift of wisdom,"* that nature gives us life but not living. Wisdom and knowledge spell the quality of life that we shall live.

The Biblical proverb: *"The tongue of the wise commends knowledge, but the mouths of fools pour out folly,"* discusses what happens when we use our words well. If we speak well of wisdom and emphasize good judgment to our children, they will pick up understanding as a critical factor in their lives. They will also internalize values that will guide them now and long after we are gone. However, if we give in to mediocrity and make pouring out of foolishness a habit, we commend the vice as the norm for living to our children.

Someone has said that *values are not taught. They are caught* because children are *good copycats*!

Broken marriages and families are a reality in our society and increasing rapidly. Broken marriages leave pain and sadness to those who are affected as well as much struggle – emotional, economic, relational, and so on. It is easy for parents to pass on their anger, anguish and sense of betrayal to their children. However, wise parents will de-link their own pain from the children's lives in a commitment to allow the young ones to grow with emotional wholeness. I have met some mothers, for example, who have ensured that their children respect and honor a drinking, abusive spouse. They remember that God's command: "Honor your father and mother," (Ephesians 6:2) is unconditional. Just like other commands that God gives, it has no "buts" or "ifs" attached to it.

Rehema learned how to de-link her children from her own marital disappointments. Her husband would hit her whenever he came home drunk. He would demand immediate service with hot food whatever time of night it was. If his wife hesitated, he would hit her again. The children were very angry with their father, but the mother cautioned them: "Please do not hate your father. He does not hit you. The differences we have are between the two of us. Please, do not let bitterness rule your hearts." The mother sought help to cope with the situation and also made sure that she protected the children's hearts and minds against the impact of their father's behavior. When finally the father stopped his drinking and abusive conduct, it was easier for the children to restore their relationship with him.

Parents should remember that their children have only one set of biological parents, and that the young ones' identity is tied to that of both their parents. Spouses may divorce one another but children can never divorce parents. For this reason, the child's image of their biological parent needs to be as intact as possible, from knowing the identity of their biological parent to preserving an ideal image of that individual. This preservation is especially important through the vulnerable period of young childhood through adolescence until the young one is old enough to withstand difficult realities, if any, about the parent. Then, from a young adult position, the young person can face the facts without being impacted negatively by the truth.

The interpretation of the reality at this point is perceived through eyes of understanding and any toxicity in the personality and parenting styles of the errant parent does not affect the youth as corrosively as it would have done through the tender years of childhood and early adolescence. This is the essence of relational protection.

THE CHILD'S SPIRITUAL PROTECTION

If you cannot be a lighthouse, be a candle.
~ North African Proverb

The fear of the Lord is the beginning of knowledge; fools despise wisdom and instruction.
~ Proverbs 1:7

The African proverb: "*If you cannot be a lighthouse, be a candle,*" is written from the premise of lighting and leading the way. Children desire to have parents act as models in matters of faith, yet some older people feel that they cannot model spirituality to their children because they do not know enough. This uncertainty may lead to neglect and so create vacuums where a child has all else but is without godliness. The proverb emphasizes that children will treasure whatever insight or modeling a parent can offer because what their parents say and do matters deeply to the young ones.

The Biblical proverb: *"The fear of the Lord is the beginning of knowledge; fools despise wisdom and instruction,"* underlines that God is the source of wisdom for parents. None of us should ever despise our knowledge of God. We communicate what we know to the children and set the atmosphere of spirituality at home so that they can learn more. We also link them to Bible teachers who know more than we do. This spiritual oversight works as protection for our children.

Parents clearly have the role of spiritual protection of their children and young people. Spiritual negligence is as damaging as allowing spiritual waywardness. This is because neglecting spiritual parenting opens up a vacuum in the child's life, and vacuums attract all sorts of practices. It has been argued that in every human heart is a void that only the true God can fill. It follows that a child who has received negligible or no spiritual parenting will long and look for anything that can fill the emptiness within.

It is surprising that some parents argue that children should be set free to choose their faith or the absence of it, and if they choose faith, they are free in the early years to worship where they will. Yet, we do not leave children free to choose whether or not they want to go to school and the kind of school they want to attend. Parental responsibility calls us to guide our children's education until at least they are able to wisely participate in decisions regarding their studies or the location thereof.

Children left to wander spiritually attract whatever promises to fill up their inner emptiness. Some youth have gotten into drugs and alcohol as these provide quick fixes. Substances have their roles of blocking pain, creating a quick rush and a spiritual high. However, the thrill is short-lived and ends up becoming addictive. Addictions obey the law of diminishing returns where more and more means less and less; that if some particular amount gave a certain level of high, next time, more is needed to give the same level of high. So, more is taken and the law repeats itself with diminishing returns of highs.

Other types of false spirituality present themselves through cults, sects, and other promises of Nirvana. A parent who does not prepare and practice holistic protection of their child sets them up for failure. Today, we have many failed young adults who were taken to Ivy-League (old, well established) schools or very good private schools, given the best in terms of material possessions, and yet they are drug addicts or alcoholics today. The reason was that they got the best in some areas but experienced neglect in others.

Let us be quick to add that even with holistic protection, some children will still stray away, just like taking all driving precautions does not rule out the possibility of road accidents or illness for health and exercise devotees. This reality means that every parent should do their best to protect their child and then leave everything else to the Creator. This is the essence of spiritual protection in parenting.

Case Study on Spiritual Protection in Parenting

Susanna Wesley, mother of two ministers: John Wesley, founder of Methodism, and his brother Charles Wesley, a prolific hymn writer, is acclaimed as an example of a tenacious mother and a pillar with a purpose. Born in 1669 to Dr. Samuel Annesley, a well-known minister in the Church of England, Susanna was molded by hardworking parents and surrounded by intellectual activity from her young years. She learnt very early that humanity's major purpose in life is to seek after godliness, and then other things would follow.

Susanna got married in 1688 when she was only 19 years old. Her husband Samuel Wesley, an ordained minister in the Church of England was unfortunately not a very organized man. As a minister he was poorly paid and they barely survived on the little income he earned. Life was tough for the young couple. The family slid into poverty. In spite of all these struggles, Susanna has been acclaimed as a stalwart woman who stood by her husband and took her place to bring up holistically healthy children.

Susanna Wesley's life gave her a lot of lemons. We have already mentioned that she married a poor man, whose salary was intermittent. Rev. Samuel Wesley never knew when his poor parishioners would get some money to pay him. Then even when some money came in, the man was a poor financial manager and the little money quickly dried off leaving the family poorer than before.

In addition, Susanna was often sickly and could not work to supplement her husband's income. It is said that Rev. Wesley was not only a poor money manager, but that the couple also struggled with marital differences, even disagreeing hotly over political alliances. Rev. Wesley had to leave the marriage for several months until reconciliation was realized.

Within 19 years of marriage, Susana gave birth to 19 children. She buried nine of these who died as infants. Among the dead nine were two sets of twins, and one baby who was accidentally smothered by a maid. One of the surviving children had an accident and was crippled for life. What sorrow for a young woman living in the days when hospitals and specialized care hardly existed! These disasters could easily have caused depression and discouragement to any woman, but not Susanna Wesley. She was committed to bring up her surviving children as best as she could. This woman had a plan and the tenacity to carry it through. She became the pillar for the children to count on.

Susanna put the spirituality of her children first, followed by their education. On spirituality, she would wake up early and spend one hour daily with God in prayer and in the study of the Bible. Then she would bring the children together and instruct them in God's word, following this Bible study class with home schooling and other instructions in the academics.

Biographer Arnold Dallimore writes: "Susanna trained her children to obey and in doing so richly molded their characters." Beyond biblical instruction and academics, Susanna taught her children to take their duties seriously, distributing responsibility and supervising them in completing their chores. Living in a large household with so many people, this was the only way to manage. Without much money, the Wesley family could hardly afford servants and other luxuries. Susanna's children were not spoilt, but learnt to work with their own hands.

Susanna was a limit-setter. She applied discipline to teach the children expectations and to emphasize consistency of responsibility. It is said that she was fair and kind as a disciplinarian. This child guidance presupposes concern for spiritual and physical needs of the child. Susanna was also emotionally engaged in the lives of her children. She developed a personal relationship with each of them though a weekly appointment with each child so as to encourage them. This kind of emotional attachment must have helped each of the children develop personal gifts and engage areas of weakness.

All these wonderful accounts may portray Susanna as a perfect, carefree woman. To the contrary, it is narrated that at 73 years of age, just before she passed away, she communicated to her son Charles that she had often struggled with confusion and doubt in regard to her faith. However, she had finally found peace and left behind children empowered to create lasting legacies in Christendom.

CHAPTER 11

PARENTING WITH PATIENCE

PATIENCE, A DEFINITION

Wisdom does not come overnight.
~ African (Somali) Proverb

A man's wisdom gives him patience; it is to his glory to overlook an offense.
~ Proverbs 19:11

The African proverb: "*Wisdom does not come overnight,*" speaks into the value of patience. Older parents who have succeeded in bringing up holistically healthy children will offer a word of counsel to young parents that patience is one of the most critical values of child-rearing. Wisdom and knowledge in raising healthy children comes slowly, a lot of it through experience. No one goes to school to study parenting skills. This means that most of parenting is self-taught, taught by God stage-by-stage through reading and prayer, or caught from other parents including one's own. All this knowledge comes slowly with much waiting and endurance.

The Biblical proverb: "*A man's wisdom gives him patience; it is to his glory to overlook an offense,*" states the outcome of learning and wisdom. The individual's behavior is controlled by what he knows. This knowledge informs him what to do if others hurt him. Can the parent overlook a child's evil doing? Does forgiveness diminish the parent's influence over her child? This verse suggests the opposite, that forgiveness and releasing the hurt and pain glorify the parent in the eyes of her children. Relationships are built and not destroyed, and resentment that comes with non-forgiveness is curtailed.

In speaking to parents, my husband, Gershon, presents a formula of the outcomes of allowing resentment to take precedence in parent-child relationships versus letting go the anger to allow for healthy relationships to blossom. Here is the formula:

R + R – R = R + R
Rules + Regulations – **Relationship** =
Resentment + Rebellion

R + R+ R = R + R
Rules + Regulations + **Relationship** =
Repentance + Resolution.

It follows that without healthy relationship, resentment and rebellion thrive because the emphasis is on rules and regulations. However, where there is communication, respect and love, people draw closer to one another. Patience plays a key factor in building healthy relationships.

One early morning I listened to James Okumu, Kenya's Hope FM radio presenter, tell a story on the way God matures his children, sometimes allowing pain for our good. A man found a cocoon of a moth and took it home on a twig. He watched the cocoon daily for readiness to open up and provide a brand new moth. One day he noticed a small crack on the cocoon. Soon after, he sensed some movement inside the hard crust as the moth begun struggling to get out of the cocoon. It would struggle and then stop, start again and then stop. At some point it stopped and seemed as though it would not make it.

The man, afraid that the poor insect would die inside, decided to help. He made an incision in the cocoon and the moth crawled out, howbeit with a swollen body and shriveled wings. The man watched, waiting for the wings to firm up and the body to come to normal size. However, it was not to be. The moth crawled around for the rest of its short life, pulling around is swollen body and shrunken wings. It never learnt to fly.

Unfortunately, the man did not realize that God's plan for moths is that struggling through the small hole in the cocoon is the activity that forces fluids from the body into the wings, firming them up and shaping them for life. In trying to rescue the moth, the man created an immature insect that would never take to the wing. Similarly, many parents do not like to see their children struggle with life. They want to rescue the young ones from the pain of the normal struggles of growing up. This rescue mentality may curtail normal development, for it is in struggling that life lessons are learned. What if we did not struggle to memorize the multiplication table? Would we know that 7 times 9 is equal to 63?

Dirt is Good!

The integrity of a person is seen, not in falling, but in rising after each fall.
~ *African Proverb*

When the shadow of a tree is bent, straighten the tree and not the shadow.
~ *African (Sierra Leonean) Proverb*

The purpose in a man's heart is like deep water, but a man of understanding will draw it out.
~ *Proverbs 20:5*

The African proverb: "*The integrity of a person is seen, not in falling, but in rising after each fall,*" is a reminder that there is nothing wrong with falling unless a person totally ignores safety rules. Life is full of struggles and sometimes we stumble and fall. A person's honor is not in remaining safe all the time but in rising after each fall. There are small falls and big falls. We all have some, but we need to look forward and keep walking. This is a life truth that our children need to learn.

The African proverb: "*When the shadow of a tree is bent, straighten the tree and not the shadow,*" is a reminder that change is a factor of the heart. If a hungry child steals food, mother should not descend on the young one with kicks and slaps. She should ask: Why did he steal food in the first place?

The Biblical proverb: "*The purpose in a man's heart is like deep water, but a man of understanding will draw it out,*" indicates that the motives of the heart are not easy to unravel. Applying this to parenting, as children mature, they come across many different perspectives of living as well as perplexing realities, some of which they are afraid to disclose to parents. Parental wisdom, unconditional love and a non-condemning attitude will aid the ability of the child to trust the goodwill of the parent enough to disclose disturbing and confusing information.

Parents often wish that they could screen their children from life's realities. However, this is not practical. Wise parents will set their children free to experience normal maturation. However, they will not stay far from young ones when they need a hand to navigate around the mines of life. One day, the little child will become a fully-grown woman and will not need the parent to hold her hand anymore.

On Kenyan television, one company carries an advertisement of children playing in muddy pools with a running theme: *"Dirt is good!"* Although the advertising company's intention is to push up sales of its detergent, it, on the other hand sends out a positive message that free, uninhibited play for young children is good even if it results in getting soiled with dirt, dust and mud. Too many children and young people are protected from pain - the dirt of life - to their own detriment. As much as the world is an unsafe place, children and young people hidden away from real life struggles grow up with shriveled wings, unable to fly on their own.

The same concern has been raised regarding the physical effects of protecting children from microbes. A recent story from Britain raised concern about young ones who live such disinfected lives that their bodies fail to develop normal immunity against disease. Parents limit their children's contact with germs. They are not allowed to play outside, climb trees, run on the grass, or handle "dirty" toys. Their hands are washed constantly and their environments cleansed with disinfectant. The outcome is that their bodies fail to develop adequate antibodies so needed for resistance against infection. Poor resistance lowers the child's immunity opening them up to opportunistic illnesses.

Another recent account in a Kenyan daily paper raised the concern that many children in urban areas do not have enough opportunity for play. They spend too much time indoors, never allowed outside the house to play, as healthy children should do. In some schools, less and less time is set for outdoor activities as emphasis is laid on academic performance. The result is children who may be competing well in class but are physically unfit, with increasing ailments such as asthma, colds, flu, obesity and diabetes. More and more children have frail bones because low physical activity reduces bone mass and poor exposure to open sunshine reduces absorption of nature's vitamin D needed for healthy bone formation.

In seeking protection of our children, we enclose them in limited physical spaces, even, for the more affluent parents, disallowing them to travel in public transportation. Too much protection and lack of patience that allows pain and exposure to normal struggles of growing up has the capacity to limit children and young people, denying them life lessons needed to make them strong and independent.

Consistency in Parenting through Adolescence and Young Adulthood

Patience attracts happiness; it brings near that which is far.
~ African (Swahili) proverb

By the time the fool has learned the game
the players have dispersed.
~ African (Ashanti) proverb

Instruction in youth is like engraving in stone.
~ African (Moroccan) Proverb

My son, if your heart is wise, my heart too will be glad.
~ Proverbs 23:15

The African (Swahili) proverb: *Patience attracts happiness; it brings near that which is far,"* used in our context is a reminder that parenting is like calling things that are not as if they were. Parents believe that, one day, their little baby will grow to become an adult. Parents dream that one day, there shall be children's graduation ceremonies, the first day at work, marriage and grandkids. To reach these marks of successful development requires hard work and focus. For those who lag behind and waste time, the African (Ashanti) proverb emphasizes: *"By the time the fool has learned the game the players have dispersed."* Fools in this context are not people of low intelligence, but individuals who refuse to live diligently.

Parents will endeavor to make sure that their children learn and do so early, because they will not forget the wisdoms imparted on them. This is emphasized by the African (Moroccan) proverb: *"Instruction in youth is like engraving in stone."* A child may not indicate that they are learning anything, but they absorb parents' instruction. The Biblical proverb: *"My son, if your heart is wise, my heart too will be glad,"* indicates the joy of any parent who realizes that his child is gaining wisdom. Wise children are a blessing to their parents.

Parenting is full of struggles that consistently test the patience of every mother and father. Adolescence is such a phase. To safely make it through this phase, young people seek out for patient parents who can allow them to succeed and even fail. Both call for opportunities to experience life and do so with parental guidance which does not deprive children of lessons learnt from life experiences.

Sometimes, parents are tempted to jealously protect their young ones, sometimes into adolescence and young adulthood, and so desire to fix their children's problems quickly. For example, they over-extend themselves to ensure the youth's success, quickly rescuing them from distress and making sure that they are happy all the time. Success can never be quick nor is life always happy. Indeed, failure is part of the road to success. Parents who lack patience give in to the youth's everyday demands and do so quickly.

A case in point is the current challenge facing many young men especially in some rural areas where mentoring of young men is experiencing a yawning vacuum, as earlier discussed. In such places, women and girls carry the bulk of household chores as well as farm work. Speaking to rural women, many of them confess waking up at 5am and finally, dropping with fatigue into bed at midnight. Their duties include milking the cows, delivering the milk to the dairy, coming back home and lighting the fire, making breakfast, serving it, feeding the animals, cleaning the compound and then going to the farm.

There, they may be planting, weeding, spreading fertilizer, pruning coffee or harvesting tea, delivering the same to the factory and making lunch. In the afternoon, the women make it to the market, or attend the *chama* – the women's cooperative group, then hurry home gathering firewood, some carrying water from the river. They get home, milk the cow again, start dinner, bathe the children and ensure that the young ones complete their homework, serve dinner, and so on. Late at night, they remember: "I didn't sit down to eat," and they finally reach out for some cold remains, wash and crawl into bed only to begin the cycle at 5 am the following day.

In such environments, girls succeed in life because they work along their mothers and are trained in the details of multitasking and running a home. Hard consistent work trains the young women in tenacity, if nothing else. On the contrary, many young men do not do as well because often, fathers fail to be role models or are absent to do so. Lack of life skills may have affected the boys' school performance and so they fail exams and do not proceed past the village. As they mature at home, they begin to make demands on their mothers. Although they do not produce much, they want to eat and dress like their peers.

The youth demand food and want it in enough amounts. Some mothers have been forced to purchase hot pots and huge vacuum flasks to keep food and hot, milky tea ready for the hungry but idle young man. The fathers of these youth are often unconcerned or absent from home. Some may be as idle as their sons, and both sets of men depend on their women folk to care for them.

These idle young men soon begin other pursuits. Physical laziness creeps into mental lethargy and school performance continues to deteriorate. Empty minds, undisciplined spirits and maturing, well-fed bodies open them up to experimentation with sex, drugs, and alcohol. Later on, when the mother cannot satisfy the demand for money to fulfill these urges, crime may creep in. Parents now begin blaming each other for the youth's behavior while others justify the lax, careless living.

These situations are also found in some progressive homes where young people may be growing up with little discipline and training, protected from hardships and cushioned like eggs between cotton wool. When parents begin failing in the art of proactive, patient parenting, they begin making demands on teachers, counselors and even sports coaches because the young man becomes a problem at home, school and community. Some parents have found themselves in police stations trying to bail out criminal youth. Others, sadly, end up in morgues, burying young people gone too soon because the protective parent could not finally rescue them from a speeding accident, drunk driving or drug overdose.

Some overprotective parents may also want to keep a tag on their children all the time. They call, text and follow their children, endlessly cushioning them from hardship, disappointment, sadness, and any other problem feelings. Why do parents become overprotective and overly demanding? Some want to model their children after their own image, while others feel that the young ones should succeed where they themselves failed. They lack the patience and willingness to allow the young ones to become what God created them to be.

The result of such pressure to perform and to conform to parental demands has the capacity to produce fearful, anxious children who lack the ability to face life's challenges. To be able to develop the ability to exercise patience so as to allow young ones to mature naturally, parents need to address their own fears and learn to gently and systematically turn over to the maturing youth the responsibility of making their own decisions. Young people need permission to correct their own mistakes and the challenge is how able and willing parents are to trust God with their children, keep silent even when tempted to speak and exercise restraint when tempted to control or worse still, rescue their young ones from experiencing normal challenges of growing up.

A television advertisement portrayed a parent teaching a ten-year-old how to ride a bicycle. The father worked long hours training the youth on balancing, the art of peddling, safety, how to keep the helmet on and so on. He would let the child ride alone for a few meters but also ran alongside to catch the youth, convinced that he might fall off any time. At one point, it was clear that the boy was trying hard to hold his frustration.

He seemed to be saying: "Dad, let go. Can I try it on my own please?" Unable to hold himself any more, the youth began to peddle faster and faster, and took off so fast that the father could not keep up the speed. As he sped away, Daddy's hand hang mid-air in the direction of the speeding bicycle while the youth waved at his father shouting: "Dad, I'm OK now. I'll be OK."

Parental Patience Tested

Patience is the mother of a beautiful child.
~ African (Bantu) proverb

Do not forget what it is like to be a sailor because of being a captain yourself.
~ African (Tanzanian) Proverb

Rescue those who are being taken away to death; hold back those who are stumbling to the slaughter.
~ Proverbs 24:11

The African (Bantu) proverb: "P*atience is the mother of a beautiful child,*" is a reminder that parental patience can be tested a lot if a child's behavior starts indicating deep life challenges like depression, substance abuse and negative influence from peers. If a parent does not recognize a teen's challenges with emotional health for whatever reason, the omission is likely to result in impatience and even anger. Young people are usually lethargic by nature due to hormonal changes and general physical challenges of maturation. The African (Tanzanian) proverb: "*Do not forget what it is like to be a sailor because of being a captain yourself,*" is a reminder that no parent should ever forget that they too were young and unsure of life in their youth. This fact will increase their understanding of their children's struggles as they walk through life.

The Biblical proverb: "*Rescue those who are being taken away to death; hold back those who are stumbling to the slaughter,*" is a call for parents to be fighters for children who are being tempted to ignore what they know to be right. If children are straying from their parents' fold, there are often signs of lethargy, loss of direction, and a *fuua* attitude. *Fuua* refers to a state where the youth loses excitement about life, complains always that life is boring, and is generally lethargic. This lethargy can easily mimic symptoms of depression such as sadness, anger, moodiness and loss of interest in usual activities. The youth may also be struggling with feelings of failure, withdrawal from family and friends, and even drug and alcohol abuse. Other young people may be truant, missing school and performing poorly in school. Most of these symptoms are usually present in a rebellious, oppositional child. However, a combination of the same may point to a likelihood of depression and desperation.

There are many factors that contribute to desperation in young people. One of the commonest reasons is emotional disconnection from parents. David, the eldest of three siblings, went into angry outbursts after his father walked out of the family. The young man adored his Dad and blamed himself when the differences between his parents culminated in violence, eventual separation and later divorce. His school performance deteriorated.

He got into wrong company and frequent fights in the neighborhood. In his anger, he became withdrawn and spent a lot of time in his room. His mother did not know what to do. However, she never gave up praying and believing that the young man would one day become able to deal with his anger and emotional wounds in a more functional manner.

This mother's patience paid off. The church's youth pastor befriended David, invited him to the youth group and generally gave him a lot of attention and care. The young man began to make friends from the youth group, joining in social activities and fun trips. Eventually, he began to engage life once again but struggled to make up for the one year of poor academic performance. Luckily, he agreed to repeat the second grade in high school and prepare better for the final high school examination two years later.

David was able to emotionally reconnect with his mother

when he realized that his anger at his father, the belief that the older man had betrayed him and feelings of false guilt and self-blame had resulted in self-loathing and depression. In her own pain, David's mother could have easily rejected the young man, but she chose to be emotionally present during his two years of difficult acceptance regarding his father's departure. Had David's depression worsened, his mother may have had to seek professional services to help her son navigate this difficult experience. All in all, parental emotional engagement and patience won the day.

Many parents lose their patience when they forget that they themselves took time in their youth to navigate their own difficult maturation. They developed their own identity over time and did not mature overnight. Indeed, we can say that children and young people are all in the process of becoming. They may be one person at home, another person at school and yet another one for their friends.

Tim was a well-behaved young man at home, soft-spoken and respectful of his family. However, at school, he was cheeky and even truant for one or two days a week. He often came back to school with a letter from his parents explaining that he had missed class because he was sick.

One time, his teacher became suspicious and asked to see his parents. They were shocked to hear that Tim had reported sick when over the past month, he had always left home daily to go to school. Finally when the truth came out, everyone was shocked. They could not believe that besides truancy, the young man also presented fake letters to explain his absence. Tim confessed that he worked as a *matatu* tout on a route in another town to "make some pocket money," he claimed.

Later on his mother discovered drug paraphernalia in the boy's room. Tim had started a habit for which he had to make money because his little pocket money could not support the growing drug use. When the addiction began to take hold of him, he had to find an alternative means of income.

Tim's father was very angry and swore to kill the boy so as to teach him a lesson. His wife reminded him that a dead boy could not learn lessons! Reason won the day. With the help of the school counselor, Tim and the family received counseling. Finally the young man made a contract with his parents to attend school regularly and to drop the drug habit. He changed his peer group by joining a community football team and finding more wholesome recreation activities. Eventually, he reformed.

The journey towards *becoming* is not easy. When parents remember their own uncertain steps towards maturation, the experimentation that almost snared some of them and the patience of their own parents, they too will provide support and steadfastness for their own unstable youth. With understanding, young people usually end up finding their feet and so building their own identity.

Beyond Parental Patience to Planned Maturation

A patient man will eat ripe fruit.
~ African Proverb

Be wise, my son, and make my heart glad, that I may answer him who reproaches me.
~ Proverbs 27:11

The African proverb: *"A patient man will eat ripe fruit,"* underlines the gains of endurance and tolerance. Parents may not necessarily receive monetary gain or physical rewards from mature, responsible, grown-up children but the very joy of watching their sons and daughters succeed in life is great satisfaction.

The Biblical proverb: *"Be wise, my son, and make my heart glad, that I may answer him who reproaches me,"* is a call for children to grow in wisdom because their maturation serves as a powerful testimony that the parent who has shaped the child is a person of worth. The failure of children easily points to the failure of parents, just as a child's holistic success points to the prudence of parents.

Healthy youth maturation demands for something more than random, haphazard parental patience that allows children and young people to make all sorts of mistakes so as to learn life's lessons. It is better to keep a child from falling into the fire than to nurse third degree burns throughout the youth's lifetime. Parenting with patience is active. It plans to train, mentor, and guide the child development through a series of fun experiences in the company of life skill trainers and mentors.

From time to time, children and young people benefit from planned time away from home, the common couch-potato practice of TV and video games, or the rigors of academics to camp sites, wilderness or bush experience, in the company of wise counselors. Every school holiday should be interjected with such rich experiences because children learn from multiple exposures. This is the purpose served by Girl Guide and Scout picnics and camps, ROPES (Rites of Passage) out-door experience and Outward Bound Schools.

In many of these programs, the young ones learn to survive with little, to be in groups where they learn how to cook for others using firewood, to fetch water, keep the camp clean, hike for many miles, study facts about flora and fauna, and even work with their hands. I firmly advocate that no child should graduate from primary school, high school or college without a minimum number of hours in community service. We have enough orphanages to construct and clean, farms to weed, hospital wards to scrub and fields to harvest, all as part of free community service.

Finally, universities should restore the one-year, mandatory national service for every young person. Where the nation does not make this provision, each parent should ensure that the child takes time off from school or college to serve the community in specific ways without expecting anything in return. This way, parental patience will meet parental planning and young people will also learn that patience is born out of hardships and difficulties.

This exposure has the capacity to shape the youth who will in turn shape others when his turn to mentor or parent someone else comes along. Just like the man who helped a pupa to pupate prematurely, many parents create dependency in their children, only to cripple them for life. Literally carried on their parents' back, the young ones never manage to crawl out of life cocoons to fly away with their own wings.

Free to Fly

We desire to bequest two things to our children: the first one is roots, the other one is wings.
~ African (Sudanese) Proverb

Whoever walks in integrity will be delivered, but he who is crooked in his ways will suddenly fall.
~ Proverbs 28:18

The African proverb: *"We desire to bequest two things to our children: the first one is roots, the other one is wings,"* underlines the outcomes of prudent parenting. It will help the child grow roots downwards for stability and steadfastness and also grow wings to rise higher and higher in accomplishing the responsibilities of adulthood.

The Biblical proverb: *"Whoever walks in integrity will be delivered, but he who is crooked in his ways will suddenly fall,"* states the outcomes of each person's investment. People of integrity are protected and do not have to beseech anyone to defend them or talk in their favor. However, people of dishonest, fraudulent ways fall very easily and sometimes suddenly, without any warning.

Planned maturation includes deliberately releasing young adults who have come of age to leave home and live independently. Many young adults are growing old in their parents' homes and even delaying marriage because they dare not leave the comforts of Mama's kitchen or the workers who cook and clean for them. Others get married only to come back home when their spouse as much as coughs or screams. Scared of conflict, or lacking skills to manage dissonance, and even worse, deluded with the "you-owe-me" entitlement mentality, they run back home to their parents' homes or leave the marriage for other freedoms.

Planned maturation urges a grown-up child to leave the parental nest and does so gently for those who are weak and afraid. Nature teaches that when an eaglet is ready to leave the parental nest, the parent watches the young one take off with its fledgling wings fearfully beating the air. The eaglet takes off and timidly lands quickly near the nest. After a bit of rest, it takes off again, and lands a little farther away. Finally, after some more rest, it stretches its wings again, and this time, lifts its head, and soars away into the sunlight.

There is, however, the scared one who hesitates to fly and sits in the nest. The mother knows that with nesting time over, it is time for the young ones to take off and begin preparing to become parents. She must urge action, so she knocks the nest upside down throwing the scared eaglet into the air. The poor darling hurtles downwards screaming and throwing feathers and limbs all over the place. The parent eagle takes off after the scared bird and spreads her wings below the falling bird, receiving it on to her wings. The parent then flies high into the sky and releases the eaglet mid air. The falling begins again. Two or three times, the saving action is repeated. Finally, the eaglet spreads its wings and takes off, never to return into the nest again. The mother eagle's planning, persistence and commitment to her task win the day. Such is the result of patience in parenting.

HELP! MY CHILD CANNOT FLY!

Life is a gift of nature but beautiful living is a gift of wisdom.
~ African (Malawian) Proverb

If you cannot be a lighthouse, be a candle.
~ North African Proverb

Speak up for those who cannot speak for themselves, for the rights of all who are destitute ...
~ Proverbs 31:8

In the last section, we discussed the need for parents to allow children wings so that they can fly. What if a child cannot fly? They may have been born without physical wings to fly like in the case of physically or mentally challenged children; or their wings may have been damaged at some stage in their lives, for example, through accidents; or they themselves may have damaged their own wings through drug abuse and alcoholism. Many parents bear the burden of living with a limited child. What can such parents do to thrive and still enjoy their motherhood and fatherhood? How can they bring out the best in their children in the face of stigma, bullying and peer rejection? Does physical and emotional safety in the home enhance the expression of the child's potential?

The African (Malawian) proverb: "Life is a gift of nature but beautiful living is a gift of wisdom," reminds Africans that life is God-given but fulfilled living is our responsibility. Indeed, in the earlier part of this chapter, we discussed that sometimes, life hands us out lemons, but we have God-given ability to choose to make lemonade. Some families with a differently-abled child report that this young one, though limited in many ways, became a source of love and gentleness in the family. The family decided to live beautifully although one of them was differently-abled. And many do.

Let us note that we no longer refer to such children as disabled, but as differently-abled, meaning that their gifts lie in other less-obvious areas. It is for this reason that North Africans give us the proverb: "If you cannot be a lighthouse, be a candle." A differently-abled child may not run and play like others or connect well with his world. She may not run the marathon or dance like everyone else. However, she can shine although she may not do so with the powerful light of a lighthouse, but with the glowing, dainty light of a candle.

The Biblical proverb: "*Speak up for those who cannot speak for themselves, for the rights of all who are destitute,*" is a reminder that all of us can do something where the needs of the differently-abled are concerned. Recently, my friend, Nkirote, told me of an organization that has been given the mandate to care for blind children. After vocational training, during graduation, the organization presents each child with the gift of a knitting machine. The goal is that they begin a knitting business and build a foundation for individual independence.

After graduation, however, one of the children, let's call her Susan, sought out my friend Nkirote, who serves as her mentor. Susan reported that her knitting machine was not working. Nkirote investigated with other students in the program, and it turned out that many of the machines were faulty. She was angry. How could they present defective machines to the students? Together with Susan, the machine in her hands, they visited the organization to demand an explanation. The answer they got was: "We are sorry we cannot help you. We gave out the machines just as we received them from the manufacturing company. If these blind students do not want them, too bad. We cannot do anything about it." My friend put her foot down and called in more support. Their tenacity won the day and the faulty machines were exchanged for good, efficient knitters.

Some tips for caring for a differently-abled child include accessing medical help, psychological services and academic advice. These will ensure that the child's abilities are recognized and developed early. As parents maximize the expression of their children's God-given abilities, they should shut down negative voices that discourage normal patterns of parenting. Limited or gifted, each child is unique and should be handled as such. In other parts of this book, we have discussed the need for partnership in parenting. Even for these special children, every parent should seek out partners and not be too proud to ask for help. Determination to be a steward of God's gift in these children will also bring a blessing.

For severely limited children, the parent may need to choose the areas to concentrate on. For example, some children can read but will not run a marathon. Let them excel in reading. Others can draw beautifully but cannot walk. Supply them with art materials, and let them draw. Sometimes providing shelter and health needs may be all that is possible. Do so with gladness. Some children may be on medication for a long time, and as much as this is possible, facilitate the same. Where the parent cannot understand the limitations of the child, there are psychologists who can assess the young one and advice. As far as is possible, seek their professional help.

Parents should refrain from pursuing explanations and prophesies regarding the limitations of their child. Trusting in God and seeking his wisdom will remove the panic of the belief that witchcraft or the evil eye has been cast on our children. Resting in God's peace and presence, and doing our best in the care of these young ones will renew us to go on.

Caring for differently-abled children can be exhausting. Taking time off to rest and replenish renews one's strength. Differently-abled children can also socialize with one another, play and laugh, and so on. Many parents are tempted to hide them away from other people, but as said earlier, "beautiful living is a gift of wisdom." This means that life should be lived as normally as possible and even differently-abled children have a right so to do.

Finally, parents should realize that negative attitudes towards disability can destructively impact the differently-abled child and expose them to bullying in the community and more so in school when the child is away from home. Some of these negative reactions could be related to the child's isolation from the more-abled children, lack of sensitivity by the other children, withdrawal from the peer group or failure to realize that bullying exists and can be so endemic. In cases like these, the protecting adult should bring up these matters with the school or indigenous community so that better intentional protection factors may be established for the school and community.

Case Study on Patience in Parenting

Parents of young children never imagine that their young ones will ever grow up and learn how to do things differently. This perception has the capacity to make young mothers feel stuck with diapers, running noses and other normal childhood experiences. "Will they ever grow up?"the mother yearns.

Looking at great men and women of the world may help humble the impatient parent towards patience. When one of my children, a quick learner was almost three years old, I was sure that I had fully toilet-trained the child. After several months of proudly showing off the *pottie* and putting away the cloth nappies that were the diapers of our day, we were at the point where we would say: "Mummy, I want to do *pottie*." We would then run and do, flush and clean up.

One day, however, with guests in the house including my father-in-law, when a young wife wants to show her best side, we showered, dressed up and came to serve the adults. In the middle of a meal, there was this foul smell and stuff that was almost falling through the clean and neat pants. I was shocked and picked up my once-upon-a-time sweet-smelling but now protesting bundle, profusely apologizing to everyone.

After we were cleaned up, changed and this time diapered for the first time in several months, we joined the group with my little one running around the room showing off the sweet-smelling clean attire. My father-in-law, a very wise man, saved the day. He told me: "Don't worry. Before children grow up, they often behave like a spiral. Three steps forward, one back; five steps forward, two back; seven steps forward, and two back; and so on till they fully learn. So, don't apologize. The child will soon be fully toilet-trained." I was relieved and validated. My wise father in-law saved the day. He gave me a lesson in patience that I've never forgotten.

On another day, my friend, our Pastor's wife, and I learned more lessons in patience. Our church, Lavington United, is a combined congregation with Methodists, Anglicans and Presbyterians who founded the church worshipping together with members from many other denominations. Every year at Confirmation when youth graduate into full church members after months of training on doctrine and tenets of faith, the heads of the three churches attend the service together and jointly confirm the graduates. Afterwards, lunch is served at the manse for this team.

Our children were young, joyful and playful, running and chasing one another through the manse. At one time, they almost ran into a bowl of food and we both called them and talked sternly to the boisterous boys. After we had set them up in another room and commanded them to be quiet, we got back to serving. One of the Bishops asked us: "What have the children done?" It was as if he was saying: "We loved having then run and play around us. Why did you have to discipline them and take them away?" Lessons in patience come in many ways.

Parents of purpose just need to be open minded to learn new ways of keeping the main thing as the main thing: purpose. This means celebrating their parenthood and yet remembering that children are like a ship that needs a rudder in the hands of a ship's pilot. The rudder is very small compared to the volume of the ship and yet it makes the voluminous vessel keep on a certain pre-determined path until destination.

Patience in large doses makes for purposeful parenting. And patience says:"We will take a shower even though we throw the tantrums."We will go to school even if we do not feel like waking up today. We'll finish our homework even though we do not like Math. We'll drop bad friends even if they are lots of fun. We'll come home early even though all our friends lie to their parents and come home late. We'll try again even if we fail. We'll persist and get out of bad habits. We may slide and fall, but we'll come up right back again."

CHAPTER 12

THE PARENT AS A PILLAR

THE MEANING OF PILLAR

A person's character cannot be washed away by the rain.
~ *African (Liberian) Proverb*

A big heart is better than a big brain.
~ *African (Ivorian) Proverb*

A good name is better than fine perfume.
~ *Eccl 7:1*

Both African proverbs we have used in this section refer to the lasting nature and preciousness of character. The African (Liberian) proverb: *"A person's character cannot be washed away by the rain,"* will remind parents that what they impart on their children in terms of character will last forever. Money can be stolen, titles abused, and college diplomas lie unused. Integrity however sustains the individual, and out of it comes stability and wellness. Integrity transforms the heart, the wellspring of all dreams, plans and purposes. The African (Ivorian) proverb: *"A big heart is better than a big brain,"* tells us again that intelligent people can lose their way but men and women of integrity will stay the course.

The Biblical proverb: *"A good name is better than fine perfume,"* underlines the lasting nature of integrity. Men and women with a good name will outlive the transient aroma of riches, power, vintage cars and other trappings of life. Good names do not fade away with age. Indeed, they outlive the owner and become legacies to offspring. In Africa, it is common to hear elders interviewing youth. One of the first questions is: "Tell me, child. Whose son are you?" This is not literal English. The question is not: "Who is your father?" That could mean: "Who sired you?" No. The answer needed is: "Who has mentored you?"

The well-mentored youth raises his head and answers with confidence: "My Dad's name is ..." Upon which the elder replies, "If then you are the son of ..., no more questions! We know you!" There is a lot of weight in this statement, because a child's character is often an extension of the parent. There are children who go astray but elders understood this too because these straying children are more the exception than the rule.

One day, I sat in my clinic with a young man who was going through a very difficult experience. He was barely holding his head above the water, and was shaken this way and that by various challenges. He narrated how difficult he was finding it to hold on. His father was dead and he had just lost his mother. The eldest of eight siblings, some of them still in school, he could not imagine how he would cope with the burden of care that had just been thrust on his shoulders. We tried to explore the alternatives he had, resources that he could use to cope.

At some point, I asked him: "What memory do you have of your parents, something that you can hold on to as an intangible yet powerful resource that can help you to hang on in times of discouragement?" This question and the memories it provoked brought a smile to his handsome face. "Let me tell you, Doctor. The greatest memory I have is of my Dad. I can say that although that man did not have much money or hold an important position in some company, my father was my pillar. He was the rock of my life, indeed the solid support for all of us. He taught me the secret of steadfastness, holding on and standing strong in spite of life's challenges. I remember my father's strength and presence now, and I am sure we'll make it." What a testimony!

In reference to a person, a pillar is defined as an individual who is a main support of an institution, in this case, a family. The young man also referred to his father as "the rock of my life." In this context, rock suggests stability, strength, especially a firm support; a refuge. What a tribute! Over the subsequent sessions, we built the young man's coping skills around the theme of the pillar that his father had modeled and in so doing, left as an unspoken legacy to the youth, standing strong through the seasons of life and demonstrating stability against life's tsunamis. Through the subsequent sessions, it was as if the young man felt his father's voice whispering over his shoulder with encouragement and with the words: "Keep on son. You are doing OK and you'll make it."

This is the legacy of a parent who determines to walk with consistency and purpose, guided by an inner core of values. Such is a parent's internal locus of control that is not dependent on the external trappings and life's circumstances.

John Courson, a renowned Christian speaker, once told a story of a prominent swimmer who was once questioned on his award-winning Olympic performance. One day, while the man prepared to jump into the pool for a swimming competition, someone asked him: "While you stand on that platform, what goes on in your mind?" Perhaps the speaker was looking for a great answer like: "I must win again!" However, he was surprised when the athlete answered without hesitation: "You know what I'm thinking? Even if I blow this swim and so lose my medal, my mother will still love me."

This answer portrayed the swimmer's mother as a pillar, a rock for her son whose love was not dependent on the medals he brought home. There is a high probability that even his climb to stardom was because he knew that his mother's love was always present, unconditional and unquestioning. The constancy of this love must have made him feel like flying, because he did not have to succeed to have this woman as his best cheerleader. These are some of the results of being a parental pillar in children's lives.

Pillars and Purpose

Two steps forward to advance, a step backwards to check.
~ *African (Cameroonian) Proverb*

Be a mountain to lean on.
~*African (Somali) Proverb*

Steadfast love and faithfulness preserve the king, and by steadfast love his throne is upheld.
~ *Proverbs 20:28*

The African (Cameroonian) proverb: "*Two steps forward to advance, a step backwards to check,*" implies that any project of worth will need planning, monitoring and evaluation. Parenting is such an enterprise. Vigilant parents keep emotionally and physically close to their children encouraging progress and celebrating success. To be able to keep on learning and growing in character, children need an environment of security and quiet strength. Loving parents provide this. In our context, this certainty is the meaning of the African (Somali) proverb: "*Be a mountain to lean on.*"

The Biblical proverb: "*Steadfast love and faithfulness preserve the king, and by steadfast love his throne is upheld,*" summarizes the reality that a virtuous king who is benevolent and kind endears himself to his people and encourages them to be dedicated subjects. Besides God and the nation's political ruler, children do not have another king. Indeed, they desire to have parents live like heroes and royalty before them, so entrenching themselves as pillars that uphold and stabilize children through the journey of maturation and into adulthood.

Pillars have purpose. Their object for existence is to stand upright and to support a structure. Pillars lose their definition if they are not positioned in one place fulfilling their role of support whatever the weight above them may be. The consistency of pillars is such that even if storms come shaking the very foundation of the building, pillars continue to remain strong.

Invited to speak in a ladies' meeting, I gave an analogy that mothers are called to hold the family structure together and to keep it steady through prayer, care and strength. Indeed, she holds up the ladders of life while her family members climb up. This does not mean that she does not climb her ladder herself, but as a parent, she takes the responsibility to pray, wait, encourage and to motivate others as they climb. "The temptation to give up," I said, "sometimes comes due to the fact that supporting the family structure often becomes difficult because some situations become too difficult to hold up. Some children are so heavy that the parent may feel like letting go. Some of these young ones do not appreciate how much it is costing the parent to keep holding up the ladder!"

At the end of the meeting, many ladies stood up as we recommitted ourselves to God to make us strong so as to hold on as pillars of support for our families. At the end, a woman came to me with tears in her eyes and narrated that she had been on the verge of letting go her support of her family. Her husband was not bothered about her and the children. He had taken off with another woman. Her teenage son was rebellious and her daughter had gotten a baby out of wedlock and refused to disclose the identity of the baby's father. Although the young woman was in college, she was not performing well, added the mother.

"I had decided to give up," she continued. "Why try helping people who do not care? As I listened to you, I asked God to forgive me. I have now decided to hold on for the sake of my children. I know they were so angry when their Dad left. They felt that he did not love them anymore because if he did, he would have stayed. I will be there for them and pray that through me, they'll realize that our heavenly Father has not left us. He will see us through."

Among the Meru people of Kenya, traditional huts were constructed with a pillar at the center to hold up the trusses on which rested the grass thatch. I remember that the pillar in my grandmother's hut was so bright, shiny and glossy that it looked as if it was polished with layers of varnish. It was an old pillar that had held up the hut for many years. The worn-out thatch was changed every year. We would come to help as women replaced the thatch before the long rainy season. The old thatch would come down and new fresh grass would be fitted into the rafters.

I still remember hunting with other children for huge, fleshy caterpillars that made their home in the old thatch and feeding the grubs to hungry, plump chicken that came to feast whenever the thatching was in progress. The point is that off came the old, rotten thatch as well as any worn-out rafters and on came the new thatch smelling of the aroma of freshly cut grass. However, the pillar stayed on from year to year holding everything up.

Why did the pillar look shiny, glazed, and polished when no one applied varnish on its surface, let alone clean it? Children and even the adults I knew did not have towels or handkerchiefs. We would wash our hands, and wipe them dry on the pillar. Muddy hands were wiped on the pillar. Food remains would find their way on to the pillar, as would the millet porridge that remained on your hands as you ground the grains on the grinding stone in grandma's hut. All on the pillar! This pillar was the receptor of everything, even the most gross. Yet with the years, the pillar did not have on it layers of dross. Instead it shone, all varnished and standing strong with age.

Similarly, parents are supposed to be pillars that stand strong receiving all, the good and the bad, and modeling the fact that parenting does not go on vacation, not then, now or ever. Pillars have purpose and they fulfill it year after year until God calls them home. Then they pass on the baton to their children to continue as pillars in their own homes. However, pillars do not work alone. They support roofs and buildings in partnership with the rafters, beams and even the solid ground on which they stand.

Pillars and Partnership

Wisdom is like a baobab tree; no one individual can embrace it.
~ African (Akan) Proverb

As iron sharpens iron, so one man sharpens another.
~ Proverbs 27:17

The African proverb: "*Wisdom is like a baobab tree; no one individual can embrace it,*" reflects the reality that true wisdom is not personal but shared. We learn, internalize, share it and pass it on. It follows that no one can parent from an isolated position. The Meru people of Kenya emphasize this truth with the words: "*Uume bwa muntu umwe ni gacigo,*" meaning that the wisdom of one individual is just a part of the whole. Africans believe that parenting is partnership. The parent leads the enterprise but also ensures that there is room to seek out and listen to the wisdom of others regarding the youth's development.

The Biblical proverb: "*As iron sharpens iron, so one man sharpens another,*" emphasizes that other people mold our character, knowledge and wisdom. Parenting is so critical that it should not happen in isolation. How do we use partnership in parenting?

Kaluki was widowed early and left by her husband of 10 years with two children: a boy aged seven and a three year-old girl. In many parts of Africa, widows suffer much from neglect or in-law trouble. Financially, many are also disabled. Kaluki was devastated because the death was so sudden. She, however, made a decision that her children would not lack anything.

She began by making the memory of their father strong and present in the children. First she tried as much as she could to explain to them that their father was gone, never to return. He had died, but, one day they would all see him again in heaven. However, for now, they had their lives to live and he would want them to succeed in life. Kaluki printed a picture of her husband and placed it on the mantelpiece where everyone could see that the dead man was still present in his home.

She worked hard in her profession and was steadily promoted, beginning to earn a good salary. She also made up her mind to remain true to her husband's memory and to spend her life for her young children. Men soon learnt that she was not interested in romance. Her life was focused. However, in the absence of a father, she decided to develop a friendship and closeness with her father-in-law whom she requested to assume a male supervisory role over the maturing children. The older man felt honored and went ahead to befriend each child. Whenever he was in the city, he stayed in her home and emphasized to the children that he expected them to obey their mother and make their father proud.

Kaluki was active in church, and there she identified several couples, invested in a close relationship with each one and went ahead to socialize her children with young ones from these families. With some, she planned regular meetings where over a good meal, the children and youth present could ask the adults questions about anything that baffled them.

Her children became young adolescents, did well in school and moved on to university. They navigated the confusion of young adulthood but finally made their way to good careers relying heavily on their mother, grandfather and adult mentors picked from the families the mother had selected to help parent her children.

Later on in their own homes, each child would tell stories of how their mother was their heroine and she in turn would tell how her partnership with God, her father-in-law and many friends contributed to the family's safety. Although she may not have laid much weight on the influence of her late husband on the children's maturation, people knew that her honor of his memory allowed him to parent his children from the grave. He too became a partner and will continue to be even after his wife leaves the world. Pillars realize that true parenting happens in partnership with meaningful members, carefully selected to fit into the structure.

When a woman has ten children, there is nothing that happens in the night that she does not know about.
~ *African (Nigerian) Proverb*

For lack of guidance a nation falls, but many advisers make victory sure.
~ *Proverbs 11:14*

The African proverb: "*When a woman has ten children, there is nothing that happens in the night that she does not know about,*" underlines the fact that whatever the number of children, mothers know them by name, are aware of their different personalities, likes and dislikes, can discern their thinking and intent and can even predict how each child may turn out. Many mothers are so committed to their children that they hang on even when some stray. They love on, believing that one day the prodigal will be restored.

The Biblical proverb: "*For lack of guidance a nation falls, but many advisers make victory sure,*" underlines the role of partnership in parenting. In Africa, many women sit in *chamas* – women groups that meet on a regular basis to pray, read the Bible, transact table banking or carry on development projects together. A lot of prayer goes on in these groups, most of it regarding families, more so children. There is mutual thanksgiving for the ones that are doing well, those preparing to sit for examinations, the ones looking for jobs or getting married and a lot of travail for the floundering. Wisdom is exchanged and suggestions provided.

It is common to see groups of these women handing over gifts at their children's weddings or graduation ceremonies or at coming out events when an initiate is received back to the community after the isolation that follows rites of passage, for example, male circumcision. Child development is a shared process and many advisers are at hand to ensure safe passage.

God is one of the most important partners in the business of supporting one another. The Almighty works through prayer, a practice that invites his presence for wisdom and strength. He provides parents with tenacity. Tenacity refers to the ability to hold firmly with cohesiveness, toughness, persistence and courage. Tenacious parents are actually purposeful pillars. They focus on a goal, work at it and stand strong against any odds that challenge this purpose.

Someone has said that if life gives you lemons, learn to make lemonade. I remember once speaking to a group of teenagers at All Saints Cathedral in Nairobi. The topic I was given was not easy. The Provost had asked me to speak on how young people can cope with violence, abuse and difficulties in their families. We discussed skills of emotional self-care, safety, prayer and so on. I then decided to explore matters of perception because when other people hurt us and make us feel helpless, the devil is able to take hold of our thinking and color the whole of life with darkness.

Desiring to communicate that the youth are never alone or helpless, that they can make a choice on what to think and how to translate the events in their lives, I gave them an analogy.

"If someone gives you several lemons and tells you that you must eat them, how would you do it?" I asked. One young lady raised her hand: "I would just slice the lemons like oranges and eat them." The young people made faces imagining how sour a lemon slice would taste. Another youth added: "I would slice the lemons and sprinkle sugar to remove some of the acid." Someone else said: "I have a better idea. I would slice the lemons, squeeze them, then add water and sugar to their juice and then drink it."

The discussion went on and on, with all sorts of ideas. Finally, after a lively debate, a 13 year-old young man gave a brilliant response: "I would first grate the lemons to get some lemon rind, then squeeze them for lemon juice. I would then use the rind to make lemon pie. To the juice, I would add water and honey to make lemonade. Finally I would invite my neighbor, who is also my best friend, and share the pie and lemonade with him."

Everyone applauded the youth. His was a brilliant, creative response. The lesson was that sometimes, life hands us lots of lemons, and how we consume them is a choice. We can grit our teeth and walk through them, or we can change our perception, accept the situation, and with a positive attitude, determine our response.

Parents who are determined to be strong, present pillars for their children are not necessarily spared struggles. Discouragements are normal. However, deeply-rooted parents who have solid value systems that inform their parenting will often stand strong against life storms and eventually bring up children who carry on their legacies.

Mothers and fathers who would be pillars of strength for their children are not necessarily endowed with riches, money and property. They are not necessarily extremely well educated, nor are they famous and renowned persons. As much as these attributes are important, they are not the foundation that upholds pillars and reinforces consistency. It seems that even the poorest of poor parents can be a pillar to his children and the weakest mother can uphold her child.

To become pillars of support with lasting legacies, parents need to connect the young ones to eternal values, and then the rest of the attributes, for example, education, property, money, and so on begin to have meaning. Parenting with purpose refers to the upbringing that moulds children to become young men and young women, who mature to become adults able to model values and so pass them in turn to their own children. This indeed is the essence of parenting with purpose.

Case Study on Parenting with Purpose

My husband, Dr. Gershon Mwiti shares how his parents and community shaped his life and character through purposeful role modeling and shared values. For example, values of hospitality and respect for guests were taught and practiced, as was etiquette, respect, honesty and so on.

When Gershon was growing up, families would work in the gardens or herd animals during the day while the children went to school. Everyone gathered home in the evening and cooking began. Preparation took long, involving as it did the shelling of beans or peas, peeling of bananas or potatoes, shredding of vegetables, and so on. The meal, cooked over an open fire with pots placed over three stones, would take several hours to be ready and many hungry mouths would be waiting. The children knew that they were to patiently wait for dinner. This was not easy. Everyone sat by the wood fire warming themselves and waiting.

Yams are a delicacy in Meru. The underground tuber is roasted in the fire and prepared as a snack while the family waits for food to be ready. One day, relates Gershon, a guest came visiting and everyone gathered around the fire waiting for the meal. Gershon's mother roasted yams and served the guest first as was the family practice. Children would wait for the next round. The guest held the yam and Gershon's young cousin grabbed the piece and ran outside with it. Later, the young lady was punished for demonstrating lack of courtesy to a guest. This way, respect was demonstrated and modeled.

Etiquette was also taught through modeling. For example, if adults were having a discussion, it was bad manners for anyone to stare at them fixedly. This behavior was described as *kwaga nthoni* or lack of good manners. Similarly, there were scenes where a child was required to look away! For example, old men did not wear underwear often. They might sit carelessly and the blanket would slip over their knees sometimes revealing their private parts. A child caught staring at the old man's nakedness would be punished. This behavior was described as *kugumuka*, meaning bad manners that have been allowed to run wild.

In the same vein, no child would be allowed to insult an elder person or shout at them. Adults modeled all these behaviors. No parent expected a child to do what mother and father were not ready to do. Open defiance, rebelliousness and strong-headedness were all behaviors punishable through discipline.

Asked what methods parents and adults used to shape child and youth behavior, Dr. Mwiti gives such examples as the use of the rod of discipline; denial of special treats such as ripe bananas or some other sweet fruit, or honey; being left behind when others went to visit grandma or other important relatives; or being denied play with peers. Among the Meru, both parents were present and both exercised the discipline.

Rules and limits were not only modeled but also clarified. For example, one had to respect people's property: when herding animals, the herders, mainly children, ensured that the goats and sheep did not stray into people's farms because they might destroy crops. Another rule was that children only ate food that was offered to them. For example, when out in the fields, it was wrong to pick food from people's gardens - ripe bananas or sugarcane that was not offered to you. This was considered theft. One could gather and eat to their fill wild fruit and berries but never steal from somebody's garden. The difference between gathering and stealing was clearly spelt out. When at home, they were not to pick and eat food left in storage. It might be what was set aside for a meal to be shared with everyone. They were also never to lick honey from the vat. Rather, they were to wait until they were served when the parents decided that they could have some.

It was common knowledge that in families where good behavior was not modeled, honey stored away in a vat and kept, may be to be paid as dowry, would be stolen a little at a time by undisciplined children, each sneaking in when no one was watching. In one such home, when the father went in to bring out the *full* honey vat, it is said that he braced himself to lift the heavy 60-pound tub, picked it up and fell backwards on his back because the container was empty! The children had licked it clear over several months while in "safe" storage.

Parents also shaped and modeled socialization by selecting and identifying the families with whom their children could socialize. Children were not allowed to visit certain homes because of possible wrong peer influence and parental role modeling.

The adage *"It takes a village to raise a child,"* was well practiced as adults took it upon themselves to remind a child what was expected of them, to *gukaanukia* or punish wrong behavior, and to report to the young one's parents if one was caught hanging out with the wrong crowd. This meant that if a youth was caught bad-mouthing adults, talking carelessly, behaving irresponsibly or mistreating young children, the lame, blind and disabled, the adult would discipline him first and then report the matter to his parents later. Parents would often add their own discipline just to emphasize the other adult's correction.

Gershon shares that among the Meru, in addition to parental training, role modeling was also ensured and reinforced by the children and youth within an age group. For example, boys formed themselves into age groups from 10 years of age and above. Those aged 10-12 played together.

If any of the boys misbehaved by disregarding behavioral expectations dictated by the parents and the community, the group would deal with such disobedience because the culprit had dented the image of the group. Here, parental standards were similar to the group's standards.

When the youth turned 13, each would have to enter the age group of *kigumi* by passing the age group-set examination. This would prove that the boy was ready to become an adolescent. Each boy took an oath to behave well. For example, he swore never to lick his mother's cooking pot however hungry he was, and never to spend time in his mother's kitchen sniffing out leftovers or pinching ripening bananas.

This order instilled etiquette and discipline in matters of food. Boys like these would wait to be served, with the emphasis on wait, not service. This is because since they socialized in groups, visiting each others' homes and eating together, the young man whose home was visited would be expected to pick up served food from his mother and dish it out to his friends.

They also swore to observe cleanliness and hygiene,

a difficult feat. There was no running water at home but there were and still are many fresh water springs and rivers in Meru. Such a vow required that the young men visit secluded parts of the river early in the morning to bathe. Along the way teeth would be brushed clean using fragrant twigs chewed soft for the purpose.

Peer discipline was also expected in the presence of young women, and rebellion was punishable by *kuingua* where the erring fellow was denied association with his age group for a period of time, forcing him to walk alone. Such social exile and alienation quickly brought repentance, and at the end of the period of excommunication, a fine was paid and the person would be allowed back into the fold.

After childhood and youthful years were over, the young people were all set for the coming of age initiation at age 15 where age-group rules and regulations would now take over from parental training and role-modeling. However, this childhood shaping would form the foundation for role modeling at another level because adults always remained engaged with the young people's lives, howbeit at another level.

After circumcision, the initiates now became warriors, trained to fight for and defend the tribe. They went into a kind of boot camp with its own rules and regulations where part of the training was care, respect and protection for girls, and personal discipline in all dealings with parents, community and peer group. The warriors were taught how to become men and live purposefully. They learned how to work and behave as a team, and how to model responsible conduct to the younger members of the community. Indeed, the Meru *muthaka* or warrior was a picture of respect, personal discipline, morality, integrity and courage.

Parenting the Parent-less

When you take a knife away from a child, give him a piece of wood instead.
~ African (Kenyan) Proverb

Water does not stay in the sky forever.
~ African (Kalenjin) Proverb

If a man shuts his ears to the cry of the poor he will cry out and not be answered.
~ Proverbs 21:13

The African proverb: "*When you take a knife away from a child, give him a piece of wood instead,*" underlines the fact that many children carry elements they have no business bearing. One of the heaviest burdens carried by homeless and orphaned children is anger and despair against a world they do not understand. Some of these children fall by the wayside into crime, substance abuse, street living, and so on. What is the role of each African adult in helping one, two or more of these children change for the better?

Orphans, are defined as children who have lost one or both parents. In Africa, many of these have lost their parents to the AIDS pandemic. It is a disaster to lose a parent when one is so young and vulnerable. However, we know that losing a parent is not a sentence for disaster that stalks one through life. A parent-less child can be parented by adults who care, and turn out successful. This is the meaning, in this context, of the African proverb: "*Water does not stay in the sky forever.*"

The Biblical proverb: "*If a man shuts his ears to the cry of the poor he will cry out and not be answered,*" is a reminder that God cares passionately for the poor. One morning, praying over breakfast, I ended with these words: " …. and, Lord, in your mercy, please supply food for so many hungry in our world."

After the "Amen," my husband Gershon said: "Usually, I do not say 'Amen' to such a prayer!" I looked at him and he was very serious.

"Why?" I asked. "I am praying for the orphans and the poor who have nothing to eat. I mean – God, send help."

"That's' OK," he said. "Question is, what have YOU done about it? God cannot rain manna from heaven. How many pray like that and then push the needy out of their minds and lives and then continue living as if there are no widows and orphans around them?"

Somehow, God's answers to our prayers are related to how much we hear the cries of the poor. Someone has observed that it does not matter what religion people adhere to. This principle is obeyed all the time. Give to the poor and you will be blessed. Care for the orphaned and God will care for your needs.

In Chapter Five, we discussed the case of Isaiah, the orphan boy who was killed by his uncle for having a HIV+ status passed on by his mother who had died of AIDS-related illnesses. Isaiah needed a caregiver and a home. He got neither. He was killed by the very hands that were supposed to be caring for him and creating a safe place for his maturation. Our society is full of orphans and vulnerable children. There is nothing that is as lonely and devastating as the helplessness of a child who feels alone in the world.

When our daughters were still very young children, my husband went for a walk with them in the neighborhood. Someone was building a big house nearby and they walked through the building, playing hide and seek. At one point, my husband ran off and hid quietly away from the girls and would not answer when they called. They called him several times: "Daddy, where are you? We know where you are. Come out!"

He did not. They decided to look for him. "Daddy, where are you? We are lost. We can't find you!" The excitement of play started to change into fear. Finally, one of them asked: "Where do you think he has disappeared to?" "I don't know. We are also lost. Aren't we?" answered the other. "How shall we now get home?" she pursued. "And it's getting dark. Can we find our way home? We're all alone now!"

The babies were almost in tears. The father continued to listen to the anguish of the scared children, and eventually, made his way out. There was joy but also anger. "Daddy, why did you hide? We were scared!" He assured them, saying: "Let's go home now." As they walked along, they held on tight to their father with the little one telling her sister, "Let's hold on tight to Dad now so that if we get lost again, we get lost together!"

The emptiness, the loneliness, the fear of the present and future, the helplessness of orphanhood must be overwhelming. Besides emotional pain, there are physical needs: food, shelter, play, school, clothes; as well as the psychological need for society to allow these helpless ones to be children. Many grow up too quickly as they parent their siblings, boys become men too fast and little girls take over as mothers when they can hardly blow their own little noses.

In addition to needy orphans are grandmas whose backs are breaking caring for babies of bereaved daughters, the aftermath of the AIDS pandemic. Gershon, my husband, and I run a slum school with up to 200 orphans and vulnerable children. Here, the children are fed two hot meals a day and instructed from kindergarten through class eight in preparation for high school.

Our most difficult time of the year is January as many grandmas will come with little ones in tow. The children look frail and hungry and their grandma is no better. These old women almost weep, beseeching us to admit the babies into kindergarten or class one. One of them recently brought two little 4 and 6 year-old girls and said: "Please, take them. Their mother is dead. I need to look for casual labor in the farms to get some food for them. While they are in school, I can look for work. We have no food at home. They'll be safe here." When the class is full, we often turn away such need, and our hearts bleed in the process.

WHO CARES?

The tears of the orphan run inside.
~ African (Mafa – Cameroon, Nigeria and Niger) Proverb

He who oppresses the poor shows contempt for his Maker, but whoever is kind to the needy honors God.
~ Proverbs 14:31

A generous man will himself be blessed, for he shares his food with the poor.
~ Proverbs 22:9

The African proverb: "*The tears of the orphan run inside,*" comes from the Mafa people who live in northern Cameroon, northern Nigeria and southern Niger. This region is very dry with scanty rain that falls for only four months in a year. People struggle to eke out a living and in their hunger during dry spells, may forget to feed the orphans among them, especially if the family is a large one. The neglected children cry with tears flowing inwards because they cannot demand for the care they ought to receive.

The Biblical proverb: "*He who oppresses the poor shows contempt for his Maker, but whoever is kind to the needy honors God,*" is indirectly implying that we have no option but to care for the needy among us, in our context, the children with no parents. To show contempt is to despise the fact that we have what many around us do not or may never have had. To seek to know the needs of the orphan is to obey God and to show our thankfulness for whatever he has endowed us with. None of us merits having more than others, as much as we may have labored for it and continue to work hard.

The Biblical proverb: *"A generous man will himself be blessed, for he shares his food with the poor,"* is a reminder that caring for the needy is partnership with God who "defends the cause of the fatherless," (Deuteronomy 10:18). He will surely bless the hands that bless the helpless. Many people often flock to churches praying for blessing. This is a good thing, but another way to be blessed is to become a blessing, for "he who waters others will himself be watered," (Proverbs 11: 25b)

Once I had in our clinic a man from another country. He was now an adult struggling with a troubled marriage. He found it very difficult to express love to his wife and sometimes, went into bouts of depression. We talked about his past. His father had died when he was about nine years old. His mother worked hard to care for the young children, but soon she fell sick with terminal cancer.

When he was 13 years old, his mother became bedridden as a result of the disease. It was decided that the children go to live with an Aunt and that the mother be placed in Hospice, the place for terminally ill patients. The young man, however, refused to be separated from his mother. He nursed her and cooked for her until her death three years later.

Apart from intermittent visits, their few relatives left the boy alone as he juggled school and care for his mother. He juggled shopping, cooking, cleaning and homework. The parentified young teenager had no time to be a child anymore. Those were the darkest days of his life. He told me that he often felt so alone and cried himself to sleep on many nights. After his mother's burial, no one helped him to deal with the pain and loss. The deeply buried grief was affecting his marriage now, many years later.

The Aroma of Care

If you have a lot, give some of your possessions;
if you have little, give some of your heart.
~ *African Proverb*

He who gives to the poor will lack nothing,
but he who closes his eyes to them receives many curses.
~ *Proverbs 28:27*

The righteous care about justice for the poor, but the wicked have no such concern.
~ *Proverbs 29:27*

The African proverb: "*If you have a lot, give some of your possessions; if you have little, give some of your heart,*" is encouragement that all of us can give something to the needy. As much as the parentless children and youth have physical needs, the greatest essentials go beyond the tangible to the emotional, psychological and spiritual. Many orphans struggle with issues of identity: "Who am I? What am I doing in the world? Where am I going? Why do I have so many problems?" Giving these children the heart refers to listening to them to identify their true needs.

Stories are told how street children rehabilitated into children's homes keep running away back into the streets. Why aren't some of them attracted by clean beds, good food and a roof over their hands? Why should they run back to eat off the rubbish bins? They are looking for someone to give them a heart.

The Biblical proverb: *"He who gives to the poor will lack nothing, but he who closes his eyes to them receives many curses,"* lays emphasis on the blessings of caring for the poor, in our case, the parent-less child, and the fact that neglecting them is going against God's command to mind the vulnerable on his behalf.

According to the Biblical proverb: *"The righteous care about justice for the poor, but the wicked have no such concern,"* indicates that those who care for the poor have God's commendation. However, those who do not care what happens to the poor receive God's disfavor. This is a strong verse that communicates God's disapproval of those who care only for their own children, forgetting that the world has many orphans.

A story is told of a teacher, we shall call her Mrs. Musyoka. She was the class six teacher, instructing the 11-12 year-olds and proceeding with them to the final class eight examination. At the beginning of the school term, she received a new group who were in class five the year before. In that class, she noticed a sad, bedraggled boy, named Mutiso, who sat quietly each lesson without saying much and often with a far-away look in his eyes.

Mutiso's performance was not good and it continued to decline through the school term. His homework was poorly done and he never offered to answer questions in class. Each end of term report was worse than the one before. She wrote things like: "He can do better. Absent minded. Mutiso spends a lot of time alone. The boy does not seem to want to play with others," and so on. When other parents came to school on Parents Day, Mutiso's parents never did. Mrs Musyoka was too busy with the other children to ask the boy why nobody ever came. Eventually, the boy's performance deteriorated so much that Mrs. Musyoka had to report the case to the Headmistress.

As she narrated her frustration with her student, the Headmistress asked: "All through this school year, have you gotten to know Mutiso?" "What is there to know? He is not just motivated to learn," she responded. The Headmistress asked her Secretary for copies of Mutiso's report forms all the way from class one. She handed the file to the teacher and said: "Just go through these for a bit."

Mrs. Musyoka read about a brilliant child who had exemplified sterling performance since Class One. However, along the way, his mother, the only parent, fell ill. As she got weaker, battling terminal illness, the child became more and more morose and his performance began to deteriorate. Other teachers had written comments like: "Mutiso's performance has continued to decline. He says that his mother was hospitalized again this week," and so on. Mrs. Musyoka felt so sad that she had failed to get to know the boy better. Soon after, just before the end of the school term, his mother died.

The term came to the end. On the final day, and as was the practice, the children brought small gifts to their teacher. Although other youngsters brought new items purchased by their parents, Mutiso brought her an old bracelet with some missing beads and a half bottle of perfume. The boy explained that these items belonged to his mother. "Please wear the bracelet and put on the perfume, so that whenever I come to school, I can see the bracelet and smell my mother's perfume and so remember that I have another mother here now." From then on, Mrs. Musyoka gave special attention to the orphaned boy. She listened to him, mentored him and encouraged him to study hard. She have him her *heart*. Eventually, his performance improved and he moved on to high school a few years later.

Mrs. Musyoka followed his progress with encouragement and the young man sought her advice often. She organized to assist him with school fees. He passed well and went on to university to study medicine. On his graduation several years later, he had a special chair reserved with the name "Mother." As Mrs. Musyoka , now an older woman, sat in that chair of honor, she was a fulfilled teacher, happy that she had not denied a helpless, grieving boy her *heart* those many years ago. For, the lonely, confused child in Mrs. Musyoka's class was now Dr. Mutiso.

CONCLUSION

In this book, we have discussed twelve characteristics of men and women who wish to parent with purpose. Purpose means that we start the journey with the end in view. We first listen to wisdom from God, the Creator, who has given each parent the task of stewardship: taking care of children on God's behalf. This means that we ought to seek his knowledge on how to partner with him to raise them in order to fulfill the plan he has for each one of them.

We also partner with the child, identifying and growing their unique gifts and listening to them express their life's desires. We partner, one parent with another, in guiding the children as they make life's choices. We also create a home environment that motivates the children's growth and maturation.

Parenting is a global task, as well as ancient undertaking. Just before completing this book, my daughter drew my attention to Tirukkural, ancient wisdom on the science of human behavior and parenting in particular. Written more than 5,000 years ago by Tiruvalluvar, a Tamil poet and writer, it reminds us that in spite of modern education and technology, the challenge of training children remains largely the same and will persist while there is life.

Tiruvalluvar's wisdom does not necessarily suggest causation. Psychological research states that no single construct can be said to "cause" another. There can only be a relationship or a correlation. For example, we cannot say that child neglect causes delinquency in the child's adolescent years, or that youth are angry and rebellious because of strict punishment received when they were growing up. Each one of these constructs can contribute to the other but there is no direct effect because many other factors could influence outcomes.

This means that we should be light in Tiruvalluvar's use of the word "because." However, the wisdom here might help parents to re-examine what we have discussed in this book and remember that good parenting is sowing wisely and consistently, and then believing that the harvest will be good. This ancient wisdom teaches truths that remain relevant most of the time. It remind us that:

1. If your child lies to you often, it is because you are harsh and over-react when he behaves inappropriately.
2. If your child is afraid of exploring new ideas, it is because you do not encourage her to make mistakes.
3. If your child has poor self-esteem, it is because you advise him more than you encourage him.
4. If your child does not stand up for himself, it is because from a young age you have regularly disciplined him in public.
5. If your child takes things that do not belong to her, it is because when you buy them things, you do not let her choose what she wants.
6. If your child is cowardly, it is because you help him too quickly.
7. If your child does not respect other people's feelings, it is because instead of speaking to your child, you order and command him.
8. If your child is too quick to anger, it is because you give too much attention to his misbehavior and too little attention to good behavior.

9. If your child is excessively jealous, it is because you only congratulate her when she successfully completes something and not when she improves at something even if she does not successfully complete it.
10. If your child intentionally disturbs you, it is because you are not physically affectionate enough.
11. If your child is openly defiant, it is because you openly threaten to do something but don't follow through.
12. If your child is secretive, it is because he does not trust that you won't blow things out of proportion.
13. If your child talks back to you, it is because they watch you do it to others and think it is normal behavior.
14. If your child does not listen to you but listens to others, it is because you are too quick to jump to conclusions.
15. If your child rebels it is because they know you care more about what others think than what is right.

(Cited by R. Srinivasan; https://swamanthan.wordpress.com/2015/03/07/parenting-ancient-wisdom-for-modern-parents-thirukkural/).

Children are like plants. Within a rich atmosphere full of light, air and food, they blossom. Where these elements lack, they shrink and shrivel. Parental presence motivates children to blossom and genuine love fires motivation.

"Let no debt remain outstanding, except the continuing debt to love one another, for he who loves his fellowman has fulfilled the law. The commandment 'Do not commit adultery,' 'Do not murder,' 'Do not steal,' 'Do not covet,' and whatever other commandment there may be, are summed up in this one rule: 'Love your neighbor as yourself.' Love does no harm to its neighbor. Therefore, love is the fulfillment of the law," (Romans 13:8-10). Our family members are our first immediate neighbors. Let

love flow in our marriages and families for partnership and shared goals.

In African wisdom, partnering with others in parenting is critical. We ask ourselves: "Who will travel this road with me? I need friends whose children are almost the same age as mine, people with clear values so that my children do not ape behavior that is different from my beliefs and way of life."

Beyond the act of parenting is the act of *being*. I need to be careful in all that I believe, think and do because whether I am aware of it or not, my child will follow me closely. I need to pass on lasting values as legacies. If I value money, property and prosperity above all else, when I pass on one day, I'll leave my children with money and property but little else that makes for virtues of living. Money and property without wisdom and character will destroy them and they will destroy one another.

Beyond passing on values, children need to internalize self-discipline by learning how to set personal limits in terms of peer influence, habits, behavior and character. They need to develop the virtue of temperance: the practice of self-control against passions of life. My child should not allow pleasure, drunkenness or addictions to run his life. For my children to observe self-discipline, I am their role model for they *"hear" more what I do than what I say!*

For them to model themselves after me, I must be present, because children are not machines to be operated by remote control. I can only mentor and coach them while I am near and reachable. As I teach them, I need to motivate them through praise and appreciation, protecting them from anything and anyone who would want to steal the God-given identity in each of them.

Then I pray that God may give me patience to build a healthy marriage and family for the married; and a healthy family for the single parents. My children desire that I become a pillar of consistency so that they can develop security to build stable identities. I am not sufficient, so I will lead them to faith in God as the guide and master of their lives, and then link them to adults of virtue who can mentor them alongside my parenting.

Lord, I need help to own and celebrate my own indigenous cultural roots and the positive values therein because this is the identity you chose to give me. Being African means upholding many positive values that you have instilled in us: our faith in God who is always present among us; our love for family; care for and protection of life, babies and children; gift of hospitality; respect and care for the aged; celebration of my belonging to community; protection of the weak and vulnerable; stewardship of our beautiful land, animals, wind, weather and waters; and excitement to live out African wisdoms, passing them on in our proverbs and folktales. Help me to hand over these precious legacies to my children so that firmly rooted in who they are, they can grow up to become who you created them to be; finally passing on the same treasures to their own children, generation after generation.

Beyond my own children is a world full of lonely, needy orphans. Lord, I know what you want me to do as your hand of blessing towards them. Let me work not only for my biological children but for others too who do not have parents. Help me in my busy time to include some of these children in my family circle. Bless me to bless them with food, education, shelter, spiritual mentoring and life coaching. I know that I cannot claim to love you or to know you when my heart does not bleed with what bleeds the heart of God, and each lonely, confused, hungry orphan bleeds your heart.

Finally, write it down in my heart Lord Jesus, that rightful parenting is the greatest investment that I will ever make in my children's lives. God, teach me to teach my kids, guide me to guide them. Become my pillar so I can become their support along life's way. For honor begets honor. This is the essence of *Parenting with Purpose and African Wisdom*.

AFRICA
STUDY
BIBLE
NLT